DRIVING BY MOONLIGHT

Happy Birthday Bets!

Much love,
Annie

DRIVING BY MOONLIGHT

Betsy —
Joyful journey!
Kristin Henderson

A JOURNEY THROUGH LOVE, WAR, AND INFERTILITY

KRISTIN HENDERSON

SEAL PRESS

Portions of this book first appeared in different form in the *Washington Post*.
"The Quaker and the Marine," January 6, 2002
"Joy Ride," September 1, 2002
"Down the Drain," September 29, 2002

DRIVING BY MOONLIGHT: A Journey Through Love, War, and Infertility
© 2003 by Kristin Henderson

Published by Seal Press
An Imprint of Avalon Publishing Group Incorporated
161 William St., 16th Floor
New York, NY 10038

Library of Congress Cataloging-in-Publication Data is available.

ISBN 1-58005-098-0

9 8 7 6 5 4 3 2 1

Designed by Jennifer Steffey
Printed in the United States of America
Distributed by Publishers Group West

for my husband

CONTENTS

SHIPPING OUT

*Starting date 9/19/01 . . . new moon . . .
odometer 124,054 . . . route: north from
Camp Lejeune, North Carolina, to Norfolk,
Virginia, then on to a pit stop in Richmond,
Virginia = two days, 358 miles*

The cop pulls me over at 1 A.M., just after I leave Norfolk, right at the start of my cross-country road trip. In a car designed to roar along at 130 miles an hour, I'm doing fifty in a sixty-five zone. My right turn signal's been *gedinking* away for no apparent reason. I look like a drunk trying to appear inconspicuous.

My dog, Rosie, is barking six inches from my ear. She's a German shepherd, a big dog with a big mouth in a small car. The cop flashes his light in my face. He has to shout so I can hear him. "Everything all right here?"

Everything all right? The World Trade Center's a week-old mountain of smoking rubble, the Pentagon has a big black hole in its side, I just put my husband on a ship full of Marines bound for the other side of the world, and my old Corvette's freaked-out alternator has been boiling the battery for the last four hours. But it got me to Norfolk, by God, where I've just managed to see my best friend, my husband of sixteen years, one last time before he leaves.

"Yes sir," I say. "Other than my alternator, everything's all right."

One week earlier, we all watched that jet explode into the south tower, explode into the south tower, explode into the south tower. . . . For days that television moment replayed over and over and over in our living rooms and our bedrooms. The instinctive response: Close your arms around the ones you love and don't let go. I had to ignore that instinct. Me and thousands of others, we had to open our arms and let the ones we love go.

I'm not complaining. Frank chose this life freely and I freely chose him. But before I let him go, in a dark parking lot out of sight of the looming gray amphibious assault ship that would carry him away, I sat next to him on the curb and listened to his voice. I don't remember what we talked about. Nothing important.

I showed him the locket I'm wearing now, the first present he ever gave me, eighteen years ago. It's a cheap, gold, heart-shaped locket that he chose as his free gift when he ordered a turntable from a catalog. He could have had a calculator the size of a credit card, but he chose the locket because he thought I might like it. I didn't, but I appreciated the thought. This morning I put it on. Sitting next to him on the curb, I told him I wasn't taking it off until he came back. In the star-speckled, moonless night I saw him smile.

Then he stroked Rosie's head and hugged me goodbye. I'm a little taller than he is, but inside the circle of his arms, inside that moment, I felt small and safe, and everything was all right.

We met in Florida in 1983 when we were both in college. Oma and Opa, my German immigrant grandparents, who'd lived with my family since I was nine, had sold me their yellow 1970 Mercury Cougar for a dollar and the promise that I would drive them to their Lutheran church every week. That's where Frank and I met. I was in the pew because of a car, and he was behind the altar because of an apartment—he lived at the church in a little studio. He took care of the property and chose to help out Sundays with the service.

Sundays I'd watch him up there behind the altar because he was a cute guy and I liked cute guys. Some of my best friends were cute guys. But the cute guys I *really* liked never seemed to like me back, with the result that I'd been on two dates in my entire life. A very nice, big, goofy guy had taken me to a basketball game, where I listened to him and his basketball pals talk about great moments in basketball, of which there were apparently a lot. My other date brought along his ex-girlfriend, who sat at our table and watched him dance with me, looking bored, smoke rising from her cigarette, as if he dragged her along on his dates with other women all the time.

Driving myself home after that date I had prayed: Okay God, I give up. If you've got somebody in mind for me, he's going to have to make the first move. In fact, he's going to have to make all the moves, because I'm through looking. That was back when I still believed God was in the matchmaking business, back when I prayed to God as if God were a person, a parent in heaven who appreciated getting specific requests so God didn't have to guess what I wanted.

So the pastor was praying. Oma and Opa's heads were bowed—tall, graceful Oma's gray perm a little higher than short Opa's pink baldness. In fact, every head was bowed except mine. I was looking at the cute guy standing behind the altar in the white assistant's robe, enjoying him from a nice, safe distance. He was good-looking in a tough, scruffy mutt kind of way, not my usual type; my type usually wore glasses. He looked like the kind of guy who had a lot of ex-girlfriends. All of a sudden he snuck a peek at the congregation to count how many wafers he was going to need for communion, he later told me. He popped open his eyes without even raising his head and saw a whole sea of bowed heads—hairdos, comb-overs, and bald spots—and a single pair of eyeballs, mine. Before I could look away, he did something horrible.

He winked.

I was naked, blushing, mortified. It was middle school all over again, when the absolutely *last* thing you want a guy to know about you is that you like him. It gave him power over you, the power to hurt and publicly humiliate you. I was a twenty-one-year-old virgin, had never said much more than hello to this guy, and now I vowed I never would. The only difficulty was that I parked at the church every day because it was next to the campus. I took care to park out of sight of his apartment.

Days passed. I started to relax. Then I found a note on my car.

> *I've been trying to catch you for three days now, but I keep missing you. So I have to resort to a note. Is your grandfather mad at me? He brushed past me the other day like he was. Or is that just his German way? Also . . . do you watch me in services a lot? I felt someone's eyes on me during the service & saw that you were watching me. It wasn't the first time. Am I wearing the alb wrong? Is my hair messed up? My zipper down? (But how could you see that?) It doesn't bother me at all. I think you've got something very pretty in your eyes,* and behind them, inside.

I reread the note, and then the last line really hit me—I was being pursued. Now I wasn't just embarrassed, I was scared. I'd never been pursued before, not by someone I liked. If I'd just been embarrassed, I would have known what to do, gone on the attack, joked my way out of it. But romantic pursuit? I had no idea how to handle it. It was a big, dark, frightening unknown. I stuffed the note in my backpack and sped out of the parking lot through the back exit.

After that, he started locking the chain across the back exit.

Now I had to pass through the exit next to his apartment, where he'd wait inside and listen for the big V-8 engine of my one-dollar, yellow car. But I was too quick at hopping out to unhook the chain, driving through, scampering back to rehook the chain, then roaring off.

So he locked that chain, too.

I arrived at my car in the middle of a tropical downpour one afternoon to find a note instructing me to knock on his door so he could let me out. I considered walking the five miles home in the rain instead.

But, I told myself, all I had to do was knock, then leap back into the car and wait there while he unlocked the chain. I wouldn't have to say more than a couple of words to him.

I pulled up to the exit and left the engine running. I ducked through the downpour to tap at his door, huddled beneath a covered walk. No answer. I tapped again. No answer. I pounded on it. Still no answer. I was turning away, annoyed and wet, when a nearby door to the church banged open. It was him.

"Hey!" He seemed a little out of breath. He was smiling.

"I got a note saying I had to get you to let me out."

"Right, sure." Very friendly, very helpful. He looked out beyond the covered walk at the solid wall of rain. "Can you give me a ride to the chain in back?"

Sit within two feet of him for the time it would take to drive thirty yards? That would be very bad. "What's wrong with this one?"

"The key's locked up in the church office."

I didn't know it was a lie. We drove the thirty yards to the back chain in silence.

He put his hand on the door handle. "After I get the lock open, would you mind giving me a ride back and then, like, you know, relocking the chain behind you when you leave?"

Another endless thirty-yard ride? No way. But the rain was pounding on the car. Making him walk back wouldn't be nice. "Well. Okay."

When he jumped in again, he was wet to the skin, hair plastered to his head. He cheerfully declared his leather boots ruined, and I, relieved to have something to talk about, told him how he could save them with newspaper and saddle soap. I stopped the car outside his apartment. He didn't get out. He just sat there, slouched on one elbow, looking up at me. The rain on the car roof was like a drum roll, and there was something about the way he was looking at me—suddenly I got a bad feeling.

And then he said, "Did you get my note?"

My heart was thudding. I gripped the wheel hard. "Yes, I got your note." I focused on evening up the balance of power. "That was the rudest thing! That was the most embarrassing moment of my life!"

"Getting the note?"

I should have said something sarcastic and funny, but I couldn't think of anything. "No! That you thought I was looking at you!" I could feel myself blushing.

"Weren't you?"

"Of course not! I was just looking around!" My face was on fire.

"Oh. Sorry."

For a long moment we just looked at each other, and, as we did, my anger and embarrassment drained away, leaving only nervous fear. I looked down and waited for him to get out. Instead he asked me if I could take him to the post office. I was still uncomfortable, but he was a good-looking guy, he hadn't said a word about basketball, and no ex-girlfriends were in sight.

We spent the rest of that rainy afternoon together.

He told me he had a little inertia problem. He'd been in college seven years. He'd been Navy ROTC, had nearly been commissioned an officer in the Marine Corps.

"You?" I asked. He had a lot of hair and a mustache and big sideburns. I grew up during the Vietnam War, in a liberal family. For me, the military was General Westmoreland lying about body counts, it was My Lai, it was a little girl running naked after napalm had burned off her clothes along with her skin. Frank didn't look like my idea of the military. But then he showed me his old military ID: no hair, no smile; he looked like he could kill. I raised my amazed eyes from his old picture to him. "What happened?"

"Got sick," he said. He'd passed out once during boot camp for officers, gutted his way through on willpower, and, after graduating from Officer Candidates School, wound up in the hospital. By this point in his story we were back at his tiny studio apartment that smelled of running shoes and French fries, and he got down on the floor to demonstrate the position he'd had to assume for an old-fashioned diagnostic colonoscopy. Rain pounded on the pavement outside. I'd known this guy all of two hours and there he was on the floor with his butt in the air. I started to laugh. I'd never met anyone like him.

He got his health back, but the Marines had already given him a medical discharge. He told me now he was feeling called to become a Lutheran minister and wanted to go to seminary once he finished college. Oma had spent her life as a minister's wife; I knew I didn't want to be one. And I didn't trust military men. He might be cute, he might make me laugh, he might even pray to God like a personal friend, the same way I did, but after he told me about his inertia problem, I told him I wanted to drive across the country and back, leaving behind other people's expectations and controlling each day's destiny with a map and a car. Clearly we weren't meant for each other.

Two and a half years later we were married.

He'd been the first one to say, "I love you." I'd never said that to anyone outside my family. Months after he first said it, when I finally whispered it back, he pounced on it. "What? What did you say?"

His look of delight made me nervous, as if I'd just revealed a secret I should have kept to myself. "You heard me," I muttered.

"Say it one more time," he begged.

Only when he stopped begging did I finally say again, "I love you." He didn't say anything then. He just made me lie down beside him, and held me.

After we were married we fought daily the first year, every other day the second, every third day the third. Mostly I can remember the fights but not what they were about; we really were just wrong for each other. Our family backgrounds and personalities were too different, our expectations didn't match. I tried to storm out once and he grabbed me, pinned me to the floor, both of us crying, me refusing to look at him till he realized he couldn't hold me down forever. I drove around for a few hours before going back.

"I'm sorry," he said.

"Thank you," I said, and started to cry again. My nose was red, my eyes puffy. I turned my head away. "Don't look at me, I'm hideous."

He put his arms around me, gently. "I think you look pretty. Sort of vulnerable." And he turned my face to his and kissed me and then made love to me. I always loved the feel of his body against mine, how different it felt from my body, the otherness of him. Sex always made things better.

The next day we had another fight about something else, money probably, or dirt. Cleaning was an issue. I had always thought my father wanted me to be a modern career woman while my mother wanted me to be the perfect wife, so I was trying to be both. I'd work all week, then I'd spend the weekend buzzing around vacuuming and trekking to the laundromat. I cooked dinner every night. I even ironed.

Frank's Saturday mornings were devoted to cartoons, the afternoons to naps. He'd wistfully pat the couch beside him. "Sit with me?"

"I have too much to do," I'd snap, playing the martyr till I couldn't take it anymore, and then I'd yell at him for lying there while I worked like a dog. It was years before I realized he didn't care if the apartment was spotless. It was a few more years before I realized I didn't either. It was one of those things I had absorbed growing up, like a natural law: If you throw a brick in the air, then it will come back down and hit you in the head; if you hit your sister, then you will get in trouble; if you're one of the little children, then Jesus loves you; if you're clean, then you're good. "They are good people," Opa would say about neighbors he admired, "everything always in order."

Later, at the seven-year mark, Frank an ordained Lutheran pastor, me a pastor's wife in the middle of nowhere, living a life that had yet to take me any of the places I'd dreamed, I told him I thought it was over, that we should get a divorce. But by then it was too late. By then, in our wrestling, without us noticing, our marriage had divided, and divided again. It had emerged apart from us and part of us, half him and half me, the truest parts of ourselves curled together into a living, breathing thing that kept him from sinking and me from floating away.

I'm trying to pay attention to what the highway patrol officer is asking me, while at the same time I'm hunting for my identification. He hasn't asked for it, but I'm sure he will and I can't find it. I'm trying to hunt very casually. I know I just had it at the naval base in Norfolk. Security was extra tight because of September 11. I had to show my ID and explain what I wanted. My husband, I wanted to see my husband. This wasn't the departure I'd planned for.

When we started out, both Frank and I believed God had a plan for us.

Since then nothing has gone according to plan.

Marriages, like people, are shaped by the turns in the road they travel. Some of the turns you see coming, some of them you don't—like the baby I expected to have but Frank didn't want. We nearly wrecked on that turn. Then there was the religious faith Frank expected us to share for life, until I turned my back on it; that nearly wrecked us, too. And three years ago, in 1998, a call came from the Navy: After nearly twenty years, they wanted him back, this time as a chaplain.

The Marine Corps, as part of the Department of the Navy, uses naval support personnel, including doctors and chaplains. This was Frank's chance to rejoin the few, the proud, the Marines, the military's smallest branch, the tip of the spear, 125,000 men and women organized into vertically integrated expeditionary units that are able to deploy quickly, with all the equipment and supplies they need, anywhere in the world—America's emergency 911. The Marines had a reputation for inspired leadership, and were the only service never to suffer a shortage of recruits. This was Frank's chance to be part of that elite group again, to get his surrogate family back. Because that's really what the Marine Corps was for him. The all-for-one-and-one-for-all family he'd never had.

"But I'm worried about you if I do this," he said, drawing back his arm and throwing Rosie's ball across the park. She exploded after it. Watching her, he admitted, "I'm worried about us." Because while Frank now hoped to once again become a member of the United States military, I was now a member of the Religious Society of Friends. I had become a Quaker.

I watched Rosie's flat-out pounding run, neck outstretched, ears tucked back, eyes on the ball as it hit the ground ahead of her and bounced high. Her head came up, ears up too, anticipating the ball's arc; she launched herself after it and plucked it out of the air. I've always been a pacifist. I have always believed if you combined a commitment to justice with the courage to look ahead and act on what you saw, all wars could be prevented. All wars. Period. I've always believed war is the easy way out. I've always believed the massive military machine Frank now wanted to rejoin just made the easy way out even easier.

It was true that as a chaplain Frank wouldn't be a combatant. But he would help make combat possible. He'd help Sailors and Marines wrestle with spiritual questions, solve personal problems, prevent them from being hazed by their peers or abused by bad officers. As a chaplain, he'd help make sure none of that got in the way of their readiness to make war.

And so he said, "I'm worried about what effect this will have on us."

Rosie rollicked her way back to us, chomping the ball in her mouth.

"Well, you know how I feel about the military." I whipped the Frisbee out over her head. She spat out the ball and whirled after it. "But you also know how I feel about marriage. It's a partnership." I picked up the ball and handed it to him. "We're supposed to support each other, help each other achieve our dreams." He took the ball and my hand and didn't let go. I smiled a small smile and said, "I would never stand in the way of your dreams."

After Frank put on a uniform, I struggled with being a pacifist and being married to a military man. But I can't say I struggled very hard. The struggle involved relatively abstract questions with no clear answers, like: Am I compromising my pacifist principles if I go to the doctor, whip out my military dependent ID card, and let the Pentagon pay my bill?

Last week American Airlines Flight 77 roared in low over the white headstones of Arlington's dead warriors, banked hard, and slammed into the Pentagon. The struggle isn't abstract anymore. But way still has not opened. That's what Quakers call it when you can't seem to move forward: Way is not opening. I still have no answers. With my own eyes I saw that shocking serpent of smoke roiling down the Potomac from where I knew the Pentagon to be, from where I knew a friend had made his way out and a friend of a friend had died. Does being a pacifist mean you have to believe it's never too late to prevent a war, or that it's wrong even to defend yourself? On TV, I saw that huge plane magically pushing its way into and through a New York skyscraper, metamorphosing along the way into a blooming poppy of fire. I watched tiny, fragile human figures standing at those broken windows a hundred floors up, someone's daughter, someone's son, all peering down and surely hoping against hope, not knowing there was no hope. Every time I see them, recall them, I want to seize something, anything, on the other side of the world and smash the hell out of it. I know I won't be satisfied until I see whole towns on the other side of the world destroyed.

I horrify myself. I want to run away from myself. Instead, for the past week I've been sitting in front of the TV, watching helplessly, listening to a continual whisper at the back of my mind: You have no power to change what happened, you have no control over what might happen next. Your country is mobilizing for war. Your husband is heading for God knows where. Your leaders may screw up. . . .

I wish I could be like Rosie when she rides in the car. Rosie, reclining on the bed I've rigged for her on top of the folded-over passenger seat, hooked into her safety harness, zones out like a Zen master. Sometimes she rests her chin on the dash, nose pressed to the windshield, eyes half closed. Sometimes she looks out the passenger window with a serene gaze to nowhere. Sometimes she falls asleep that way and her head starts to bob. Nothing keeps her from enjoying the moment, nothing disturbs her sleep, no regrets about the past, no worries about the future.

I need to be like Rosie. At the very least I need to anesthetize myself against the helplessness and the horror I feel, and motion is my drug of choice. I need to take a trip, leave the confusion behind, and find a road to that kind of peace. By coincidence, on September 11 I already had a trip planned, a big one—that cross-country road trip I had told Frank I'd been dreaming about since I was a teenager. Finally I had put work and the rest of my life on hold. Frank and I were both scheduled to ship out on our respective journeys September 19, and in spite of September 11, because of September 11, we're both still going. As Frank's ship prepares to slip its moorings and disappear with the tide, Rosie and I rumble away into the dark, off to see America.

Except I have alternator trouble.

The mechanic's diagnosis: The alternator is dying. Usually dying alternators simply stop converting a small portion of the engine's power into electricity to run the car's accessories and recharge the battery, and eventually the car will no longer go. But on rare occasions a dying alternator instead sees the Grim Reaper coming and freaks out, cranks out so much juice the battery overcharges, boils over, pops its top, and spews acidic water everywhere. Even many motorheads do not know this can happen—this according to my mechanic when he answered the call I placed to him earlier tonight from the side of the road. He assured me there was a solution, which there would not have been if the alternator had died in the usual manner, though I can't say I was all that grateful for my rare, so-called good, luck.

The mechanic's solution: First, reduce power. Slow down. The faster you drive, the more power the engine sends to the alternator, which in turn dumps it into the battery. Second, siphon off excess power. Turn on every electrical accessory. Full blast. As in, not just headlights, but headlights on high beams. Air conditioning on arctic wind setting. Wipers scraping back and forth across the dry windshield. Radio on. Hit the cigarette lighter every few minutes as needed. Also as needed, run the electric windows down, which motivates Rosie to stick her head out, and up, which forces her to immediately yank her head back in. Down-out, up-in. I am driving down the road in Crazy Accessory Car . . . but I am driving.

I'm telling a skeptical highway patrol officer the parable of the alternator, trying to explain why I'm driving a Corvette fifteen miles below the speed limit, with the blinker on, in the wee hours of the morning. I'm shouting over Rosie, who's on her feet, back against the roof, hackles up, barking across me like she wants to eat his liver. She never barks like this at dogs. It's people she doesn't trust.

The officer ignores her. He flashes his light around inside the car, squints at the evidence—windshield wipers scraping across the dry windshield, a/c blasting, blinker flashing—and raises an eyebrow. He's not interested in my ID, which it turns out I'm sitting on. He tells me he hopes I don't have far to go.

I'm hoping to go as far as the West Coast.

I get as far as Richmond.

IF RELIGIONS WERE CARS

Starting date 9/21/01 . . . waxing crescent moon . . . odometer 124,412 . . . route: north through Virginia to a pit stop in Washington, D.C. = one day, 123 miles

With a new alternator under the hood, Rosie and I are back in motion, headed north toward Washington, D.C. I have always been restless. In one of my earliest memories of growing up in Florida, I'm four or five, sitting next to my still and silent mother, surrounded by other still and silent grownups. It's a typical Quaker meeting for worship, the silence broken only occasionally when the Spirit moves a member to stand up and deliver a spontaneous, presumably divinely inspired message. I'm feeling pretty self-righteous about how still and silent I'm being until my mother leans over and whispers, "If you don't stop squirming, you'll have to go back outside with the other children."

I can't remember if that was before or after one of the grownups rose to his feet to break the silence with this message: "Stop the world! I want to get off!" I just remember my broad-shouldered, big-voiced father later boiling over in the car. "That meeting's a joke. I am not going back." And he didn't. Since my father was the Quaker, my mother didn't go back either—Oma and Opa had raised her as a Lutheran.

From my father I inherited the skeptic's open mind; from my mother, the seeker's open heart. Without even trying I can rebel against both of them at the same time, opposing my mother by practicing the wrong religion, and my father by practicing any religion at all. I count myself so lucky. Frank counts the number of times I've changed religions and just shakes his head.

Frank, a Lutheran minister, grew up the son of a Lutheran minister; he was born a Lutheran, baptized a Lutheran, confirmed a Lutheran, married a Lutheran, ordained a Lutheran, and will be buried a Lutheran. Lutheranism is the Ford sedan of the religious world: practical, roomy, tasteful, nothing too flashy. In my religious journey, I've ridden in a somewhat wider variety of vehicles.

I began life a Quaker.

The Pacer

If Quakerism were a car, I could see it as a Pacer, that odd compact from the seventies, an eye-catching, wide-bodied bubble that was easy on the gas. It made a quirky but sensible everyman statement driving down the road, but like the Religious Society of Friends, it wasn't for every man.

Friends, also known as Quakers, emerged out of the social turmoil of mid-seventeenth-century England, when the big, established churches served the needs of the people with money and power, which left the poor and powerless hungry for a church that was on their side. About that time a cobbler named George Fox rejected the materialistic hierarchy of both society and the church, and began to preach about a democratic God who lived inside every man and woman, a friendly, accessible God who would lead each individual from within, eventually guiding all of humankind toward Christ's heavenly kingdom right here on earth, a kingdom of equality, community, simplicity, integrity, and peace. With a God like that, you didn't need clergy.

That's as close as Fox's religious movement ever came to any kind of official doctrine. Instead of codifying their faith, Friends lived it. The first Friends numbered the months and the days of the week—Sunday was First Day, Monday was Second Day, and so on—because simple numbers were plainer than the old pagan names, plus, numbering the days and months reinforced the idea they were all equally holy. Friends wore simple, unadorned clothes even if they were rich, though most of them weren't. They refused to remove their hats in the presence of their betters. In an age when you addressed your betters as "you" and everyone else as "thee," they addressed everyone the same way in the name of equality, but instead of being smart about it and promoting everyone to "you," they stubbornly insisted on bringing everyone down to the level of "thee," a demotion their betters didn't appreciate. When Friends were hauled into court, which was often, they refused to swear before heaven to tell the truth since they believed that their commitment to integrity required them to be truthful all the time, not just in court, and that what they said in court deserved no more attention from heaven than what they said anywhere else, a stand the judges didn't appreciate, either. When Friends were physically attacked for their insubordinate faith, which was also often, they refused to take up weapons to defend themselves because they had noticed that all the violent revolutions in England's recent past had failed to make the world a better place. They spent a lot of time in the stocks, and a number of them died in prison.

Convincing the average Joe to join such a bunch of hard-headed, badly dressed misfits was a bit of a tough sell. As with the Pacer, most people decided they'd rather point and stare than buy into anything that odd and homely, so Quakerism never really caught on on a large scale. These days there are fewer than one hundred thousand Quakers in America and just over three hundred thousand worldwide, most of them in Africa thanks to the proselytizing of evangelical Quakers who, unlike my brand of Quaker, have ministers and pre-planned worship services that feature hymns and sermons.

Quakerism didn't catch me either the first time around, except for the part about pacifism, which was clear and simple enough for any child to understand when soldiers were tromping through the jungle every night on the evening news. "They're fighting the Viet Cong gorillas," I told my little sister. I remember first my father then my mother sitting on the edge of their bed one night, each with a scrap of paper in one hand and the phone in the other. "You have to either be quiet now or go out," my mother said.

"Why?" I asked.

"Daddy and I are calling the White House to tell President Nixon to stop bombing Cambodia."

I was impressed my parents knew the president well enough to call him.

All the cool kids at school wore peace symbols on their bell-bottomed hip-huggers and flashed the V-fingered peace sign to other cool kids. War was hell, it was bad; peace was good, peacenik pacifists were simply *right*. Martin Luther King, Jr., was a pacifist, Gandhi was a pacifist, my very own Quaker ancestors were pacifists. I was pleased to be a pacifist, too, a descendant of a small, elite group among the world's do-gooders—the few, the proud, the Quakers.

The paint job on the Quaker Pacer would be simple silver-gray, of course.

The MG

After my mother followed my father out of the meetinghouse, we were peacenik atheists for years, worshiping in the Church of the Sunday Morning Tennis Game. Atheism, for me, was like driving my father's little white MG. Smart and sophisticated, it looked great in the driveway, which was fortunate, because after each repair it worked just long enough to drive it home from the garage and park it there. If we wanted to actually go somewhere, like the public tennis courts, which in the South in those days were always available on Sunday mornings, we had to pile into our other car, the old fifty-dollar Chevy with Saran Wrap over the place where the rear window should have been.

For the record, I was never very good at either tennis or atheism. I just wasn't able to look at the intricate beauty and pain of the material world and believe it was a random accident.

The VW Microbus

I was ten when my parents split up and my mother began seeking in earnest. It was 1972, a psychedelic Day-Glo VW Microbus sort of phase. We careened through the catalogued readings of Edgar Cayce, psychic, preacher of reincarnation, reader of minds or of wishes I cannot say. I remember my personal astrological chart, which mapped my life with spooky precision from the moment of my latest birth, and my sisters and me squinting to see each other's auras but seeing only each other.

We beep-beeped head-on into the saffron teachings of the Paramhansa Yogananda, his photo on the flickering altar in my mother's bedroom, his gently greasy smile, sticks of incense exhaling themselves from one state of being to another. I sat cross-legged next to my transcendental meditation teacher on her waterbed, waiting for bliss to come. My secret mantra, which I was warned to tell no one lest it lose its power to exhale me into another state of being, rhymed with Gleem toothpaste, which was how I remembered it: *Eem. Eem. Eeeeeeem.* Now you can't tell anyone either.

The Custom Van

When the Microbus ran out of gas, we hitched a ride in one of those really big custom leisure vans: sculpted multicolor carpet on the floor, walls, and ceiling, faux-wood dash, tinted glass behind window treatments of ruffled curtains and miniblinds. The born-again, fundamentalist church we joined came equipped with everything but taste. Great ride though, very comfortable, very easy. From the captain's chairs way up high, you could look down on the rest of the traffic, a nice, confident view.

We'd pass the hours with ecstatic singing, clapping, and dancing, arms raised to Jesus. This was where I fell in love with Jesus, where I came to believe God had a personal one-on-one interest in *me.* As we sang, one voice would leave the song to sing in tongues, then another and another until the flow of singing broke up in the whitewater rush of syllables, the eerie thousand-part harmony of Babel. But my sisters and I were silent, our mouths open like baby birds, waiting to receive the gift. One helpful woman told us she just started speaking in tongues on the toilet one day. "It can happen *anywhere!*" she said. "When you *least expect it!* Because *that's how God works!*" Sure enough, it happened to me while driving.

I became a teenage Christian conservative. But the fundamentalists' obsession with prophecies about the horrifying period of tribulation that would precede the end of time as the world spiraled toward judgment day and Jesus' second coming was a little unsettling.

So was the claim that the only people who go to heaven were the ones who'd asked Jesus to be their personal Lord and Savior and invited Him to live in their hearts. I asked: What happens to a pygmy deep in the rain forest who's never had a chance to hear about Jesus Christ? Is God going to condemn him to the eternal fires of hell?

Fundamentalist Christians who answer this question with a sincere yes fall into one of three categories: those who are brokenhearted over this injustice and so are driven to try to save the world; those who are too lazy to go to all that trouble for a pygmy preordained to hell anyway and hardhearted enough not to lose any sleep over it; and those who are both brokenhearted and lazy. I was of the third type, and the only way I could live with myself was to answer the question differently: No, God's not going to condemn him. Surely God makes exceptions for the spiritually uninformed.

But what about someone here in America who's heard the "good news," but due to the emotional scars of, say, an abusive father, can't accept any father figure, including God? Surely a God who would suffer and die for humanity would understand such pain and make an exception for the spiritually wounded, too.

And what about Democrats? Does God make an exception for Democrats? It was 1980. On my eighteenth birthday, my father sent me a telegram: *Congratulations! Don't forget to register to vote!* He didn't even

21

have to include the word "Democrat." In our family, it was a foregone conclusion. Even as a teenage Christian conservative with all the answers, it never occurred to me to register as anything but a Democrat. I just didn't tell my father when I voted for Ronald Reagan, and I didn't tell Oma and Opa either, because they'd starved through the German side of World War I, had both lost brothers to it, were opposed to all war, and were afraid Reagan would get us into a big one with the Soviet Union because, as Oma said, shaking her finger, "That Reagan talks just like the Kaiser did." But I voted for Reagan anyway because he was for all the family values good Christians were for.

Then one day I was watching the news with Opa. A spokesman for the newly organized Christian Right was talking about the duty of every good Christian to support the Republican agenda of trickle-down economics and missile defense, when the interviewer asked if a person could be a good Democrat and also be a good Christian. The spokesman said, "No."

I sat there with my mouth open. No? No ifs, ands, or buts, just *no?* I gaped like a fish until Opa, a retired Lutheran minister and a Democrat ever since he became a citizen decades earlier—a man who never had much money and gave away most of what little he did have—muttered in German from his easy chair, "That's stupid."

Back to the Ford Sedan

After that, Opa gave me the gift of his car (for a dollar and a promise), the yellow 1970 Mercury Cougar, which he'd bought new the day he retired, the first car he'd ever bought for himself after a lifetime of driving the modest dark sedans his congregations had always chosen for him. So I drove the Cougar away from the fundamentalists and back to the Lutherans, where Frank locked me in the parking lot.

Despite growing up the granddaughter of a Lutheran pastor, I didn't know exactly what Lutherans believed. The treasure of keys at Frank's belt opened doors I didn't even know existed around the church; their jingle, the creak of doors, our voices and footsteps were the only sounds in the sanctuary's weekday quiet.

Climbing with Frank high among the steep, shadowy forest of pipes in the organ loft, I described my disenchantment with the fundamentalist belief that you had to ask Jesus into your heart to be saved. Consigning everyone else to hell made God's love seem so stingy and narrow. Looking down at the neat, honey-hued geometry of the empty wooden pews, Frank explained that Lutherans believed as long as you didn't kick Jesus, who was God, out of your heart, God was there, and even if you acted as if you had kicked God out, you might not have, *really*, because only God knew what was in your heart, so who were we to judge?

One day, walking with Frank in the moss-draped shade of live oaks, next to a peaceful, sparkling lake laced with lily pads, I also allowed as how I kind of resented the old Bible-thumping preachers who seemed so eager for Jesus to come back and bring on the end of time. Easy for them to say, said I: They'd already had the chance to live their lives, whereas I was still hoping to have time to enjoy mine, get married, have children.

Frank said they were taking those apocalyptic verses from the Book of Revelation out of context, that the verses weren't meant to be prophetic, but rather were written in a time of first-century persecution, in an attempt to give the suffering some meaning and the survivors some reassurance that God had not abandoned them—a truth that was still applicable even if the facts weren't.

"As for the second coming," Frank said, "when each of us dies and Christ comes to take us home, that's my understanding of the second coming. It's pretty arrogant to think the end of time depends on what happens here on Earth. If time ends, then the whole universe ends. Is God going to bring the whole universe to a stop just because of the events on one little planet?" He found that possibility highly unlikely.

As we walked beside that peaceful lake, Frank's Lutheranism seemed like a generous, sensible faith, a faith I could believe in, too, a church with enough room for both my certainty that Jesus was God and the source of my own personal salvation and happiness, and my uncertainty about everything else. We walked on, while behind us the deceptively placid lily pads rippled with cruising gators.

Out beyond the lights of town on a humid Florida night, we sat behind the Cougar by the side of a dark road. Frank squinted at his star wheel by the red glow of the Cougar's taillights, then pointed at the sky. "There's the Big Dipper." His finger moved up. "The chart doesn't show it, but there's Saturn."

Where I saw only a mass of stars, Frank saw destinations. He was born the same year as NASA, a year after the Soviet Union launched Sputnik I. Growing up he had papered his room with posters of the moon, and star charts, and photos of men in space suits. In an era when astronauts were always test pilots first, he dreamed of becoming a Navy pilot then an astronaut, of escaping the gravity of his father's unhappiness to float free in space. Defective color vision disqualified him from flying so he opted for the Marines, and then even that was taken away. But he still dreamed of the endless possibilities of space.

"When was Apollo 11?" I asked. "When did Neil Armstrong step out onto the moon?"

"July 20, 1969."

"I was seven."

"Mmm. I was eleven."

"I remember my parents dragging us out of bed to watch it on TV. It was late, like eleven o'clock or something."

Frank was silent. Insects chanted in the dark grass around us.

"I knew what we were seeing was important, but I was too young to really understand why. You were old enough, though. What was it like for you to watch history happen?"

He didn't take his eyes off the stars. "I didn't. My father made me go to bed."

"Why? It was summer vacation, it wasn't even a school night." My voice rose with surprise. "He must have known what it meant to you."

Frank shrugged. "I begged him to let me stay up, but he didn't care."

The thought of a small Frank huddled alone in his moon-shadowed, star-papered room while the rest of the world had gathered together around its flickering black-and-white television sets made me want to cry. I took his hand. "I wish you'd had my parents."

He squeezed my hand hard. He didn't say anything, but I knew he didn't really need my parents. He'd found a better parent, a God who loved him so much God was willing to leave a starry heaven and come down to earth as a man, and then die for him, a God who loved everyone that much. Frank's faith in God's unfailing love gave his life meaning. It gave my life meaning, too.

Then Frank said, "I've got you." He kissed my hand. "And we share the same faith. That means everything to me."

"I was just thinking the same thing."

He looked up at the vast black canopy pin-pricked with faraway suns. "I believe in divine orchestration."

"So do I." I believed God had a perfect plan for my life; I believed everything happened for a reason. If I kept an ear tuned to God and prayed for guidance, I'd be able to follow that plan. If God steered a needy person across my path, I trusted I'd know how to help. I trusted I'd know what car to buy. I trusted I'd know whom to marry.

Frank pulled my arm through his. "You're the best thing that's ever happened to me," he said. I leaned against him.

Months later, when he asked me to go through confirmation, join the Lutheran Church, and marry him, I said yes. By then it didn't seem to matter that at one time he'd trained to use deadly force, or that the ministry he now planned to join would circumscribe my life. I loved him. My heart told me it was part of God's plan.

I supported Frank through years of seminary. My job in the video production business paid the bills but didn't have much to offer on a spiritual level. Still, I figured since Frank was in the spiritual fulfillment business, by supporting his ministry I'd find spiritual fulfillment, too.

When Frank finished seminary and was ordained, he became a pastor to a couple of rural North Carolina congregations. I became a pastor's wife.

It was like playing a role. The real me, the freelance writer and director who worked mostly with men, would go out on the road for video shoots and give as good as I got, fuck this, shit that. Back home in the parsonage next door to the church, I was onstage week after week. My actress self would drive along country lanes visiting the neighbors, who were also Frank's parishioners. She watched her language and picked greens, attended pig pickings and fish fries, weddings and funerals. She sang in the choir, taught Sunday school, joined the women's group. It wasn't as spiritually fulfilling as I had hoped. It was like traveling in a foreign country—fascinating, edifying, but eventually you just want your own bathroom.

Then Iraq invaded Kuwait. On the news each night the first President Bush said Saddam had to be stopped. Reservists were called up. Hundreds of thousands of Americans shipped out for the Persian Gulf. It came up at church, around the table in a basement Sunday school room.

"I hate that we got to have a war, but if we got to have one, let's go do it and get it over with," said one of the ladies.

"The president must know what he's doing," said another. "Those people on the TV saying he's wrong, that don't seem right at a time like this."

At the other end of the table, I kept my mouth shut—until I got back to the parsonage. "We helped arm Saddam Hussein so he could kill Iranians for us!" I ranted to Frank. "We looked the other way while he murdered innocent people, and we tried to cut *business* deals with him! Like that wouldn't have consequences?" I had just about exhausted my knowledge of that part of the world, but that had never been known to slow me down. "You could see this mess coming for ten years, yet nobody ever wants to make the hard decisions until the least creative, most violent solutions are just about the only ones left! Well Bush can just put that Ivy League brain of his to work coming up with a better idea than killing poor miserable Iraqi conscripts!"

Frank unbuttoned his white plastic minister's collar and stretched out on the couch for his Sunday afternoon nap. "Instead of yelling at me about it," he yawned, "why don't you do something about it?"

So I got in the Cougar and drove up to Washington for a big protest march. I had lunch with my father the day before. He introduced me around his office. "My eldest daughter," he said proudly, "here for the big protest march." Someone asked him if he would be marching, too. "Heck no," he laughed. "It's too cold. Besides, the Redskins are playing."

The next day I joined the crowds of people who gathered on the Mall below the Capitol. I hooked up with a group of Lutherans from Milwaukee who needed help carrying their banner, and let myself be carried along with them past the White House shouting antiwar chants, surrounded by thousands of others just as sure as I was of the rightness of our cause. Marching with them was joyous, like diving into a cold river on a hot day and kicking along with the exuberant current.

Rounding a corner beyond the White House, I saw a woman in an old coat and sensible shoes standing quietly on the sidewalk, holding a poster above her head with both hands: Quakers Believe All War Is Wrong. And I thought, Yes! Yes that's me! That's me! I too believe there's a spark of God inside every human being, shedding its perfect light on our consciences, showing us the road we should follow to arrive one day at heaven on earth, a world without war, without inequality, greed, or poverty. This buoyant hope for the future, this faith for optimists, that's me!

Soon after, I visited my Quaker grandmother in Iowa. Sitting beside her in the familiar stillness of the Quaker meeting where my father grew up, I realized this was my church. I had been drawn to the Lutherans' open-minded theology of salvation, but looking back, if Frank hadn't asked, I probably wouldn't have been confirmed. I joined the Lutheran Church for Frank. It was Frank's church, not mine.

At the rise of meeting, I said to Grandma, "If I weren't a Lutheran pastor's wife, I'd be a Quaker."

We walked back to the house, following the electric fence along Grandpa's horse pasture, the prairie wind at our backs. Grandma blew her nose on the hanky she kept tucked in her bra inside her dress, which, like most of her dresses, she'd sewn herself. She was a woman of efficient talents and thrifty habits. "Well, that's nice for your grandmother to hear," she said. "But I've always thought the Lutherans do have a lot to offer."

"I'd still rather be Quaker."

"Why do you suppose that is?"

I thought for a minute. "It feels like home."

Washington, D.C., has always felt like home to me, too. Inside the Beltway, after driving up from Richmond, the interstate runs Rosie and me straight up through the great suburban encampment surrounding the city, the strip malls and apartment towers and rolling hills of neighborhood roofs among green trees. Eventually the Washington Monument arrows up over the horizon from the far side of the Potomac River and the glowing white helmet of the Capitol dome. But that's still in the distance when all of a sudden, just before I reach the river, the highway curves and rises and the Pentagon emerges to my left.

I'm a Washington resident, but this is the closest I've been to the Pentagon since it was hit. For some reason I'm expecting the usual pale hulk of a fortress I always see; I'm expecting it to look as solid and unbreachable as ever. For some reason, despite the smoke I saw from down the river a week ago, I'm not expecting the charred, top-to-bottom gash in its southern wall, the long expanses of blackened stone on either side, the American flag hanging from the roof like a brave, perky Band-Aid on a mangled body. I stare, gliding by, uncomprehending.

Yesterday in Richmond, while the Vette was getting a new alternator, I sat on my sister's kitchen floor and played a convoluted child's card game with my seven-year-old niece. In between telling me which card to play, Annali asked, "Did you hear about the big traffic jam up there?"

"Where?" I asked, frowning at my inscrutable hand of cards.

"In Washington and New York. They had really big traffic jams. People had to walk home. They even had to walk across the bridges, I saw pictures. They had to walk for *miles*."

I put down my hand. I said carefully, "You know what caused those traffic jams, don't you, Annali?"

"Oh yeah, the bad people crashed planes into the buildings. But then there was a traffic jam, a really big one."

She's had firsthand experience with traffic jams; she's sat in them herself. So have I. Traffic jams we can understand.

But this. I stare at that smoking gash as I go by.

Ten years ago, when I came back from protesting the Gulf War before it happened, I said to Frank, "All wars can be prevented."

"Well, what do you do once bad guys are out of control?" Frank had asked. "Saddam's over there killing innocent Kuwaitis, right now."

"Because we were short-sighted and self-serving."

"So you're saying we just have to roll over and take the consequences?"

I gave a philosophical shrug. "Maybe if we had to take the consequences of our mistakes more often we'd work harder to avoid them."

Easy for me to say. I wasn't a Kuwaiti, watching invaders kill my children.

I still believe all wars can be prevented, but now, staring at those consequences so much closer to home, a philosophical shrug eludes me. The black hole in the Pentagon sucks me in as I drive by, and I stare at it as if it's a question that demands an answer. I cannot stop staring till the concrete embankment rises and it's gone. Then I fly out onto the bridge above the sparkling Potomac River and into the city. The Pentagon and its demanding, confusing black hole are behind me.

This is where we came after Frank left his rural southern congregations and went back to school. This is where I came back to the Quakers; this is home. I was born in Manhattan, I grew up in Florida, I rent a house near Marine Corps Base Camp Lejeune in North Carolina, but Washington, D.C., is home no matter where else Frank's calling takes us. The bone-white monuments. The V-shaped panels of the Vietnam memorial half-buried in the ground, a black-winged fossil of grief. The swirling mysteries of traffic circles that Frank and I zipped around crowing in call and response: "We live here! / And we know how to navigate!" A few blocks up from the honk and bustle of Dupont Circle, a cocoon of companionable quiet inside my Quaker meetinghouse. Down Pennsylvania Avenue from the Capitol, at the top of the Metro escalator near my house, a jumpy man with his hand out who always told me to smile. Down the street on the corner, a cluster of young Marines aglow in red and blue and gold braid, carrying a tuba, a trumpet, a flute. In the alley behind my house, the weary, rolling, fat-bottomed walk of the woman in the short, black stretch dress—sometime addict, occasional prostitute, and mother of the boy who invited himself along with me on outings to the library. The police helicopter *whumping* overhead. In the park at dawn, a groggy cluster of bed-headed consultants and bureaucrats and secretaries, gay and straight, black, brown, and white, watching our dogs romp and pee. My father lives here in the D.C. area, and some of my cousins, and the woman I call my second mom, who entered our lives when my sisters and I were children and has remained as our mother-by-affection. This is home.

Every Fourth of July Frank and I lay on our backs below the Washington Monument next to the fireworks battery and watched the colors boom and crackle and flower overhead while the burned debris rained down around us.

Our house is here, a tiny, hundred-year-old rowhouse on Capitol Hill, though we've been renting it out since Frank went in the Navy three years ago. Passing through at the start of my road trip, I stop by to clean up the yard, touch up the paint; it's between tenants. Rosie eagerly sniffs the postage-stamp yard as if it's familiar, roams around inside, toenails clicking across the floorboards in the small, hollow, high-ceilinged rooms. This is where the phone rang when the Navy called. Six months before that, this is where I confessed to Frank I didn't believe in his Jesus anymore. This is where Frank and I tried for years to make a baby.

When the first round of infertility treatment failed five years ago, I brought Rosie home to this house. She was the cheapest German shepherd puppy I could find in the *Washington Post* classifieds, some kid's 4-H project, the only shepherd puppy I could afford. She was an early consolation prize.

Three years ago, when Frank left for Navy training and I finally accepted the fact that we weren't ever going to have children, I drove the Corvette home here, my second consolation prize, the cheapest Vette I could find. It was a late third-generation model that didn't yet interest the collectors, the one I would have bought when I was sixteen if I'd been able to afford it new—a 1978 midnight-blue coupe, white leather disco interior, small-block L82 engine with the heads bored out, four-speed manual transmission, big bad rumbling mufflers with double-barreled tailpipes.

We have all these myths in our heads about the way our lives will go, the marks we'll make on the world, the successes we'll check off, the careers and children we'll have; we imagine there's this place filled with perfect little babies and it's our job to go get one and bring it back. It was a bewildering experience to discover something I always believed in wasn't true. I felt lost, as if I'd suddenly realized I wasn't on the road I thought I was, that I was on a road not even on my map.

We leave the empty house, Rosie and I, and climb in the Vette. I strap her in, my second-choice child, inside the car of my second-choice life. We get back on the road, headed for the Rocky Mountains and beyond.

The Father He Hated

Starting date 9/22/01 . . . waxing crescent moon . . . odometer 124,535 . . . route: north through Maryland, Pennsylvania, New York, and Ontario to an extended pit stop on Papineau Lake = twelve days, 752 miles

The Vette's long, swooping nose points northwest. We may be headed for the Rockies and beyond, but it would be nice if, along the way, we could escape the real world for a while. So we head for Canada. When Oma and Opa left Germany in 1930, they emigrated to Canada first, built a life and a cottage in the north woods. We still have the cottage.

The Vette rolls through the hills of Maryland and Pennsylvania. It roars under American flags hung from overpasses. I've never seen so many American flags in my life. Until last week, the only people who flew flags were crusty old veterans. Now flags hang from starter homes and apartment balconies and dorm windows. Seeing so many flags is unsettling. I was raised to distrust patriotism, that simplistic emotion—it's too easy and too easily misused. I grew up hearing from Oma and Opa how patriotic the Nazis were, and they didn't mean it as a compliment. The Vette blows past an electronic traffic-announcement sign lit up with animated waving flags and God Bless America. It's unsettling, but it's also something else. It's exciting.

There's a part of me that wants to jump into this emotional patriotic current just like I threw myself into the emotional current of protest a decade ago. They feel the same, these currents that are so much larger than my small self. I want to tie a small flag to my American-made car's antenna and lose myself in patriotism's vague illusion of purpose. But then I glance at the rearview mirror, and beyond it on the other side of the windshield, I see the stickers centered at the top edge of the glass. Department of Defense, reads one. Camp Lejeune, NC, reads another. The color blue says "officer." My fingers trace the heart shape of the locket at my throat. I don't have to fly a flag to prove my patriotism. I've offered up my husband.

I have to take a deep breath.

Query: What am I really worried about?

Quakers believe in promoting spiritual growth by querying the Inner Teacher, a.k.a. the Light Within or That of God—what more mainstream Christians might call the Holy Spirit, what atheists would refer to as one's inner resource.

Again I ask myself, hoping my Inner Teacher/Light/Spirit/resource/Whatever will guide me toward an answer: I mean really, what am I worried about? Frank may be with the Marines, but he's a chaplain, a noncombatant. Chaplains carry no weapons, they're never armed. There are others with a lot more reason to worry: the wives of the men who lead companies into battle, the mothers of the boys who carry the guns.

In Pennsylvania, far to the west beyond the horizon, in a gentle, green field, they're sifting the torn earth for bits of plane, pieces of lives. As the Vette passes through New York State, beyond the eastern horizon in Manhattan, ground zero is still smoking. Further east, a Navy battle group moves steadily away across the Atlantic—an aircraft carrier, a fast combat support ship, destroyers, cruisers, submarines, and three amphibious assault ships carrying 2,200 members of the 26th Marine Expeditionary Unit (MEU). Frank is on one of those assault ships. When I think about the smoking wreckage that lies up and down the coast they've just left behind, I can't shake the feeling they're doing the right thing.

We cross the border. The kilometers roll by. Heading west now, we pass a truck stop flying a huge Canadian flag at half-mast. I'm disturbed to find myself longing to announce to every stranger I meet—the currency exchange lady, the gas station attendant, the kid at the fast-food drive-thru window: "Hi! Lovely weather we're having! My husband's probably on his way to Afghanistan!"

Query: Is the pressure forcing me to confront my inner loser, a socially inept braggart? Or am I just looking for someone to share the weight of this burden I'm carrying?

On a backcountry road, I pass a farmhouse with a flag fluttering from its TV antenna tower. It's an American flag, lowered to half-mast. I'm not expecting to see that out here in the middle of nowhere, in another country. I'm not expecting my throat to close up.

I ease the low-slung Corvette down the rutted, mossy two-track drive to the white clapboard cottage at the water's edge. Rosie dances ahead; I let her out at the top of the track because her tail was beating me in the face while she hung out her window yelping hysterically. The clear air is spicy with the incense of evergreen needles overhead and the carpet of fallen leaves below. The late-afternoon sun slants through the towering, open-armed pines, the curly white-paper trunks of birches, the deep green steeples of fir, the branches of maple leaves turning tangerine, cherry and lemon. The last ragamuffin wildflowers bob lavender-haired in open sunny patches between the ferns. From across the lake, *ha-ha-ha-ha-ha,* the crazy, scale-singing laughter of loons. Sunlight sparkles on the water like fairy dust.

Rosie loves this place. In all our travels, it's the only place where I've had to coax her into the car when it's time to leave. If I had kids, I imagine they'd love it as much as Rosie does, as much as I did when I was a kid. In high summer my sisters and I swooped up and down the beach with flocks of cousins and neighbors, collected strips of birch bark in the woods to write secret messages, rowed around the lake flying a pirate flag. My mother grew up coming here. I grew up coming here. I always thought a child of my own would grow up coming here, too, that I'd get to experience the delight of reliving my childhood from the height of an adult, standing and watching from the shore.

Instead I watch my dog charge out onto the beach and into the lake. I watch her take big joyous bites out of the water.

Before Frank and I married, we talked about children. We planned to have children as soon as he finished seminary. I wanted one and he wanted three. We compromised on two.

Within a year of our wedding, he changed his mind about the two we'd agreed on. He decided he didn't want any. We lived next door to an out-of-control child; he discovered the child's bad behavior made him unreasonably angry. He started noticing that same unreasonable anger in himself whenever he was within earshot of any child having a temper tantrum. He wasn't on very good terms with his father and he concluded he'd make a terrible father himself.

I figured it was a phase and the phase would pass. I could wait him out. I had other things I wanted to do with my life in the meantime. I shifted away from video production and built up a freelance writing business while he was busy with his congregations. Sometimes I'd think wistfully about starting a family, but I didn't want to risk making him feel pressured so I didn't say anything.

We moved to a leafy old rowhouse neighborhood in Washington, D.C. He took a temporary leave of absence from ministry and went back to school again, psychology this time, and I, freed for a while from being a minister's wife, opened the phone book, found the nearest Friends meeting and started slipping in now and then on Sunday mornings. More and more often I thought about a baby, but I didn't want to make Frank dig in his heels so I still didn't say anything.

My thirtieth birthday came and went. Frank's "phase" showed no sign of passing. It was 1993 and the ticking in my body had grown very loud, but I seemed to be the only one who could hear it. Frank was studying for midterms at his desk in the living room of our little one-bedroom apartment when I finally threw myself on the couch and announced we needed to talk.

"I know you didn't deliberately wait till after we were married to change your mind about wanting children. But it still feels like bait and switch."

"You also know I can't help how I feel," he said.

"But this is a fundamental life function we're talking about here. It's something I've always looked forward to experiencing. It was how I expected to give something back to the world. If you'd told me you didn't want children before we were married, I probably wouldn't have married you."

"Well thanks a lot." He shoved his chair back from his desk, an angry scrape. His voice rose. "What you're saying is a baby's more important to you than me. If I don't say yes to having kids, does that mean you're going to leave me?"

I yelled back, "After eight years? Give me a break!" This was why I hadn't pressed the issue all these years; somehow I had known it would come to this. I shook my head. "Why don't you want children?"

He launched into the usual excuses: He was back in school. We had no money. The apartment was too small. He would make a terrible, terrible father. For as long as I'd known him, Frank had always resorted to over-the-top gloom when pressured. It never meant anything except that he was feeling pressured.

"Frank," I said, "there is never going to be a good time. My father was in grad school when my parents had me. Your father was in school when you were a kid. Somehow they muddled through."

He didn't answer. He just looked out the window, sagging slowly in his chair. He looked as if something inside him was curling into a very small ball.

The minutes passed. I waited, growing restless. I straightened a stack of books. I was straightening the top of the coffee table when he said through clenched teeth, "You know my father was a minister. At church he'd act one way, and people would tell me how lucky I was to have such a nice father. He was almost never home, but when he was, he was completely different."

I had stopped straightening and was sitting very still.

"He was always mad about something. I was afraid of him. When he yelled, his voice was a physical force, loud enough to make the pots and pans ring."

The whole room had grown still, as if we were both holding our breath and peering through a crack in a door that had been locked. Frank breathed in and out through his nose. "When he spanked us, he used one of those paddles, the kind that had a rubber ball attached by an elastic string, but he pulled that off. God, I could never do anything right. If I hurt myself, like you know, tripped and scraped my knee or something, I was afraid for him to find out because it would be my fault and then I'd be in trouble or he'd make fun of me."

Frank glanced at me then, and the door closed. Beyond that narrow peek, I knew, lay a whole haunted house, but he said nothing more, except, "I don't want to do to a kid what my father did to me." He looked inside again where I couldn't see, and his fist tightened hard against the arm of his chair. "The kid would hate me."

I tried to reassure him that he was not his father, that I was sure he could never be his father, but all that did was convince him I didn't know what I was talking about and would never understand what he was feeling.

Query: How do you reconcile the irreconcilable—children scarred by parents who continue to wound them, opposites like Quakers and Marines? How do you reconcile yourself to pain, or to dreams that fortune has decided to hold within view but just out of reach?

Quakers reconcile the irreconcilable all the time. We won't take any group action on anything unless the whole group is in agreement. Not majority rule, not even consensus—complete *agreement*. If the whole meeting's not in agreement, if the sense of the meeting isn't clear, the issue is laid over for "seasoning" until the next time we meet to take up the subject. This goes on until everyone comes to clearness on the issue or, if there are a few holdouts, until they willingly come to clearness that they should stand aside and allow the meeting to move forward.

To reach clearness, we Quakers rely on two things: time and the mysterious work of the Inner Light in each person, which skeptics might also call peer pressure. Late in the seventeenth century, when American Quakers took up the issue of slavery, coming to clearness on whether to oppose it took a mere hundred years.

Unfortunately, the rest of the world doesn't always have the luxury of waiting until time and peer pressure have done their work.

My early childhood experience with the Quaker form of worship had left a groove in my soul; sitting shoulder to shoulder with like-minded people in the stillness really was like coming home. I'd sit there in the silence each Sunday, which Friends still call by the plainer name First Day, and I'd pray for Frank to have a change of heart if it was part of God's plan for our lives.

Then, after the rise of meeting, I'd dash twelve blocks to slip, panting, into a pew at the back of Frank's Lutheran church, where I was still a member. And I'd pray some more while the choir sang and the congregation recited the creed. Each week the creeds laid out what I was supposed to believe, but after spending an hour in the expectant quiet of meeting—where I had felt open to the possibility of epiphany, either from within my own heart or from someone else's spontaneously spoken message—more and more often the creeds just left me feeling closed in.

Still, I gladly skipped meeting one Sunday when the pastor was on vacation and Frank filled in. I listened to the careful, compassionate symmetry of his sermon and, as he chanted the service, to his pure tenor echoing ancient and sweet from the high, curved ceiling and

stained glass. Along with the rest of the congregation I filed to the front
for communion, watched out of the corner of my eye as he moved
down the line in his white alb and colorful, poncholike chasuble, laying a pale wafer on each person's open palm, murmuring over and over,
"The body of Christ, given for you." When he laid the wafer on my
palm, he squeezed my fingers and smiled. "The body of Christ, given
for you." Then he was on to the next. "The body of Christ . . ." Frank's
presence was the only part of the Lutheran form of worship that I
missed when I went to meeting instead.

"I'm thinking I'd like to get more involved at meeting," I said.

We were on our way across town to one of my cousins' for dinner.

"The committee I'm interested in handles family and worship
issues—marriages, family crises, clearness committees, and also anything to do with the worship service."

"You'd be good at that."

"The only thing is, since that committee handles things that are fundamental to the life of the meeting, you have to be a member to be on
it. It's not like grounds committee or something, where you can be an
attender and still do weeding."

"You're saying you want to join the meeting?"

"I'm thinking about it."

"You may have trouble maintaining membership in two churches."

"You think so?"

"Yeah."

"Oh."

After a stoplight's worth of silence, I asked, "Are you okay with that?"

"I look at it this way. The Quakers have done a lot of good in the
world. They're part of your family heritage. It makes sense for you to
join them, and God's still first in your life, so nothing's changed really."

I was about to tell him how lucky I was to have him when he added,
"Besides, deep down inside I'll always be a PK."

"A what?"

"A PK, a preacher's kid. We're troublemakers because we're always torn between devotion and rebellion. We love the familiar ritual but we hate the expectations. As much as I like the comfort of you being a Lutheran, I'm going to enjoy confounding everybody's expectations with a Quaker wife just as much." He slapped me on the thigh. "You sure got lucky the day you met me."

"If only you'd agree to a baby so easily." I said it lightly, with a laugh, so I could pretend I didn't mean it, but he knew better. His smile vanished into a thin, resentful line, and my moment of feeling lucky was over.

Later, in the kitchen before dinner, my cousin was telling me he and his wife had just found out they were—oops!—unexpectedly pregnant with number three, when he asked, "So what about you and Frank? Any plans?"

"No." Only many intense discussions that ultimately went nowhere. "He doesn't think he'd make a good father."

My cousin looked at me blankly. Then he leaned around the corner and took a good long look at what we could hear in the living room— Frank thumping around on the floor with my cousin's two little kids, laughing, "Aaah! You got me!"

In the car on the way home, we picked up where we'd left off and fought to a silent standstill. The glow of the dashboard shadowed the knot in Frank's jaw, the shine of my eyes. I was incoherent with aggrieved anger.

After a long period of nothing but engine hum, the words started slipping into place and I heard myself say, "I supported you all through seminary. When it came time for your first call, I followed you to Middle-of-nowhere, North Carolina. When you realized parish ministry wasn't for you and said you wanted to go back to school, I supported that decision, too, even though it put all the financial pressure back on me again. But I just wanted you to be happy. Do you remember how unhappy you were at the end there in the parish? Now you want to specialize in pastoral counseling, you're back in school, you're doing what you have to do to be more fulfilled, and I'm supporting you in that. And I'm glad to do it. You know why? Because I love you and I know it's important to you. But I'm just asking for the same thing. I'm just asking you to support me because even though having a baby isn't important to you, it's important to me."

After a moment he said, "It is, too, important to me. If we have a child, and it hates me, I'll have to live with that for the rest of my life."

We drove the rest of the way home in silence.

I didn't get around to officially joining the meeting, not for a while. I kept putting it off. I wasn't sure why. I joined a spiritual support group instead— two Quakers, a Catholic, and me, still the semi-Lutheran. Once a month we "spiritual friends" would get together, and each of us would have fifteen minutes to talk while the others just listened in silence; it was presumed to be a three-way communication between the speaker, the listeners, and the Inner Light. For fifteen minutes you could ramble on about anything, examining it through a spiritual lens. I spent my quarter-hours rambling on about possible strategies for overcoming Frank's resistance.

It's uncomfortable at first, talking for fifteen long minutes while three other people just look at you or stare off into space. But it's also moving, to be heard so profoundly without argument or judgment; and surprising, what you hear yourself saying as one thought leads to another, as the still, small voice of the Inner Teacher leads you, perhaps, to some new insight, or even clearness. After mulling over strategies, I found myself wondering aloud whether or not I was supposed to even try to become a mother, whether it was part of God's perfect plan, or as the Quakers would say, whether the Light's inward leading was guiding me in that direction. Was God using Frank to tell me no? Or was Frank's "no" just God's way of teaching me patience?

Unlike me, Frank doesn't need to think out loud in front of an audience. Frank is a spiritual support group of one.

One evening, when I was at the computer in the closet we'd converted into my office, he walked up, stood at my back, and said, "Well. I guess I've resigned myself to this baby thing. I wouldn't want you to leave me over it." He said it with mock woefulness. At least I think it was mock. "Since it's so important to you, you know . . ."

It had been weeks since we'd last talked about it. I'd had no idea it was on his mind, but that's how it is with Frank. The feelings are right out there in the open where you can see them, while the thinking goes on underground. With a thinker like him, it's what you can't see that matters most. I almost jumped up and hugged him, but I didn't want to spook him with any sudden moves. I stuck to my chair and just looked up at him. "Thank you," I said.

He crossed his arms. "Just now I was imagining checking under the bed for monsters for my kid, and then pretending to be dragged under."

For me, the fantasy was taking our child to the car wash, gliding through the wall of soapy water, watching the oversized pom-poms shimmy against the windows. It was clear. On motherhood, I had my marching orders from God.

While Rosie dashes along the edge of the lake, I unload the Vette. Oma and Opa built this cottage back in the forties. Inside, Opa paneled the walls with pine that has darkened with age. In the early fifties one of my uncles painted the kitchen cabinet doors with Pennsylvania Dutch–style birds and flowers and one very masculine mermaid. In the living room, upholstered bamboo chairs, circa 1968, circle the picture window that looks out across the lake. The cottage has no insulation, no central heat, no radio, and, best of all, no TV. Just plenty of mice, and on the walls, Oma's appliqués of the Holy Family; at the windows, the curtains my sisters sewed; in the bedrooms, the beds Frank built; in the living room, the fireplace where my sisters and cousins and I toasted marshmallows and huddled under towels after a nighttime skinny-dip in the freezing lake. Here, I'm surrounded by my family even when I'm alone.

There is a phone jack in the kitchen, installed in the eighties, the cottage's one concession to the outside world. I light the stove, pull out my laptop computer and plug it in. I've got mail.

> We are now on our way east. Nothing in
> sight except other ships every so often.

Frank can send me email from the ship, as long as the ship's out-dated computer system isn't overloaded. As I read, a window opens inside me. It must have been much, much harder for military families in the days before email.

> We are starting to feel the rolls of
> the ocean. It is pretty calm out
> here right now but we have been
> rolling enough that it wakes me up
> sometimes at night.

I picture him stretched out on his bunk in his so-called stateroom, which he shares with two other officers—a tiny, windowless, metal cubicle painted a color he calls puke, lined with two stacks of metal bunks the same color, metal cabinets that open into desks, and squeezed in between, a sink, metal chairs.

> Not sure exactly where we will be
> going. Got to see some of the pres-
> ident's speech the other night. Did
> you notice he specifically mentioned
> Afghanistan as the foe?

I noticed.

Afghanistan, graveyard of empires. Afghanistan, playground of Osama bin Laden, whom I picture crouched in an Afghan cave, waiting, like a spider.

I write back, a long screed about how little I trust Frank's Republican commander in chief, ranting about how the president risks dragging us all through a long, drawn-out disaster that may just get a lot of people killed, none of whom the president will know personally since they're not the heads of corporations and never likely to be . . .

"I'm sorry," I tap into the computer. "I hope I haven't bothered you going on like this." Frank hates it when I declaim as if my opinions are gospel. He's never felt much allegiance to any party. "It's just that the life of the man I love is in the hands of people I'm not sure I trust to do the right thing. It's very surreal having your husband carried off by forces larger than any of us. I feel helpless, which makes me feel a little frantic. Other than that, I'm fine."

A day later I see he's written back.

```
Your love seems to come through better
in email when I am away than when I
am around.
```

Maybe that's because it's always easier to love someone when the real person isn't around to distract you from your fantasy of who he is.

I drag the canoe into the water, strap life preservers on both Rosie and myself, and paddle out. Through the clear water, the sandy bottom passes below—in the shallows, a synchronized school of small flashing fish, the loopy sand trails of clams. Farther out, where the bottom begins to drop away into darkness, I can dimly make out the clawed hands of broken tree limbs reaching up from where the lake's currents have left them.

When I was a kid, this shadowy zone between the translucent shallows and the invisible deep was where I swam the fastest. Somewhere in the primal shiver down the back of my neck I was waiting to feel those scratchy, branchy claws close around my kicking feet. Once I could look down and see my pale, blurry legs treading over nothing, I always felt better. Better to see everything or nothing at all; I wish I either knew exactly where Frank is going, or else had no idea. It's this in-between guessing, and waiting, and trying not to imagine the worst that's the hardest. I don't have children. All I have is Frank.

My paddle leaves a string of widening circles in the dark water. Then twenty feet away, a tiny splash. A big loon breaks the surface and coasts. Rosie doesn't get up from between my feet, though her ears, her whole body, lean forward into her nose. I rest the paddle across my knees and look around for the other loon. There's always another loon. Once they choose each other, they dive and swim together, sometimes as close as a few feet, sometimes a hundred yards apart. They never look at each other; they don't need to. It's as if they're tied together by an invisible elastic string that stretches freely but always, quivering, draws them back.

The second loon pops up about fifty feet away on the other side of the canoe. Rosie's head snaps around to watch. The two loons cruise as if by magic, necks arced to hunt the water beneath them for fish. Then one by one, they're gone again. The lake's surface crinkles in a chilly breeze.

The weather turns on me, a cold, windy Canadian autumn rain.

Nights, I snuggle under the covers in that unheated cottage with my canine furnace and a little light reading: *On the Origins of War and the Preservation of Peace.* When I poke my head out from under the covers in the mornings, I can see my breath.

Days, as gray curtains of rain move in waves across the hazy lake beyond the window, Rosie and I curl up in the kitchen, near the hiss of the wood stove. I log on and surf to the CNN website, click to the *Washington Post,* the *New York Times.* They're offering crash courses in recent Central Asian history, explaining how, over the last twenty years, events on the other side of the world fell like dominoes straight toward the twin towers.

Query: Why is it that reading all these historical treatises and news articles doesn't have the same overwhelming effect on my emotions as those television images? Is it maybe because by limiting myself to printed news I can intellectualize it, keep it at arm's length, control how it affects me?

I've always read when I'm emotionally at sea. Books are my rudder— knowledge for the skeptic, enlightenment for the seeker. Whether or not real life is just a random series of events, if you take those events and turn them into a story, they take on meaning. In the shape of a book, it all makes sense.

I finish one book and start another. I now understand why September 11 happened. I understand how decades of American mistakes, some well-intended, some selfish and unjust, caused people to hate us, how our size and wealth drew envy and resentment like a magnet. It doesn't justify the violence of September 11, and intellectually I don't believe September 11 justifies more violence from us either. But in my heart, my supposedly Quaker heart, it still feel like it does.

⚍⬧⚎

We are near the top of our great circle route across the pond. We are coming up behind a low-pressure system that has some bad storms associated with it, and have been warned to prepare for rough seas tonight.

Right after Frank sends that message, the ship's email system crashes. His emails will continue to stream across the ocean to me, but mine to him will stack up behind an electronic dam. For him, tossed in the gale winds of the North Atlantic, there will be nothing but silence for nearly a week whenever he checks his mail.

> I miss hearing from you. I had a weird experience the other evening when I was falling asleep. I heard you call my name. My knowledge of what the brain does when it is slipping down into the shallowest levels of sleep should offer me some comfort, but the knowledge of you being up there in Canada all alone has made me wonder if something has happened . . . I guess I am tired and hungry for some contact. Especially since I have not heard anything from you in so many days. As I write this, I keep clicking over to my "in box" to see if anything has arrived.

I write back, even though I know he won't be able to read it, at least not till the system is fixed. I write: "I'm reading *A History of Warfare*. Have you read it? I can hardly put it down."

The next day, the ship's system is back up again.

> Tried to read *A History of Warfare* once, but the guy's writing style made it difficult to follow. Gave up on it.

Sponging up war, war, war has had two results.

I feel more knowledgeable and therefore more on top of the situation, more in control.

I am also paralyzed, unable to write, can't even journal. Query: What can I do with all this knowledge besides hope for the best? And what is the best I should hope for—what I know or what I feel? Even the queries provided by my regional Quaker organization to my local meeting, which we Friends are expected to ask ourselves regularly, aren't helping.

Query: Do you endeavor to live "in virtue of that life and power which takes away the occasion for all wars"? (No, I drive a car that increases my country's need to fight for oil. I drive it a lot.)

Query: Do you weigh your day-to-day activities for their effect on peacekeeping, conflict resolution, and the elimination of violence? (No, I just drive my car a lot and worry.)

Query: Are you working toward eliminating aggression at all levels, from the personal to the international? (No, I just drive my car a lot, and worry. Well, I don't fight with my husband as much as I used to.)

The rain has stopped. Snow flurries are on the way, which reminds me that winter comes early in the mountains and I need to get across the plains and over the Rockies before the first snows hit. I'm outside the cottage in the predawn, a wash of stars and half-seen clouds overhead, shadowy autumn leaves drifting down around me in the breeze as I drag the cover off the Vette. It gleams at me in the moonlight in all its curvaceous, bodacious, wasp-waisted glory. Let's go, it purrs. I load it up, then look around for Rosie.

She's watching me from the beach. As I approach her, she lies down and looks out at the water. I lower myself beside her.

The moon has set. The lake is calm; the flat stillness mirrors the hills tipped in gold from the rising sun, the black outline of trees on the stony point at the end of the beach, the pink and purple clouds. Mist rises off the water and the pair of loons call to each other, long and soulful. Some people think it's a lonely sound. To me it's the sound of companionship. I can see them out there in the early light, those two dark specks separated by a broad expanse of water.

Rosie doesn't move until I get in the car and crank up the engine. Then she trudges up from the beach and slowly, one paw at a time, climbs in. She turns around once in the tight space and bumps me hard with her nose before dropping onto her side. As we jounce our way up the track to the washboard road, she rests her muzzle on the dash with a sigh. We crunch slowly up the dirt road to a paved one, then out to the highway, accelerating southwest through the candy-colored forests of a northern autumn, back to the real world, back on our way across the continent.

```
Don't forget to send me the jockstraps
I forgot, whenever you return home.
Also, I mentioned that you were trav-
eling about in the early part of
deployment. Chain of command is asking
that you provide the battalion's volun-
teer coordinator with your locations.
```

This is because if something bad happens to him, the military has a policy of only delivering that kind of news in person. I've called the coordinator and given her my cell phone number. If they ever need to, now they can call me and tell me to stay put until someone can get to me. I picture myself answering my phone on some long empty highway across the prairie, pulling over and waiting there with the wind blowing till a distant speck slowly, slowly grows larger, and closer, a speck growing into a car that grows into a nondescript sedan that grows into an official government vehicle that slows and finally stops.

I imagine the sound of wind blowing. That is a lonely sound.

The Illusion of Control

Starting date 10/4/01 . . . waning gibbous moon . . . odometer 125,287 . . . route: west through Ontario, Michigan, Indiana, and Illinois to a pit stop in Chicago, then on west through Illinois, Wisconsin, and Iowa = five days, 1345 miles

My plan is to drive the Vette as far as the Canadian side of the border. My plan is to spend the night. In the morning, my plan is to cross the border and go on to my cousin's place in Chicago. My plan, all plans, they shimmer with the hopeful, reassuring symmetry of thin blue lines on fragile rolls of architectural paper.

I like to make plans and unfurl them into the future. Not nitty-gritty detailed plans, which just make me gasp for air, but big-picture plans, like the plan Frank and I made once we decided to start a family. We'd move out of our one-bedroom apartment into a place with two bedrooms. A nice, big-picture plan. Such plans give me a feeling of accomplishment. So I drive to the border. We spend the night. Now on to Chicago.

We cross the border north of Detroit, leave behind endlessly cool, homogenized Canada and hurl ourselves back down into the messy holler of America, the plan rolling us smoothly down to Detroit, Motor City, Motown USA. The Vette roars past whole armies of union-made cars massed around assembly plant fortresses and windowless malls like temple mounts. Above the engine's din, Aretha Franklin's on the radio singing about respect as we flash from brilliant sunlight to shadowed underpasses seething with graffiti, grubby row-houses sprouting antennae that give way to mowed suburban acres hooked to underground cables. These, in turn, give way to rolling green fields and yellow-tinged forests and frame farmhouses with satellite dishes pointed at the air, where on the radio, a panel discussion between a priest, a rabbi, and an imam calls for tolerance and understanding, and a press conference live from the Justice Department claims that in this time of crisis we Americans must be willing to give up our rights in order to defend them.

The search for certainty in an uncertain world. Voices crackling through the static, wafting like smoke across the continent. A DJ rants, "Nuke those camel jockeys!" a news report declares the curious have made the Koran the most requested book in America, and a preacher prophesies the inevitability of the coming apocalypse and the certainty of spiritual warfare between the sons of Isaac and the sons of Ishmael. A retired general speculates on the likelihood that American planes will soon start dropping bombs on Afghanistan. A rabbit goes still when it senses danger; I go still inside.

You can't bring a country like Afghanistan to its knees by bombing transportation corridors and power grids it doesn't have. If bombs start falling, it will be for one purpose—to soften up any opposition before sending in the Marines. Frank is the combat chaplain for the 26th MEU's Marine Battalion Landing Team.

My plan is to go to my cousin's place in Chicago. My plan is to go to Chicago. My plan, my plan. Organize, synchronize, rationalize, and actualize the things I can control. I turn off the radio, watch my travel plan unfold as predictably as the well-mapped highways I'm following: Michigan giving way to Indiana, rolling green giving way to old, gray industrial workhorses, rusting, hard-working plants that hunker along Lake Michigan's southern shore. The closer we get to Chicago, the more cars join us on the highway, humming alongside clanging kluges of corrugated sheds and covered conveyors wrapped in grimy tangles of muscular piping, smokestacks that belch steam at the sky.

Rounding the lake, wind buffets the Vette with muffled nudges. This crisp autumn wind has swept the sky clean, rushing three hundred miles down the length of Lake Michigan, driving before it swirls of puff-chested sailboats like white confetti. The wind sweeps across the aquamarine vastness with nothing to stop it till it breaks like an invisible wave around the skyscraping ridgeline that is Chicago—the quarter-mile-high Sears Tower, the hundred-story Hancock building. The skyscrapers set their shoulders against this wind that can sink ships and uproot trees and even carve rock, but can do no more to these giants than sway them a few inches, glass and aluminum and steel and concrete and thousands of human beings looming sun-washed and exposed high above the rest of the Windy City, immense, immovable, and, since September 11, looking as if they have great big bull's-eyes painted on their sides.

My cousin Mary's apartment is one of three stacked on top of each other, a three-flat squeezed between tidy old houses in a neighborhood of American flags and new immigrants. A Korean family lives on one side, Lebanese on the other, Mary's mother in the flat overhead, and her brother in the flat below. In Mary's flat, *Sesame Street* is on the television, her two-year-old daughter, Hanna, is pushing a tricycle up and down the hall, two fat cats are looking for places to hide, and standing solid and stubborn in the middle of it all is a big, tough Akita-mix named Sweeny. He and Rosie check out each other's tail ends.

When dogs meet for the first time, it's not unusual for one to try to hump the other. Who winds up the humper and who the humpee has nothing to do with gender and everything to do with who's in charge. Dogs do this because, like people, most are happiest when the outlines of their lives are clearly defined.

The world according to Sweeny is simple and clear: He is a humper, the rest of creation, humpees. His body language says this with such black-and-white conviction that most other dogs believe it must be true. One look at him and they consider themselves humped. Rosie, on the other hand, lives in a grayer, more flexible world. She's a middle-of-the-pack dog. She has no interest in being the alpha, but I've never seen her roll over like a submissive omega either. She gives Sweeny no reason to hump, no reason to question his faith in himself. She ducks her head and gives him coy sideways glances—hey, big boy—when he's looking, and chews up his toys when he's not.

I am pleased to consider myself more like Rosie than Sweeny. She and I have achieved an advanced state, really, far superior to all those people on the radio looking for certainty.

In Mary's living room, I plug in and check my email.

> This past week it sank in that on this trip you will be going from one person you know to another. That gave me some peace of mind. But I am still a little wary when I think about the possibility of your old car giving you trouble. Please be careful. And please be sure not to let Rosie get into any dangerous situations on the trip. It would sicken me to get a message from you telling me she had been hurt or killed.

He's looking for certainty, too.

A cousin has forwarded an email announcing a march to protest America's rush toward another preventable war. I know from my reading that the recent attack and coming war were and are just as preventable as the conflict I protested ten years ago. But at the thought of protesting now, with a black gash in the side of the Pentagon and lower Manhattan still covered in the dust of thousands of people, I hang back.

Another cousin has forwarded an email petition. I have a lot of cousins. I read the petition, pacifists rhapsodizing about what an amazing message it would send to the world if America were to respond to September 11 with gifts of food and clothing instead of bombs. This time I don't just hang back inside—I roll my eyes.

I catch myself. Why did I roll my eyes? This is what I believe, isn't it? That the only way to stop violence is simply to stop it? There are certainly millions of people in Afghanistan who had nothing to do with September 11, people who need food and clothing and a whole lot more help dropped on them, not bombs. If we bomb that country, bombs will inevitably go astray. Innocent people will die. Before he left, Frank said, "What we need is a Marshall Plan for the Third World," and I nodded my head like a dashboard dog. If we were to do for Afghanistan what we did for Germany after World War II, we'd go a long way toward preventing another war involving the Afghans.

But the starving people of Afghanistan aren't the ones who caused those planes to fly into the twin towers and the Pentagon and a field in Pennsylvania. What do you do about those people, who are hiding among the starving? When I imagine the kind of people who could dream up a plan to wipe out three thousand innocent lives, and the Taliban government of Afghanistan that's protecting them, dropping food and clothing anywhere near such people seems not just naive. It seems foolish.

My aunt says, "You look like you need a glass of wine," and hands me one.

My cousin Mary picks up the book I just unpacked, *Acts of War: The Behavior of Men in Battle,* cheerfully tosses it aside and says, "What you need is a little romance."

Mary is a lapsed Lutheran, a six-foot brunette in her mid-thirties with perfect bone structure—a registered nurse with a specialty in critical care, a single mother who went all the way to China to find her tiny daughter, and the proud owner of the biggest collection of paperback romance novels I've ever seen. They fill the better part of one entire wall in her bedroom. She tells me to take as many as I want. "Just send them back when you're done."

"What do you want them for?"

"I reread them."

"You're kidding."

"You wait long enough, it's like reading a new book. The embarrassing part is that sometimes I don't realize I've already read it till I'm almost to the end. There are only so many ways to tell the same story. But they're great stress relievers."

I ditch the heavy academic treatises on war and select a dozen romances. The embarrassing part is, I select them carefully. As if it makes a difference.

I'm curled up on the couch with a paperback romance in one hand, the head of a wet, stinking, stuffed toy bird in the other. Stinky Pheasant is Rosie's favorite toy, lovingly licked and chewed to a rich ripeness, to the point that even I could sniff it out if it were hidden. Stinky's head is in my hand because Rosie shoved it there. Its tail is clamped between her teeth. She squeaks it at me in lieu of words, saying, *"Whee-ee, whee-ee."* Over the edge of my book I see her tail, a slow, hopeful wag. I wiggle Stinky's head. The tail wags faster. *Whee-ee.*

Sweeny is following Mary around the apartment as she picks up toys and wipes down the highchair; he's cleaning up the crumbs. Three evenings a week Mary hands off the baby monitor to her mother and works the twelve-hour overnight shift, then at dawn drives her minivan home from the hospital with dance club music blasting to keep herself awake behind the wheel. She's there when her daughter wakes up, sees her off to the sitter, sleeps a few hours, and is there again when her daughter returns home in the middle of the afternoon. Mary's commitment and self-sacrifice seem Jesus-like to me. She knows why she goes to work on the days she works, and why she stays home on the days she doesn't. Children are a ready-made way to fill your life with certainty and purpose. Raise a happy, compassionate child, fulfill your potential for divine creativity, and leave the world a slightly better place.

I haven't quite figured out yet how I'm going to do that without the requisite child. So far I've bought a puppy and a car. I can see where the dog has some possibilities for divine virtue, but the Vette gets fifteen selfish miles to the gallon, though on a good day, going downhill with a tail wind, it can get as many as sixteen.

War, too, can fill you with certainty and purpose, even if all you do is wave the flag to support it or march at a demonstration to oppose it, the way I did on the eve of the Gulf War in 1991. But on the eve of this war in Afghanistan, the only thing I'm filled with is aimless uncertainty. I feel as if I'm in the Vette at night with no headlights and I can just barely see the road to find my way. I feel as if I'm driving by moonlight.

Rosie sighs through Stinky's tail. I reinvigorate my absent-minded end of our game of tug. I'm a little distracted by the plot of the book I'm reading, which goes like this: A brilliant and single scientist wants a baby, but she doesn't want her progeny to have the same miserable childhood she had growing up as a genius freak. So she conspires to get herself pregnant by the stupidest man she can find, an NFL quarterback who, under that dumb-lug exterior, is unfortunately one smart cookie.

I roll my eyes at this, too. Please. I would have been happy with any baby, even a genius freak baby. Except that's not true. I could have adopted like Mary. But I didn't.

In the darkened bedroom next to Mary's, I look down at her daughter. Hanna is sprawled on her back, her cover kicked off, as fearless asleep as she is awake. Her first word was a command, "Sit!" She still says it before handing you her Elmo book to read aloud.

Rosie clicks in behind me, checking to see what could possibly be more interesting than Stinky Pheasant, who's been left on the living room floor. Mary follows Rosie in with an armload of laundry to pack away.

I whisper, "So why didn't you just seduce an NFL quarterback?"

She whispers back, "Actually, I originally thought about going to a sperm bank."

"Why didn't you?"

"Well, you know, there are enough children without fathers. I didn't want to be responsible for bringing another one into the world. Being the child of a single parent isn't exactly ideal." She's silent in the darkness. Rosie clicks out of the room. Mary adds, "But it's better than having no parents."

Mary chose to adopt a child who otherwise would have had nobody. She spent years finding the money and putting the necessary plans in place to transform an unknown mother's sadness into this joy. I wasn't even that altruistic with my dog. I didn't go rescue an abandoned older animal from the pound. I bought a puppy from a wannabe breeder.

Rosie clicks back into the room. I feel the wet head of a stuffed bird bump against my hand.

Before reading myself to sleep, I check my email again.

```
Morale seems good on the ship. This
morning, Marines were crowing like
roosters when reveille sounded over
the ship's PA system.
```

Their average age is about nineteen. They're kids. Frank's kids, all twelve hundred of them, on three different ships. Pretty ironic for a man who didn't want children—or maybe these are the children he really wanted. But back in 1994, for my sake, he agreed to try to conceive a child with me.

I went off the Pill. My ovaries groaned back to life. We bought a house, nine hundred miniature square feet in a marginal Capitol Hill neighborhood. It had three things going for it: a cheap price and two bedrooms.

I laid plans to conceive in September and give birth in June. That way I wouldn't be so large over the winter months that I'd have to invest in an expensive cold-weather maternity wardrobe that I would never use again. I also wouldn't be pregnant at all over the summer months, when it would be too hot to wear the heavy-duty support hose I planned to wear to prevent varicose veins from popping out all over my legs. Additionally, by June, spring semester would be well over. With no time pressures and no finals, Frank could spend a stress-free summer bonding with his new offspring.

I swore off alcohol. I gave up chocolate. I munched on raw carrots, but not too many—excessive vitamin A can have a detrimental effect on a developing embryo. I meditated, popped folic acid, drank fruit juice, ate garbanzo beans. With natural childbirth my goal, I took up power walking, huffed through abdominal crunches. I calculated our budget, decided on an education track—public school to start, maybe a private Quaker high school, college—and figured out how much money to save each year. There it was, neatly planned out, unfurling into the future, as good as done.

Back then, I still believed. I believed if you set a goal for yourself, if you mapped out the route to reach that goal, if you were resourceful, if you worked hard, if you trusted God, if you wanted it badly enough, eventually you'd get there. Then as now I believed you reap what you sow. But as September 11 proved, you don't always realize what you're sowing.

I'm walking the dogs. Sweeny struts ahead, Rosie prances behind. The part of my day spent walking a dog used to bore me, but over the years it's become a relief. This is Rosie's gift to me, like the silent meeting for worship on First Day mornings, the only other part of my life that's not about producing something, crossing something off a list, getting from point A to point B.

Overhead, sunlight flares through the trees that line the street. A silvery plane passes through the blue open space between the branches, on its way to O'Hare. A nearby playground sends up childish shouts, the metallic squeal of a swing's chain. There are children everywhere, so many children. How many of them were planned? Mary's daughter was originally an accident. I was an accident, conceived on my parents' honeymoon. My youngest sister, Erin, was an accident, too, conceived in spite of an IUD. Only Ingrid, my middle sister, was planned, and when she and her husband started thinking about children, she wound up pregnant a couple months before they'd planned to start trying. Given all the unplanned babies in my family, it never occurred to me I'd have trouble conceiving a baby I'd actually made plans for. I figured all Frank and I had to do was raise our eyebrows at each other and, *boom*, I'd be knitting booties and craving grotesque food combinations.

The first month, I announced, "I've entered my fertile period!"

"What does that mean?" Frank sounded suspicious.

"It means we should have sex every other day for the next week, starting right now."

This did not inspire him. During that week we didn't have sex once. I learned to be a little more subtle. For a long time after that, Frank had no idea where I was in my cycle. But I knew. My reactivated body reminded me daily. Without any guidance from me, my body waxed and waned as predictably as the moon, mucous slickening, ovaries twinging, breasts swelling, lining of the uterus thickening with a soft, clotted bed of blood before melting out of my body unused and starting all over again, slickening, twinging, swelling, thickening, melting.

Eventually, though, Frank learned to recognize when my body was beginning to melt. One month he found me sitting on the toilet, biting my lip. Another lunar cycle and he came upon me in my great-great grandmother's rocking chair, staring out the window, my hands on my stomach. Cycle again and I was in the shower, the water running red around my feet before circling down the drain, my face turned up into the spray so that if you didn't know me, if you weren't Frank, you wouldn't have seen the tears.

All across the universe uncountable numbers of spinning galaxies raced toward their destinies. Within each galaxy, planets swept their way around stars, moons ticked through their orbits around planets, a woman woke up each sunrise and before getting out of bed placed a thermometer under her tongue and charted the minuscule rise and fall that proved her body's clockwork exertions.

If God could explode the universe in all its complexity, set the galaxies spinning, time the whirl of stars and planets and moons and the cycle of ovaries, surely such a God left nothing to chance. In a universe created by such a God everything must happen for a reason; God must have had a plan. I just had to figure out what it was. Maybe God's plan didn't include my getting pregnant; maybe this road was a hopeless dead end. But if that were true, why had God given me such a strong desire for a baby? Why didn't I *feel* hopeless?

I decided to stick to the road I had chosen, as planned, at least until I could clearly see where it was taking me. So I bought that basal temperature thermometer and began to plot the optimum morning, afternoon, or evening to begin having sex. It became impossible even to pretend the sex was spontaneous. It became a job. Frank would glance over my shoulder as I made my scientific measurements and learned to spot the upswing of the do-it-now temperature spike.

"Let's get it over with," he'd say.

Once, I said, "A little more enthusiasm would be appreciated."

"I'm not the one who wants kids. I'm just doing this for you."

I knew that of course; I'd realized it long before. But instead of filling me with appreciation for his efforts on my behalf, hearing him say it out loud left me feeling lonely and sorry for myself. "What happened to wanting to play monster games with a child of your own?"

"Did I say that?"

"Yeah, you did."

He assumed the position. "Well, that's not how I feel most of the time. I'm sorry."

We did what we had to do, as erotic as the coupling of two dogs. And I mourned the lover I had lost somewhere along the way.

After sex I would hug my knees to my chest, he'd wedge a pillow under my hips, and there I would lie, curled on my back like an egg. I'd visualize his sperm bumping into my ovum. I could see it dividing. "Thank you, God," I'd whisper.

And still, no matter how diligently I measured, plotted, and planned, no matter how much I prayed, still, each month I melted.

Sweeny and Rosie lead me back to the three-flat. I may not be able to plan my whole life's journey, but I can at least plan a six-week road trip. Another day in Chicago before moving on to my relatives' farm in Iowa, then to the South Dakota Badlands and Yellowstone National Park, then over the Rockies, across Idaho, and on to the Pacific coast, then back the other way. The reassuring lines of it shimmer before my eyes.

When the dogs and I burst into Mary's apartment, Big Bird is no longer on the television. He's been replaced by the president. Bombs have started to fall on Afghanistan. My first thought is of Frank, waiting on a ship. My second thought is of the people who brought down the twin towers: That'll show them. Quickly, I turn my thoughts back to Frank.

Frank is in the middle of the Mediterranean, in the middle of a worship service, when the word comes over the ship's PA system that the Air Force is bombing Afghanistan. He continues with the service.

```
One of the guys asked me if he was
becoming nuts or morbid. He wanted
to leave a letter to his loved ones
```

with someone who would mail it home
for him in the event he is killed
before he returns. I assured him
there was nothing wrong with his
concerns and told him similar ideas
had led to the invention of the dog
tag. He asked me if I would hold the
letter and I said I would, but also
asked what would happen if I were
killed. We decided I should hold any
letters in my safe here on the ship
with a note from me saying that if
I am killed, only the letters of
others who had also been killed
should be sent home.

There was a combat chaplain in Vietnam who crawled out under fire to get to the wounded and dying. If the injured Marine was lying on his back, the chaplain raised himself up on his elbows to speak or pray with him or to give him first aid. Other Marines yelled to him to get down, that he was making himself a target. But maybe the way he saw it, he had to look those boys in the eyes and make sure they saw the love of God. His Marines loved him; they knew he loved them, would do anything, give anything for them. He received the Congressional Medal of Honor for his love. Posthumously.

I'm curled up on Mary's couch with Rosie and the scientist and the quarterback. I can't seem to put this silly romance down, though I know I will learn nothing new. My fingers mindlessly rub the heart-shaped locket around my neck like a lucky rabbit's foot. I know exactly how this story, how all these stories, will progress and how they will end. I know the heroines will always be shorter than the heroes. I know the lovers will never fail to contrive—and the more contrived the better—to give in to temptation by page thirty, with more amazing sex occurring every fifty or so pages after that. I know they will suffer from childhood traumas, financial reversals, social slights, and shipwrecks. But most of all, I know no matter how extreme the suffering of the foregoing pages, they will always, *always,* arrive at a happy ending.

I wedge my thumbnail into the locket, pop it open, close it. *Click.* I take a cue from the paperback romances. *Click.* I remind myself that despite the bombing it's still entirely possible Frank could spend the entire deployment waiting on the ship. *Click.* He may never go ashore at all. *Click. Click. Click . . .*

The next day, as planned, Rosie and I are back on the road, now with a dozen paperbacks added to the Vette's load. I wanted to get an early start, get out of Illinois, up through the southeast corner of Wisconsin, and then across Iowa by late afternoon. So we're leaving during morning rush hour, which is why we've been leaving for over two hours now and still aren't out of Chicago. I'm shifting in my seat with frustration, but Rosie likes going slow. It gives her time to hang out the window and eyeball the drivers in the other cars, speculate on whether she can scare the pee out of them, and bark.

When we finally leave rush hour behind, I lose more time by taking a wrong turn, heading south when I should head north. We're a few hours behind schedule by the time we reach Prairie du Chien, Wisconsin, and cross over a narrow, unassuming river. I hardly notice it between the bluffs. Ten miles later I look at the map and realize we're in Iowa now, and that was the not-very-mighty Mississippi. Like most celebrities, it seemed much smaller in person.

In Iowa we hit road construction, creeping detours that lead to washboard roads, lumbering tractors, elderly caravans of Airstream trailers. The endless day leaves Rosie plenty of time to zone out. It leaves me plenty of time to brood. I brood about the ship Frank's on, engines thrumming east through the waves. I brood about the leaders I don't trust to do the right thing and the boys who may die for nothing if those leaders do the wrong thing—if, for example, they choose the easy way out, bomb the hell out of Afghanistan, send in the Marines to kick some butt, fight a shortsighted war, then walk away without fixing the poverty, desperation, and First World exploitation that led to this mess in the first place, so that we just have to go back in someday and do it all over again. I brood about my own mistakes, how they've combined with circumstances beyond my control to undo my travel plan for the day, a longish but easy drive transformed into a grueling marathon. I realize I'm not as flexible as I like to think I am. I don't care. I am still determined: We will make the northwest corner of Iowa tonight.

Flexible. Ha! Who am I kidding? I'm no different from those people on the radio searching for some little bit of reassuring certainty to cling to. The Quakers' moral certainty is what drew me back to them in the end, their commitment to make the world a better place. I was smugly proud of my Quaker heritage; it was easy and comfortable to share their certainty that all war is wrong. At least it was when my principles weren't actually put to the test.

The sun has set while I've been brooding. A pale dirt road rolls out of the dark into the headlights, flat and straight and gray. In the rearview mirror, dust billows red in the taillights. In the black fields on either side, tractors harvest soybeans with their floodlights on, industrious little islands of light inching through the night. Watching them is like watching a candle. Watching them, I'm suddenly living in this moment of the road's white noise and no other. I'm not where I was and I'm not where I'm going. I'm not dwelling on the past, I'm not fretting about the future. I'm just here, Zen-like as the dog. When I hit a bump ten seconds later, it's like waking from a flying dream.

FRIENDLY WAYS

Starting date 10/9/01 . . . last quarter moon . . . pit stop at my family's farm in northwest Iowa = one day

etween 1994 and 1996, my world swelled with babies; everyone was giving birth, it seemed: my sister, my coworkers, my
coworkers' wives, my other sister, my best friends, my best
friends' wives, my neighbors, my cousins. Meanwhile, a bewildered
voice inside echoed in the emptiness: What about me?

The second year of trying to get pregnant wore on. With every passing month I needed more and more consoling when my period came.
I began to cheer myself up by listing all the things I couldn't do if I were
pregnant. Toxic, hazardous things.

Things I Couldn't Do If I Were Pregnant
drink beer
drink wine
drink scotch
eat chocolate
paint walls
strip furniture
spray insecticides on shrubs
shimmy into crawl spaces
haul armloads of bricks
go bungee jumping

I never actually did go bungee jumping. But it was heartening to think I *could* go bungee jumping, as inside me the voice grew shrill, a hyper little dog at the window frantically trying to dig through the glass and yapping, Yoo hoo! God! Where are you? Where's the Light? In case you hadn't noticed, I'm down here dutifully having sex on a schedule *and nothing's happening!* I'm in the dark! What do you want me to do about this? What do you want me to do?

All that helpless, frustrated energy spurted out into my freelance work and gushed into our old house. This is how it came to pass that, in the midst of trying to have a baby, we gutted our one and only bathroom.

It was a perfectly functional bathroom, but a prior owner had subjected it to an unfortunate makeover back in the era of polyester bell-bottoms. That owner had moved on, but the bathroom remained trapped in time with its single groovy but dim light globe, black floor tile, black sink in a dark brown cabinet, and a wall between the sink and the toilet, which all together managed to make a forty-square-foot bathroom look like four square feet.

The black floor tiles were a little loose, so one day, too distracted by my lack of a baby to do anything at my desk but spin my wheels, I pried one up. It was so easy I pried up another tile, and then another and another, thinking how lovely it was to finally gain some traction on *something*.

"What are you doing?" Frank asked when he came home from school.

"We've been talking about renovating the bathroom since we moved in."

He looked a little stunned. "But we have no money."

"Yeah, but after class you have time." He was between after-school jobs at the moment.

He protested he didn't know how to renovate a bathroom, but I respected his know-how. He was one of those self-taught, innately handy guys whose favorite bathroom reading is *Fundamentals of Electricity,* although "electricity," as he pointed out while reluctantly measuring the bathroom, "is not plumbing." Still, most of the floor tiles were gone and I was gazing up at him from the bathroom floor with an expectant look on my face.

Realizing he had no choice, Frank joined me in cautiously prying up the last of the tiles. With increasing confidence we dismantled the sink cabinet, then gleefully sledgehammered the nondescript thirty-year-old bathtub into easy-to-carry-out pieces. We ripped out the drywall, discovered the old lath-and-plaster wall behind it and ripped that out, too. We staggered into the back yard with armloads of debris, followed by billowing clouds of drywall and plaster dust.

The empowerment of destruction! All my life I'd been told, Be gentle, don't break, handle with care. Wantonly wrecking part of my house, I felt like a biker chick, rebellious and free. After two years of trying to have a baby on our own, I finally realized what the Light was leading me toward: I needed to break out of passively waiting, month in and month out; I needed to take charge of the situation, take some serious action. Medical action. I was determined not to wind up like the guy in the joke who finds himself trapped by a flood and, as the waters rise, keeps turning down offers of rescue, first from a passing SUV, then a boat, even a helicopter, each time saying, "Oh no, I'm trusting God to save me," until he finally drowns. When he gets to heaven, he demands to know why God didn't save him, and God says, "What are you talking about? I sent you an SUV, a boat, and a helicopter!"

So as we paged through home décor magazines looking for the ideal bathroom design to transplant into our little house, I said, "Frank, I don't know how to bring this up, but I've read that if you haven't gotten pregnant in a year, you officially qualify as infertile."

Two years of failure had left Frank looking like a man who had dodged a bullet. "Well, we tried," he said cheerfully. He gestured dismissively at the magazines. "I don't think any of these bathrooms are going to work."

The bathrooms we were flipping past were all the size of our entire upstairs—Taj Mahals with toilets. Any one of them would turn our house into a no bedroom, one bath. "Actually," I said, "all we've tried is a basal temperature thermometer. We should probably talk to a doctor. It might be something simple."

He raised his hands. Now he looked like I'd just pulled a gun on him. "I don't want some stranger poking around my private life."

"But I need some answers, and only a doctor can give them to me."

"Maybe God's giving you your answer."

"I might agree with you if God hadn't also given us doctors."

"Why can't you accept that this is a sign we aren't meant to have children?"

"How do you know it's a sign and not a lesson in patience and persistence?"

"I don't have a good feeling about this."

"That's not good enough for me. I need proof."

"I'm telling you, this is going to end in disaster."

Frank and his under-pressure gloom. I rolled my eyes. "That's a real supportive thing to say," I muttered and backed off for a while.

This went on for days, back and forth, in and out of the tile show room, the fixture store, the salvage warehouse full of old sinks and tubs. He did not want to talk to a doctor, didn't want to be tested, didn't want anything to do with it. I didn't want to go on living with the uncertainty, couldn't take it, had to know.

"Look," Frank said, "if we go to a doctor, we're going to keep on trying and that just prolongs the uncertainty. If you want certainty, you should decide to stop."

"I can't just *decide* to be certain. I have to feel it."

On it went, through the lighting displays, the plumbing aisle, and back in the bathroom itself as Frank continued to gut it each day after class, growling, "All this waiting and wondering if we're going to have a baby is wearing me out. You like rearranging the furniture. I don't."

"Change is healthy, it's energizing."

"It sucks me dry." He was stomping on slats of wall lathing, breaking each lath into more manageable pieces. "I've still got a couple years of school left, and I don't even know if I'll be able to find a job at the end of it."

"Of course you will. You're good at what you do."

He looked at me sadly. "Your optimistic nature is very much a part of who you are, and I love who you are, but it means you're not always realistic." He stomped a slat in two. "I'm not even sure I'm going to be able to put this bathroom back together." He stomped again. "I'm afraid of what happens the first time the baby won't stop crying and I lose it."

"Everybody says it's different when it's your own baby."

He burst out, "Why can't you just respect my feelings?" and stomped a slat, and a nail sticking out of it drove straight up through his boot into his heel bone.

We escaped the blood-splattered demolition zone for a brief respite in a comfortable dust-free walk-in clinic. I kept my eyes on my knees. Why *couldn't* I just respect how he felt? "You know how it is in my family." My voice was so low I could barely hear myself. "We all want the best for each other—we want the one with the greatest need to win. But the only way to figure out whose need is greatest is to see who pushes hardest. Of course, with my sisters, the neediest one doesn't usually have to push so hard before the other two get it."

He was quiet so long I thought maybe he hadn't heard me, or had decided to ignore me, until he said in a weary voice, "I do want the best for you." He winced as he shifted his throbbing foot. "Well, I guess I have no choice."

I wanted to nod. But I didn't.

"I will not go to extremes on this. No heroic measures."

Now I did nod, and he squeezed my shoulder. I took his hand. "I don't want to go to extremes either, Frank. I don't want to spend obscene amounts of money that could be better spent on starving children in Africa or something."

I promised him then—no heroic measures. I told myself that once I knew the facts I would be able to make a rational decision. If we found out we couldn't have children, it would clearly be God's plan and I would let go of this desire for a baby. Life would go on; I would find other ways to fulfill myself and give back to the world.

After his tetanus shot, we pitched the glossy magazines, came up with our own bathroom design, ordered our do-it-yourself tile and fixtures, and charged it all to our credit card.

The sun has set and the waning moon hasn't risen yet. From out of the darkness the Vette's headlights sweep off the graded dirt road past a painted cartoon pig that points the way down a gravel drive filled with pickups and boxy sedans, and, beyond them, a low-slung ranch-style house. I kill the lights and the engine. Against the blackness of the countryside the windows glow with the promise of warm food and recliners and a round of hugs. I let Rosie out to sniff around.

The front door opens, spilling a golden carpet of light down the front walk. "Kristin? Is that you?" calls my aunt.

My uncle's right behind her. "By Joe, I believe we could hear that car coming from three counties away. Come in! Bet you're hungry!"

Inside, a dozen of their fellow retired farmers are gathered around the extended dining room table, playing board games and drinking coffee. While they get back to their games and I pile a plate with potluck leftovers and Rosie sniffs around the work boots at the back door, Frank and the rest of the 26th MEU prepare to leave their ships for ten days of military exercises in the Egyptian desert. There's word they face a possible terrorist threat. None of this is public knowledge; I'm not allowed to talk about it. Surrounded by people who've commiserated with my family in tough times for sixty years and more, I stuff my worries into a cold, unspoken lump in my chest that sometimes makes it hard to breathe.

Members of the Iowa half of my family were willing to go to prison rather than do what Frank is doing. They were Quakers, pacifists, even a

Methodist who married into the family and became a convinced Friend. Their parents and grandparents came to this country mostly during the late nineteenth century, mostly to escape poverty and the draft in Scotland, Norway, and Denmark. During America's wars they declined to participate.

They were not wispy intellectual idealists. Most were farmers, solid practical men who fixed tractors, milked cows, slaughtered pigs, and drew a line between right and wrong in the rich black earth they plowed, a line they would not cross—war was wrong, all war was wrong, and they would not take part in it. So when the U.S. Army called, they stood up and said they wouldn't fight. Some wound up serving in other ways. Some wound up in prison. The wars, and the harvests, went on without them.

The corn harvest was over weeks ago. The cobless stalks have been left standing in the fields that surround my aunt and uncle's house, the long, broad leaves dry and brown, rattle-flapping in the constant wind, tens of thousands of stalks raising up a hissing roar. The Greek word for wind is "*pneuma*." The same word means breath. It also means spirit. Sculptor of stone, shaper of landscapes. Wind, the breath of God.

It's early morning and I'm lying under a quilt in a tall wooden bed in the basement, listening to the stalks through the open window. I shift and Rosie gets up from her dog bed by the dresser. She puts on her performing-seal persona—ears slicked back, body wriggling, tail wagging— so she can tell me what a blue-bird-singing morning it is now that I'm awake. I scratch her back and listen to the wind, scratch the sweet spot just at the top of her tail. She humps her spine and half-closes her eyes, and outside, the wind never stops. Across the vast open prairie between Chicago's towers and the Rocky Mountains, there's nothing to stop it.

Between the initial primal urge to procreate and the final goal of a baby in my arms, there was no obvious place to stop either. In my quest for a baby, I kept watching for a clear line where, once crossed, I could stop and, even though I hadn't reached my goal, say, This is far enough. After two years, with the monthly failures piling up, with the ultimate goal beginning to look smaller and bluer and more distant on the horizon, the best I could do was squint into the future and draw an arbitrary line somewhere out ahead.

That's what I was doing when I promised Frank that even though I wanted a baby, in fact inexplicably needed one more with each passing month, I wouldn't insist on taking any heroic measures.

The trouble with drawing an arbitrary line is, when you reach it, it's hard to find a reason to stop if you still feel the breath of God at your back.

Upstairs Aunt Beth has breakfast on. She's my father's sister, the eldest, like me. We both grew up in charge, which means we're in the habit of telling people what to do while putting those people's needs ahead of our own. It has made us excellent, if slightly bossy, caretakers. We're both named for my great-grandmother Lora: Lora Beth and Kristin Lora. When I was a gangly, buck-toothed teenager and feeling my homeliest, Dad would cheer me up by saying, "You come from a family of late bloomers. Look at your Aunt Beth. Now *she* has matured into a very handsome woman." It's still true. Now in her late sixties, her red hair graying, her freckles fading, she is beautiful, her high cheekbones lined with laughter. Beth grew up on a farm, married a farmer at age eighteen, raised four children, quilts by hand, paints, reads smart books, and during the Cold War went to the Soviet Union as a member of a peace group, building people-to-people links with Russian farmers. Hog farmers, she says, are pretty much the same everywhere.

I'm just sitting down to breakfast with Aunt Beth and Uncle Ernie when Ernie glances out the window and says, "By Joe, got us that possum." He gets back up, heads for the door.

"It'll wait till after breakfast, won't it?" asks Aunt Beth.

"Don't want him to suffer," says Uncle Ernie.

I crane to see out the window, and sure enough, there beneath the bird feeders is a possum pacing back and forth inside a Have-a-Heart humane trap. How sweet, I think, pacifist farmers worried about the suffering of even a brainless little possum.

"That one's been getting into my feeders till there's nothing left for the birds," says Aunt Beth as she passes the potato pancakes, the homemade applesauce and strawberry preserves, the fresh raspberries, the made-from-scratch muffins, the bacon from their own hogs. I'm reaching for a muffin, feeling nourished already, when Uncle Ernie appears around the corner of the house with a rifle and blasts the possum in its cage.

In the mind of a farmer, a possum falls clearly on that side of the line over which humans have dominion. I grew up in a suburb where the meat came wrapped in cellophane from grocery store refrigerators; by contrast, Uncle Ernie is a man with no illusions about where his meat comes from. Not that Ernie's going to eat this possum. But rural electrification didn't reach his family's farm till the 1950s. Until then, the best way to keep meat fresh was to keep it alive until you were ready to eat it. If you wanted fried chicken, you went outside and chopped its head off.

Both Beth and Ernie maintain no illusions about a lot of things. They're both birthright Friends—they were born Friends and they've been practicing Friendly ways all their lives. I came here intending to ask them about September 11. I was hoping with their lifetime of accumulated knowledge and wisdom and conviction they could help me sort through my confusion and distress, help me figure out the proper Quaker response to naked aggression. I was hoping to learn where to draw the line.

But now that I'm here sitting at the table with them, I can't do it. I can't bring it up. It feels too messy. When September 11 does come up, as it inevitably does, I can't bring myself to take it any deeper than our mutual cluckings about how sad and awful it all is. I get the impression September 11 has left even them as confused and windblown as I am.

I came to this farm, to this table, to this aunt the last time I felt this way, when I was in the depths of my struggle to have a baby. I wasn't able to bring that up, either. Yet these were people I could just *be* with—not talking, not analyzing, just being normal. I had absorbed solace through my skin. I left feeling nourished, my feet firmly on the ground. This time, if I can't leave with answers, I hope I can at least leave with that.

Aunt Beth takes me visiting in her roomy four-door along the straight, flat, dusty roads through the corn and soybean sea. Our destinations, small mounded islands of trees that slowly rose up a century ago wherever a newcomer chose to stop and build a life, hammering together a frame house, planting a bulwark of trees to shelter against the wind.

Inside one of those frame farmhouses, around a dining table, I sit with Aunt Beth and eight or nine other women in cardigans and dresses. All of them are farmers' wives, most of them are Quaker. There's a homemade pie on the table, and coffee cups, and lists of serious books. They read biographies and histories and discuss them. This month the discussion starts with a book about a pioneer woman who homesteaded alone on the prairie and ends with a story that's not in that book, that's not in any book, a story about a doctor they all know at a small hospital in a nearby town. He's an Indian Sikh.

"You know my daughter works for him."

"He's such a wonderful doctor."

"This county will be in a pickle if he ever leaves."

"Well, he walked in to work the other morning and my daughter didn't recognize him at first."

"What? With that turban and beard of his?"

"They were gone."

"What on earth?"

"Don't they wear those for life?"

"Yes, she couldn't believe her eyes. Well, he said he'd received anonymous threats."

"Oh dear. Someone thought he was a Muslim."

"Yes, thought he was a Muslim and that all Muslims are to blame for September 11."

"Oh dear."

"He said he prayed with his wife and children about what to do. Then he just took off his turban and shaved off his beard. Karen said, 'Mother, I couldn't help crying.' It's so disturbing. He said he just prays no one back in India ever sees how he has forsaken his faith. Or the visible parts of it anyway."

In the long, sad quiet that follows, as I picture hatred as a pair of glaring anonymous headlights roaming the dark prairie, random and blind, the familiar grind of a tractor lumbers by on the two-lane highway outside.

"There goes Bernie," one of the women says.

They know every tractor that goes by, and most of the cars and pickups.

Quakers know what it's like to be a lightning rod for anger and fear and resentment. In this small community where everyone knows everyone—Quaker and Catholic and Lutheran—during wartime the neighbors slathered a Quaker family's house in yellow paint. A drunken mob showed up at the house of another Quaker family, demanding to get its hands on the yellow-bellied son inside until the father came out on the porch and called his fellow farmers by name, asked what on earth they were doing and suggested perhaps they should go home, which sheepishly they did. Another mob tried to drag a Quaker girl into a truck outside her meetinghouse, till the men of the meeting ran out and pulled her to safety.

In town during World War II, German Americans spat sharp words at my grandfather, or refused to speak with him at all, resentful that their sons were fighting their own brothers overseas, dying for their new country, while my grandfather went about his business in safety.

At the elementary school, the children of those German immigrants beat up my father's older brother to prove their patriotism, and the teacher singled him out for humiliation because he was the only one who hadn't bought war bonds, ruining the class's perfect record. My father was younger and didn't experience harassment by his peers till the McCarthy years. Then, as he likes to say, he had to fight for his pacifist principles.

Aunt Beth's four-door sails us through the fields past the old frame farmhouse where she and my father grew up with their brothers and baby sister, a square two-story box now sprawling with another family's additions inside its windbreak of trees. Beyond it sit the barn where they burrowed tunnels in the hay mow and the silo they helped fill with corn every fall. Further up the road we skim past the plain white clapboard meetinghouse where my family has sat in the First Day silence for more than a hundred years, where Beth and Ernie still sit down with Friends each week. Beyond it lie the low rows of simple headstones where all the names are familiar, my grandparents and an aunt, great aunts and uncles, cousins and neighbors.

"Does your meeting have a peace committee?" I ask.

"Oh yes," Aunt Beth nods. "Though we haven't been too active lately I'm afraid."

"My meeting back home actually laid down its peace committee a while back for lack of participation. Some people were pretty shocked, like, hey, how can you have a peace testimony without a peace committee? I guess the peace thing is what most people think of when they think of Quakers. That and those flat hats like on the oatmeal box."

"I suppose so," Aunt Beth laughs. Half a mile later she adds, "Well, the peace testimony is concerned with more than war in any case."

"Like what?"

"How you raise your children, how you resolve your differences with your neighbors, that sort of thing. It's always been a matter of individual conscience."

That's true. When William Penn became a convinced Friend, he was a young courtier in England's royal court. Custom required him to wear a sword. But now that he believed the Light lived in everyone, he wondered, how could he continue to wear a weapon designed to snuff out that Light? The answer he got from George Fox, the founder of the Religious Society of Friends, was enigmatic: "Wear thy sword as long as thou canst."

Nearly a hundred years later in the American colony Penn founded, when Native Americans attacked settlers on the frontier, the settlers pleaded with the Pennsylvania legislature to send an army to protect them. The settlers were not pacifists; the legislature was dominated by pacifist Friends. Those Friends decided they could not in good conscience support a violent defense, but they also decided they could not in good conscience force others to live and possibly die by Friendly principles. So the Quaker majority voted down a resolution to raise an army, then the entire Quaker majority resigned from the legislature, leaving nonpacifist legislators free to call for the army they wanted.

A couple miles straight up the road at an empty crossroads we turn right and sail another couple miles toward a steeple and a grain elevator. The prairie is wide, and the streets of town are, too, pickups parked diagonally in front of the hardware store, the five-and-dime, the diner, the library, the gas station, the farmers' co-op. A dozen blocks and we re-emerge into the fields on the other side, headed for the tree islands where two of my cousins live with their families a mile or so apart as the crow flies.

Dan and Colin are both sunburned and lean as hunting hounds as they pass through their wives' kitchens between chores. Dan's the quiet one, his younger brother Colin the talker. "Mom couldn't talk y'into taking the Corvette drag racing today?" Aunt Beth protests and laughs with her sons, their midwestern voices confined to the backs of their throats and noses, their humor as dry as the wind, as shielding as the trees.

Dan and Colin farm hogs together. Unlike a lot of hog farmers these days, they've chosen not to cram their hogs into sheds on bare concrete floors where the animals never see the sun, where they thrive only if pumped up on drugs, where the raw manure has to be constantly flushed from the concrete floors into waste ponds so toxic that any accidental release kills fish for miles. No human being can live downwind from the stink of those kinds of farms.

Corporate agriculture insists such factory farming is the only way to raise hogs profitably. Yet Dan and Colin support two families totaling fifteen people on hogs that stay healthy without drugs because the hogs spend summers in fields and winters in roomy sheds with fresh air and fresh straw bedding that continually composts the manure into fertilizer that gets spread onto fields of crops. The sheds and fields surround my cousins' old tree-shaded frame houses and smell the way farms are supposed to smell, rich and earthy and green.

Dan and his wife have five children. Colin and his wife have six children, five from India and one from Haiti. My cousins' lives are outlined by a moon that waxes and wanes each month, snow that gives way to bare earth that greens over till harvest and then gives way to snow again, lines that cannot be crossed and lines that shouldn't: Animals shouldn't be made to suffer needlessly; children shouldn't be unwanted.

I hook my fingers in the wire of the poultry pen and admire the chickens one of Colin's sons is raising. Caleb is eighteen, tall and lanky and handsome in his overalls, peering through wire-rimmed glasses over the last edge of childhood.

"So what are your plans?" I ask.

"My dad says he needs me here." His face is solemn. "But I'm thinking about being a fireman. They really need firemen right now, you know, since so many firemen died in the World Trade Center. More than three hundred."

I'm not sure that means they need more firemen in northwest Iowa, but that's beside the point. I compare my smash-anything response to Caleb's earnest sweetness, my need to flee to his desire to serve, and I am ashamed. A month before all those firemen died, Caleb was driving home late one night and pulled over to check on something rattling in the back of the car. While he was bent over the trunk on the side of that quiet, dark road in a rural county where no one locks their doors, a pair of headlights stopped behind him. A man got out. He shouted filthy names. He beat Caleb bloody, beat him in the head. The man was never caught. No one knows who he was, just that he was big, and drunk, and white. Caleb, who has lived here on this farm since he was two, was born in India; his skin is dark. For that one reason he may never again have peripheral vision in one eye.

I wish hatred and evil really were like a pair of glaring, anonymous headlights. But I know they're not. From the Quaker side of my family I have learned evil always wears a face that I know, that *somebody* knows. From my German Oma and Opa, I learned sometimes the face it wears is my own. Because there's a Nazi in my closet.

Germany bears most of the blame for two world wars and the deaths of tens of millions of people. This is a heavy load to carry. Even I feel the weight of it, and I'm only half German, born in America a generation after the killing stopped.

I used to deal with the guilt by telling myself that *my* family's hands, at least, were clean. Before Hitler took power, Oma and Opa were on a ship bound for Canada, and none of the rest of the family who stayed behind actually joined the Nazi party. I repeated the story of my great uncle, a young Lutheran pastor, an anti-fascist, a man who believed in doing the right thing. The Nazis interrogated him in the late thirties for publishing a flyer with excerpts from *Mein Kampf* that didn't make Hitler look too good. But as he pointed out, he was only quoting his *Führer* so all they could do was cite him and let him go. Not long after that he developed sepsis, and in his delirium he took the wrong medication and died. But if he hadn't, so the story goes, the Nazis probably would have seen to it eventually.

I've seen old photographs of him—tall, blond, achingly handsome. Behind his old-fashioned spectacles the outer edges of his eyes sigh downward, both kind and sad. He was my image of the German half of my family, golden, compassionate, quietly heroic. I couldn't be accused if they couldn't be. And how could they be? They sprang from the same familial womb as my Oma, who had raised up a foster child in addition to her own three children, and had taken in a cantankerous, bedridden old woman with nowhere else to go, caring for her for years until the old woman's death. There was nothing to feel guilty for there.

The first hint that there was a subplot to this story came when I was a teenager, visiting Germany with Oma. In a small apartment in a cobblestone town, as Oma drank coffee with her sister and brother-in-law, I sat on the floor and leafed through old photo albums. I came to a page that was nearly empty, all but two of the black-and-white snapshots torn out. In one, a little girl sat in a garden. In her hand she held a tiny swastika flag. Next to that was another snapshot, the same little girl caught up in the arms of a man wearing the gray uniform of the regular army of the Third Reich.

I stared at these pictures as the rest of the world fell away, the clinks and murmurs of my great aunt and uncle having coffee and *Torte* with Oma across the room, the bells of the old walled city. My heart was pounding. I recognized the man hugging the little girl with the swastika in her hand, the man in the uniform. It was Onkel Ernst, the now elderly great uncle having coffee across the room, one of the gentlest men I'd ever known, an ordinary man who worked as a gardener all his life. The pictures floated alone and inexplicable in their half-empty page. I closed the photo album. I said nothing to anyone.

But Oma and her sister saw me staring at the album, and, later, sitting on a train that rocked us back and forth, Oma told me this story: As World War II dragged on, the German draft pulled in more and more German men until one day a thirty-something gardener named Ernst was ordered to put on a private's uniform and go to war. The tiny swastika flag his daughter held as he hugged her goodbye was one of many the neighborhood authorities shoved into the hands of children that day. The camera clicked. Then Onkel Ernst, who had never fired a gun in his life, marched off and surrendered to the first Allied soldier he saw.

I nodded as I listened to this description of a person like me, who wasn't heroically good, but wasn't evil either. Those inexplicable pictures suddenly made sense. I pushed them to the back of my mind and forgot about them, until years later, when I went home to Florida for Christmas.

I sat with Oma in her sunny room of memories and photographs framed in pressed flowers. The clock on the wall ticked. Beneath it lay the crèche Oma constructed every year, five long feet of mossy hills and miniature sponge trees, molded plastic sheep, painted tin angels, carved wooden kings—a motley little world united only by its adoration of a tiny wooden ball tucked into a minimalist manger. That was the baby Jesus.

We were looking through an old photo album, talking about Oma's first visit back to Germany in 1965. She'd left in 1930. She told me about the church bells she'd missed hearing for so long and the tearful reunions with her sisters on train station platforms. "And also my Tante Emmi," she said.

"Tante Emmi?" I asked. "Who's Tante Emmi?"

"She was the wife from my mother's brother."

When Oma was a child before the war—that would be the First World War—her mother had fallen sick and Oma had been sent to live for a while with her uncle and aunt, Onkel Richard and Tante Emmi, and their daughter and two sons. Onkel Richard had had a short career as a missionary in China, but he was more interested in birds than souls. Oma remembered an aviary behind his house in Germany, aflutter with birds. I listened, fascinated. This was a story I'd never heard before. No one on this side of the Atlantic had.

Half a century later, when Oma arrived for her visit, the aviary sagged empty and desolate. Inside the house, Oma sat in the dark, lace-curtained parlor with Tante Emmi, the only one still alive. "Oh how hard that must be," Oma said, and bitterly Tante Emmi agreed, describing how each had died—the daughter lost to cancer, Onkel Richard gone before the Second World War, one son during. The other son went missing in action on the eastern front near the war's end. And that's when all of a sudden the family closet burst open and Oma's missing cousin came tumbling out head over jackboots into the middle of the room. He was all duded up in a snappy black uniform with a pair of silver lightning bolts gleaming from his lapels. Because he was not just a Nazi. He was SS.

"Tante Emmi, she told me this." Oma's voice dropped as if she was tired. "She told me proudly."

SS is short for *Schutzstaffel*. Literally, it means protection squadron. By the end of World War II there were 1.6 million of them. They were Hitler's bodyguards. They ran the concentration camps. They followed behind the regular army when it invaded Eastern Europe and the Soviet Union and they murdered Jews, gypsies, communists, and partisans; they murdered women, children, and old men. That was the SS. And I was related to one of them.

My face felt stiff with shock. I tried to find words. "Were *you* shocked?" I gasped at Oma.

If she was, she didn't look shocked now. She just looked sad. She lifted her shoulders, a stiff, hesitant shrug. "Yes and no."

This shocked me even more. "Your own cousin, and you weren't shocked?"

"His brother, too. They both have joined the Nazis."

I didn't know what to do with him or his brother. Onkel Ernst, drafted into the uniform of the regular army, hugging his daughter with a tiny swastika—that was one thing. This was another thing entirely. How did the same family that produced my Oma and the brave, anti-fascist great uncle also produce a monster in an SS uniform? He made no sense to me. He was as disconnected and meaningless as an uncaptioned photo on an empty album page.

Oma went on. "At the time when I have lived with them, those boys weren't always the nicest. Martin and Mathias were their names. Mathias was a little bit handicapped somehow. Well, so, being away from my mother, I began to wet the bed, though I was long since potty trained. Tante Emmi made up a bed for me in the bathroom. That hurt my mother to hear about later when she recovered, that they would stick me in the bathroom. So, one night a voice comes: 'I am the Bad Man, and if you wet the bed I will get you!' I screamed and screamed. It was Mathias. His parents came running to comfort me and were very mad at him."

I never did get straight which brother became the SS officer, Martin or Mathias. So I was free to comfort myself by labeling that uncaptioned photo in my mind: Mathias. The Bad Man. Bad from the very beginning. I was free to make up a scene and set it in his father's aviary after dark, imagining a boyish shadow slipping in among a blizzard of startled wings, the snap of small neck bones, the silence of feathers that drifted down like Russian snow.

Oma covered her mouth with her hand and shook her head. "The enemy from outside is not the worst. The enemy inside is the baddest one, is the fight that we—all of us, all of us—we have to fight."

At twilight, in my aunt's darkened basement guest room, I stand at the window and gaze out at the lawn and the wide world beyond it. I'm down here to feed Rosie before we sit down to supper. I listen to her beside me, crunching her supper out of her bowl. My line of sight is at ground level, about the level of a possum.

I've had five or six years now to get used to the idea of Nazis in the family. The shock has worn off. Maybe that's why, as I stand at the window and recall Oma's words about the enemy inside, way opens for me to remember something that happened when I was seven.

Despite my family's Christmas traditions, as a child I had only a vague knowledge of the guy who was born on Christmas. I knew the basic story: He was born in a manger and later a mob got carried away and yelled for him to be killed. In my child's heart I believed that if I had lived back then, I would have spoken up in Jesus' defense. That way, the mob would have come to its senses—because sometimes all it takes is one courageous person—and a nice guy like Jesus wouldn't have had to die. I had missed the Sunday when Christian children learn to believe Jesus had to die, had to take our licking for us because we're all equally, hopelessly sinful and sin has to be acknowledged and paid for.

One summer day when I was seven I was playing with three neighbor girls at a house beneath a mossy live oak down the street. It was a house like all of ours, pastel cinderblock, mildew-proof terrazzo floors, aluminum crank windows, a typical 1960s Florida tract house. The girl who lived there, Melanie, we all agreed, was spoiled. A few months before, we'd heard there was a pony in Melanie's front yard, so we all ran down the street and, sure enough, there it was—a real, live pony. I would have given a major organ for a pony, or even just for a ride on one. But all any of us neighbor girls were welcome to do was watch Melanie preen atop her new pony before she ran back inside to the birthday party to which none of us was invited.

In addition to a pony, Melanie also had a closet stocked with dress-up clothes, including a fabulous pair of glittery high-heeled mules with puffy white pom-poms on the toes. On that rare day that I was there playing in her bedroom, one of the other girls was clacking around the terrazzo floor in those fabulous mules when Melanie demanded she hand them over.

"But I had them first," the girl protested.

"So what," Melanie said. "They're mine."

We all watched in silence as Melanie stuck the mules on her own feet. She teetered upright. She clacked around the room. And the girl who'd had to give them up hissed to the other girl, "She's a Jew. The Jews killed Jesus, didn't they?"

"Uh huh." The other girl narrowed her eyes at Melanie. "You killed Jesus."

"I did not."

"Did too."

"Did not!"

"You killed Jesus, you killed Jesus."

"I didn't!" Melanie started to cry. "Stop it!"

"You killed Jesus, you killed Jesus."

By the time Melanie ran sobbing from the room, I was chanting it, too. It wasn't that I lacked the courage to speak up in her defense. What I lacked was any desire to defend her at all. I had no idea what a Jew was, but it felt good to see her cry.

A few minutes after Melanie left the room in tears, her father threw us out of the house.

I sat alone on the swing in my back yard. I nudged the dirt with my toe, rocked the swing, just a little. I was looking down at my toe, but what I was seeing was the door I had opened inside myself when I helped make Melanie cry. I saw something bad in there, something I disliked more than I disliked Melanie. I brooded on my guilt for two days before I finally confessed to my mother, who confirmed that, yes, I had done a very bad thing. "Why don't we bake some cookies for Melanie and you can take them to her and tell her you're sorry," she said.

So the next day I trudged alone back up the hot, empty street noisy with cicadas, a plate of cookies in my hands. A maid answered the door. She called Melanie out from the kitchen where it sounded like something deliciously fun was going on.

"I'm sorry I was mean to you," I mumbled. "I made you some cookies."

She was under no obligation to forgive me; that was between her and her own heart. And, in fact, she acted as if she didn't know what I was talking about. She said cheerfully, dismissively, "Okay," took the plate of cookies, and closed the door in my face.

I was hurt. I was embarrassed. I was angry. But that was nothing compared to the knowledge that weighed me down as I turned around and trudged back home through the noisy cicada heat, the knowledge that only I could close a door in the face of my own worst self.

Outside, the twilight is nearly gone, the wider nighttime world where evil is done nearly impossible to see anymore. Rosie is still crunching at her bowl. I turn from the window to switch on the bedside light, and as I turn back to give Rosie a pat before heading upstairs for supper, I catch a glimpse of myself reflected in the window, now mirror-black. There I am, superimposed over the night. I close my eyes. Once again I picture that imaginary scene of Mathias as a boy in his father's aviary. With his thumb he strokes the head of the bird he holds in his hand before he releases it, gently, back into its cage. Then I picture him, years later, burning down a house in Russia with a mother and her children still inside.

The windbreaks around my aunt and uncle's house are on the north and west sides, evergreen sieves that sift the wind to a breeze. Rosie and I wander across the relative stillness of the lawn. We pass through the evergreens into a small grove of gnarled apple trees.

Coming out on the other side, there in front of us is a sheep pen. Rosie stops and stares. The sheep bunch up at the fence, staring back and going *baa* in their funny men's voices, their very tiny brains trying to figure out whether they should run or not. People usually bring food, for which they'd like to stick around, but the wolf they're not so sure of. After a couple minutes, though, they figure out Rosie's just another sheep, in wolf's clothing.

If the big bad wolf did show up, Rosie would run with the rest of the ewes and lambs. Running is always her first instinct. If she's cornered, like in the car, she barks in her deepest, loudest voice and raises the fur along her back to make herself look big and scary; she tries to make the threat run away so she doesn't have to try to break down the car door to run away herself.

I've heard people claim we're the only species for whom fighting to the death with other members of the same species comes naturally. But despite the Nazi in my closet, I don't think the idea that we're natural born killers is true. In a battlefield study of firing rates during World War II, the U.S. Army was surprised to discover most soldiers, even when they were being fired upon, even when their lives and their friends' lives were in danger, never fired back.

Like the rest of the animal world, when we're threatened our natural instinct is not to kill. For most of us our first instinct is to get the hell out of there. Even among those who don't run or hide, the first impulse is to try to scare off the threat, not kill it, a peaceful impulse as ancient and natural as the desire for violent vengeance. During World War II, if a hundred soldiers were in a firefight, only fifteen to twenty would actually fire their weapons, and of those, most were firing over the enemy's heads— like Rosie, just making as much noise as possible, just trying to scare off the threat. When our contradictory impulses are put to the test, at the moment of truth, our natural instinct is that of the conscientious objector.

However, with the proper conditioning, we can overcome that. Even mild-mannered dogs like Rosie who've never bitten anyone can be trained to attack. After that battlefield study, the Army changed the way it trained its soldiers, and ten years later in the Korean War the firing rate had increased to 55 percent. By Vietnam it was 95 percent. Only a few of us may be born with the line drawn somewhere on the far side of killing, but clearly the rest of us have it in us to learn to do the same.

Beyond the sheep pen, the checkerboard fields roll away to the horizon, endlessly rippling in the wind.

Surveyors used our arbitrary, manmade system of measurement to draw a neat grid of lines over this entire state. The roads were laid out along that grid running north-south and east-west, the fields in between. What did my war-resisting friends and relations use to draw the line on war?

A member of my meeting back in D.C. actually enlisted during World War II because defending innocent people seemed to him the right thing for a Quaker to do. Other conscientious objectors chose to serve in the military, too, but as noncombatants like Frank, helping the wounded. Still others felt they could not support any war effort in any way; drafted in World War I, they used passive resistance to eventually win the right to choose nonmilitary service, working on farms, in mental hospitals, rebuilding homes in war zones. And then there was my father's cousin's husband, who reached draft age during the Second World War. He searched his heart and decided he could not cooperate with the system at all, could not even register. He wrote a letter to his draft board stating his position and went to prison. When the prison inmates were ordered to do war-related work, he quietly refused and was thrown into solitary confinement in the hole.

None of these men was successful in ridding the world of war—I'm sure they didn't expect to be in their lifetimes. But each man was apparently successful in the small internal world of his own soul. Somehow each knew where to draw his own line. What I wonder is, did each know where the line was ahead of time? Or only after stumbling up against it? Were they certain, or were they as confused as I am? I'm as confused now as when I was searching for answers to my infertility, trying to come to a decision. Was theirs an intellectual decision? A gut reaction? How did they know?

I follow Rosie back into the quiet of the apple grove. Surrounded by twisted trunks and low-hanging branches just starting to let go of their leaves, I can no longer see the wind-scoured line between the earth and the sky.

One thing I'm pretty sure of: My pacifist relatives didn't draw their lines where they did because they were afraid of getting hurt or killed. Even though the verbal and physical abuse they endured paled in comparison to the intense suffering of those who were fighting and dying, they weren't trying to avoid that suffering. They were trying to nudge their fellow Americans one small step closer toward ending that suffering for everyone. They were placing their feet in the footprints left by the Quakers who had gone before them, who stood up to oppose wrongs like slavery, quietly, patiently standing their ground until eventually they were successful in helping make our world a slightly better place.

I follow Rosie as she wanders back toward the house, past the big metal shed where the combines and tractors are parked, past the bird feeder, the fading vegetable garden. Out beyond the wall of trees, the withered rows of corn stalks flap and roar.

In town the next morning, I angle the Vette into a diagonal parking spot outside the tiny post office. Inside I fill out a customs form, list the contents of the package I'm sending overseas: pictures of Rosie, batteries, and, from Aunt Beth, homemade cookies.

On board ship, Frank and the rest of his battalion are gearing up— hoisting their packs, climbing into amphibious hovercraft that crash over the waves and up onto the beaches of Egypt. It's not war yet, just practice. It should be no big deal. But in that cold, silent lump inside my chest, it is. They're wearing gas masks on their hips.

> Everyone, *everyone* in the area in which we are located knows what is about to happen. There are some among the locals who are not all that keen on our presence here, and some of them will be near us. Many of us are concerned about the things we hear. Watch the news. I'm gone. Love you forever.

He'll be out of email contact for ten days, maybe two weeks. My fingers touch the locket.

I walk out of the post office, climb into the Vette where Rosie waits, and we're gone, too. I roll down the windows so Rosie can grin into the wind that drives us on. I hit the accelerator; we really need to get over the Rockies before winter rolls in.

BATHROOMS AND LIFE'S OTHER UNNECESSARY LAYERS

Starting date 10/10/01 . . . waning quarter moon . . . odometer 126,632 . . . route: northwest through Nebraska and South Dakota to a pit stop in the Badlands, then west through the Black Hills, Wyoming, and the Bighorn Mountains = two days, 841 miles

I've never before driven farther west than Iowa. I'm finally entering a part of the country that's as unknown to me as the desert is to Frank. I try to picture him, where he is; I picture a human dot on a rippled sea of sand. I cut across the northeast corner of Nebraska, drive due north into South Dakota. I leave behind people I know.

I make a sharp left turn onto Interstate 90 and leave behind cities, Sioux Falls's few office towers shrinking in the rearview mirror. I leave behind traffic, I leave behind farmhouses within sight of each other. I drive straight west through miles and miles of nothing but grass and fields and grass and every now and then a huge billboard for Wall Drug: You'll Get Walleyed at Wall Drug . . . Be a Wall Flower at Wall Drug . . . Have You Dug Wall Drug? I don't know why the billboards are so big. Out here on the plains the eye is so desperate for something to settle on that a small, hand-painted sign nailed to a fence post would have the same effect. Back in 1961, after driving across this landscape, Ernest Hemingway committed suicide.

I leave behind hills. I thought Iowa was flat, but I was wrong. Somehow the land keeps getting flatter. Anything out here that has a third dimension is manmade. The Wall Drug billboards. Small towns.

Hunting down a grocery store in Mitchell, I round a corner and there before me is something from another dimension all together, a hayseed Kremlin in the middle of the prairie, minarets and onion domes and . . . corncobs. It's a big block of a building, and the entire thing is covered in corncobs. Red cobs, yellow cobs, they're arranged on the walls and the domes like mosaics, geometric patterns and murals of cowboys and buffalo. Nestled in among the kernels is an electronic marquee—God Bless America, it glows. Above that, spelled out in cob art, Mitchell Corn Palace.

I turn to Rosie. "What the hell is a corn palace?"

She gives me a scornful look: Like that matters.

She's right. What it is doesn't matter. It just is. The corn palace. I leave behind the need to know why.

The prairie rolls on. The radio yammers words into the engine's roar. None of the words mention a military exercise in the desert. I picture Frank jouncing in the back of a crowded Humvee, picture a small, dented taxi with a trunk full of explosives rattling toward it head-on. I erase the taxi from the picture, leave only long lines of Humvees, trucks, tanks, plumes of dust on an endless desert road.

While the radio is silent about what's going on in Egypt, it has plenty to say about the ongoing air war in Afghanistan.

I grew up believing if well-intentioned moderates like me ruled the world, all war would be preventable. The way I heard it from Oma and Opa, in 1914 extremist militarists in Germany and the rest of Europe caused the world's great powers to go tripping into World War I by accident, just another slip on the old banana peel. At the end of that war, Germany had to pay the victors impossible reparations that ruined the German economy, left the people hungry and desperate, and created an opportunity for a demagogic madman like Hitler to seize power and reignite the world war, part two.

I've always liked this explanation. It allows me to believe that people are basically rational, that only homicidal maniacs want war, that there's a reasonable, moderate solution: To prevent deliberate war, just lock up the maniacs; to prevent accidental war, just try to see the other guy's side of it and treat him fairly. That's what I want to believe. But according to the military histories I'm reading, such a sensible solution is so hard to achieve it's as good as a myth.

At the turn of the twentieth century, Germany was a new, growing nation that needed access to more raw materials and more markets for the things it produced. But the leaders of Europe's biggest imperial powers, Britain among them, had no interest in sharing with Germany and no interest in seeing Germany's side of it. This made the Germans feel like everyone was out to get them, so they decided to strike a pre-emptive blow while they still might be able to win, then set up a united European economic union dominated by Germany that would secure its place in the world. Germany's frightened, pugnacious leaders ignored the warning of Prince Otto von Bismarck, the man who founded the German nation, who said fighting a preventive war was like committing suicide for fear of death.

In Britain, the leaders who made the mistake of ignoring Germany's grievances weren't extremists. They were moderates. Soon after the rest of Europe rushed into a war that Germany was favored to win, those British moderates made another mistake. They joined the fight, and what probably would have been a quick little war turned into a world war of attrition. Nine million combatants would die in that first world war and uncounted millions of civilians, just to postpone the inevitable—a German-dominated European economic union. Inevitable because it is Germany's geographic luck to be big, and rich, and located in the heart of Europe.

By the end of the war, the British moderates and their allies had come to regret their earlier mistakes. Being anxious to avoid another war, they tried to give Germany's new moderate postwar leaders what they wanted, but only in bits and pieces that didn't satisfy anyone. By the time they offered total accommodation, it was too late. Germany's economy had collapsed and the moderates had been replaced by

Hitler, a street thug who saw accommodation as a sign of weakness, not reason.

At the time, everyone blamed Germany's economic disaster on unfair war reparations. After all, there was proof: Every time a reparations payment came due, a burst of inflation would hit the country. To buy a loaf of bread, women had to push wheelbarrows full of worthless money through crowds of demobilized soldiers who couldn't find work. But reparations couldn't have been at fault because Germany didn't pay them. From the beginning, the government missed payment after payment.

Decades later, German archives have revealed the country's moderate leaders made a calculated decision to deliberately ruin their economy to prove reparations were ruining their economy. These rational, reasonable men wanted to undo the treaty, end reparations, and free Germany to rearm and rejoin the world's great powers—many of the same goals as those of Hitler the madman. Unlike Hitler, they weren't planning another war. Yet they were the ones who started the rewriting of history, who told their people Germany bore no guilt for World War I, who subjected them to economic insecurity and social unrest, who laid the groundwork for World War II.

The good intentions of human hearts had not prevented war; in the case of both world wars, they may even have caused it. I did the hard, earnest work of peeling away the layers of myth, and this was my reward—the awful truth. I leave behind my certainty that war is always preventable.

Further down the road I stop again, at a prairie-sized outdoorsman's store, tawny grass rolling away to the horizon in every direction. Rosie watches from the Vette as I am swallowed up in its maw. Through tens of thousands of square feet I pinball from boats to taxidermy to tents to fishing vests to bows and arrows before staggering back out into the bright sunlight clutching my new solar-powered radio, which I had no idea I needed till I saw it, lest I ever be without news of the war, and a buttery-soft buffalo sandwich, which Rosie agrees is delicious.

I leave behind impatience. The interstate stretches ahead to the vanishing point of infinity—there's no hurrying the prairie. Even with the speedometer at eighty it goes on for hours. I can't imagine crossing this space at the speed of an ox. My sister once said she wondered why people settled here, but I think I know why. After a few mind-numbing weeks of this you'd settle for just about anything. You'd forget your past, forget your future, forget where you were going and why, and since one patch of prairie looks pretty much as good as any other, you'd settle for the patch where you were and you'd name it Kimball, or Reliance, or Vivian, or Cottonwood. You'd bust the sod and you'd watch the clouds, the horizon transformed into a stage for operatic clouds, burlesque clouds, clouds that linger like grazing herds of white buffalo, clouds that boil up into billowing towers until the wind smears them in banners across the sky.

The interstate stretches on.

Then, without warning, the grassland breaks up and drops out from under me, the smooth flat prairie shattering itself into the Badlands. Just like that, I leave behind the earth. I'm on the moon. The harsh rock and sand and tough grasses and shrubs are pale and gray, as if this place has stripped them to the bone, leaving nothing but their bare presence and their shadows, long and deep in the late afternoon. The road winds down into this jagged, bony scar, and I wind down with it, slowing the Vette to stare at the stone that is rough, then smooth, then jagged—rows of short, sharp peaks like the toothy jaws of prehistoric sharks.

I roll down the windows. Rosie hangs out one side, I hang out the other. I breathe deep and I'm surprised. In a place that looks so barren, the cool air smells fertile, like the manure of plant eaters, and spicy, too, a mix of fir and hay and basil and thyme.

I'm pitching my tent in the tall grass of the empty campground,

watching the setting sun turn the western sky into a shifting kaleido-
scope of neon pink and purple and orange, when I turn and notice the
sharp hills and ravines behind me to the east, and the Badlands surprise
me again. This landscape that I had thought was empty of color has
become a mirror of the sky—the sand and rocks switching on the same
neon colors, the peaks like sharks' teeth washed in blood. I stop what
I'm doing to stare at this monkish land, a survivor of terrible forces,
stripped of mortal decoration, scrubbed into that pale and shiny and
motionless state where we're all best able to reflect the glory of heaven.

It's cold and getting colder. I pull on two sweaters over my t-shirt, two
pairs of pants and socks, and jam a wool cap on my head. It's a three-
dog night, but all I have is the one I'm snuggling with. I curl up with
Rosie outside the tent. We listen to the coyotes, Rosie perfectly still
except for her swiveling ears. I watch my breath puff white, look up at
a glittering highway of stars. I've never before camped without Frank.
I imagine him looking up at the same stars thousands of miles away.
Then I remember it's daylight where he is. I imagine him beneath the
desert sun, haloed by light so bright it overexposes the sand around
him, white and featureless as a cloud. I hold him in that light. When
you pray for someone, Quakers call it holding them in the Light.

In the morning, while deer graze nearby, Rosie disappears into the
tall grass to squat and I trudge to the cold, silent toilets in the middle
of the campground to do the same. I've left behind hot water and
showers. It's not the first time. Whenever Frank and I camp, we go
backcountry backpacking and leave behind toilets, too. And then of
course there was that time when we renovated our bathroom.

When I pried up those black bathroom tiles, I began a process that
would strip away the architectural facade from one of life's most fundamental activities, one we share with every other animal on earth. I
did this casually; I did it voluntarily. It was Frank—the one who had
no choice—who most clearly saw what lay ahead. And he was afraid.

I, on the other hand, figured the new bathroom would be in place in a couple weeks.

Weeks 1–2

Within a couple weeks we had moved out. Frank had lucked into a part-time job, which was easy on the budget but hell on the construction schedule. Carrying only toothbrushes and a change of clothes in plastic grocery bags, we closed the door on a house that looked like a *Three Stooges* studio set after the big flour-fight scene. We hightailed it to the suburbs to housesit for my second mom while she was out of town.

"This is great!" I said, pleased with such excellent timing.

"This is an embarrassment," Frank said, morose about our precipitous retreat.

Meanwhile, back at our house during the daytime hours, I hunted around for insurance that covered infertility treatment and Frank hauled a large quantity of drywall sheets into the middle of our dust-covered, debris-strewn living room. While he nursed his sore back, I, humming, rid the house of the dust and debris.

Weeks 3–4

For these weeks we landed another housesitting gig, this time for vacationing friends. I remained pleased with the continuation of such excellent timing. Frank remained uncomfortable in a home not his own.

Meanwhile, back at our house during the days, Frank discovered hundred-year-old houses have no ninety-degree corners anywhere and, after cursing for a while, framed in the new space with as much exacting precision as he could force into it. I found insurance that would pay for basic infertility treatment, ran around the house waving my arms then, still humming, again rid the house of dust and debris. Also, this time I sealed off the construction zone with large sheets of plastic.

On the other side of the plastic, Frank said a prayer and started plumbing. Now and then he thumped down the stairs to turn off the water to the house at the water cutoff under the kitchen cabinets. He removed the toilet. My father, himself an incurable renovator, stopped by to say, "Doing your own plumbing? You're a better man than me, Gunga Din." I gave Frank a proud thumbs up. Frank gave me a woeful basset-hound look.

Week 5

That was the week we bunked in the attic of another friend's nine-hundred-square-foot house. It felt even smaller to all concerned by the end of the week.

Meanwhile, back at our house, standing beneath the bathroom, Frank narrowed his eyes at the living room ceiling. "Is that a new leak?"

I furrowed my brow. "I don't know. Looks a lot like the seventeen other leaks up there. Does it feel wet?"

Frank said morosely, "Water hates me."

We developed and implemented a leak documentation system, which involved dragging a chair to the middle of the living room beneath the leak-stained portion of the ceiling, climbing up and outlining each leak with a pencil and inscribing it with the date. Leaks without dated outlines could immediately be classified as new. After a while we quit dragging the chair back and forth and just left it in the middle of the room.

We trekked out to a suburban medical center to attend our first meeting with the infertility doctor. Upon learning Frank was an ordained pastor, Dr. Warner, a Lutheran like Frank, became a little too reverent for my taste. So when Frank left the exam room to make his appointment to produce a sperm sample and Dr. Warner asked about intercourse, I tortured her with unpastoral revelations about our sex life.

Afterward Frank hustled me out to the car.

"What's the rush?" I asked.

"My appointment's in two days."

"And you think it's going to take you the entire two days to produce the sample?"

He scowled at me. "It's not funny. The sperm have to be at least two days old, but no more than seven."

We hadn't had sex in weeks. His new part-time job took up his afternoons and he had class tonight. "Hit the gas," I said.

He sped our wheezing old Honda toward home because we agreed the privacy of our own deconstructed house was preferable to our friend's attic. But when we screeched to the curb, one of our neighbors was standing between us and the front door with a large hunk of wood.

"Hey Frank," he called, "can you cut this for me on your table saw?"

Frank grabbed me by the hand and blew past him with a brusque, "No, it's in a friend's basement, bye." We hopped on the dusty bed at 12:01 and by 12:04, mission accomplished. Frank even had time to dig out his circular saw, go over to the neighbor's and cut the wood. He thanked Frank profusely. "No problem," Frank said. "I've gotten so much done today already." He made it to work fifteen minutes early.

Most sperm samples are produced at the medical center's clinic in a small, fluorescent-lit room equipped with a vinyl chair and a wrinkly stack of pornographic magazines. Everyone walking past that door knows what's going on behind it. Two days later, anticipating performance anxiety in such an environment, Frank received special dispensation to produce the sperm sample in the comfort of his own home, though the nurse sternly warned me against participation. "There must be no introduction of foreign bodily fluids," she said.

"So no spitting?" I asked.

"Among other things," she said.

After a valiant solo effort, Frank produced. I leaped into the Honda with the cup and chauffeured the boys to the lab for a head count.

He had to produce another sample a couple days later, but this time I was the cup. At the clinic I climbed into the stirrups and cracked jokes at the ceiling while Dr. Warner peered inside me to see if Frank's sperm had the strength to swim through foreign bodily fluids.

Frank's sperm report came back. Four hundred million vigorous and well-shaped swimmers, four times as many as necessary. Frank was only slightly cheered by this proof of his manliness. "At least now we know it's not my fault," he sighed.

Weeks 6–7

During this phase we reappeared on my second mom's doorstep looking like bag people, I took my turn at being tested, Frank continued plumbing in between working and studying for finals, and we both spent time circling and dating new leaks on the living room ceiling.

At the lab, repeated stabs were required to obtain the blood to test my hormone levels. The venipuncturists all declared me a medical wonder, a freak of nature with no actual veins. This didn't surprise me. I tried to donate blood once, and the Red Cross worker had to stab me three times to find the vein, then kept wringing my arm to milk a pint from me before it started coagulating.

At the house, when friends and neighbors asked how the bathroom was coming along, Frank reported he was learning plumbing as he went and it was waking him up with night terrors. Touched by his humility, I listed his many handy, self-taught skills. Frank said he wasn't kidding. I pointed out we could always call in a professional. Frank pointed out the embarrassment would kill him.

At the clinic, my plumbing checked out after being flooded with dye and x-rayed. The good news about no blockages almost made up for the time spent doubled up with cramps from the dye.

Back at the house, the plastic sheeting that had sealed the construction zone began to sag. No longer humming, I again rid the house of dust and debris.

Week 8

End-of-spring-semester finals led to a bathroom hiatus during this week.

More hormone tests led me, while waiting at the lab, to jog in place and wave my arms to increase the flow of blood to my nonexistent veins, and the other patients to move to the far side of the waiting room.

"When you get the results, are you prepared for bad news?" Frank asked.

We were in the back yard, trying to clear a path to the alley through the piles of demolition debris. It was like trying to bulldoze through the Alps.

"I'm expecting an answer one way or the other." I heaved the old brown sink cabinet aside. "And either way that will be good news. If they find something clearly broken, it'll either be something that can be fixed or something that's hopeless. Either way we'll be able to move on with our lives."

"Okay. As long as you're prepared." He dragged the sink cabinet back from where I'd heaved it. "Hey, I can probably use these hinges one day. For something."

Ordinarily that would have annoyed me, but I was feeling good, I was feeling optimistic. The odds favored a nice neat diagnosis, nine to one.

Diagnostic Odds for Infertile Couples

40 percent due to female problems

40 percent due to male problems

10 percent due to both male and female problems

Only 10 percent remain completely unexplained

While we waited for the results, Frank decided he'd had enough of living the overturned life of a refugee. He longed to retreat to his own space; no matter how big a disaster that space might be, it was his and it was safe. He lobbied to move back into the house with no bathroom.

It didn't seem like such a great idea to me, but since he'd done his part to be supportive through the testing, I figured I owed him some support in return. I agreed to return to the house, even though, due to ongoing work on the plumbing beneath the floor level, the Space Formerly Known as Bathroom had no floor, just the exposed floor beams. No walls, just the exposed backsides of the neighboring rooms' walls. No sink, no bathtub, no door, just a bed sheet nailed up over the doorway. It did have a recently reinstalled toilet, hooked up to the water lines and positioned over the waste pipe, carefully balanced on one joist and two scraps of wood. To use the toilet, all you had to do was approach with caution, tiptoeing from joist to joist, and sit down slowly, avoiding wiggling, then flush gently and check the living room ceiling for new leaks. Also, we discovered it was possible to wash an entire adult human body in a kitchen sink if the operation was broken down into parts.

Soon after we moved back in, the plastic sheeting around the construction zone failed completely. This time, I didn't bother to rid the house of dust and debris. Instead, I retreated to the kitchen and settled in behind a hazy wall of plastic sheeting over the doorway.

Week 9

Still no test results. The waiting continued. The plumbing resumed. Frank uninstalled the toilet. After two months on the urban frontier, we were tougher now. The lack of a toilet no longer seemed like any reason to move out.

For basic needs, by removing the sewer-muffling rag from the waste pipe and utilizing his male advantage, Frank was still able to employ the waste pipe for its intended purpose. Utilizing three feet of rubber tubing attached to a plastic funnel, I was able to employ the waste pipe, too.

For other needs we got to know our neighbors really well. The distance from front door to front door and into their first-floor half-bath: fourteen steps, eight if running.

And for the perfect start to a Saturday morning, I would rise at 0830. I would pick up the newspaper from the stoop, proceed to the car, and drive at a leisurely pace through empty streets to the

Smithsonian's Air and Space Museum. I would park right outside—there was always plenty of on-street parking at that hour. When the museum opened, I would proceed to the freshly cleaned public restroom, select a stall, open the newspaper, and make myself at home.

Week 10
That was the week the test results came back.

I sat up very straight next to Frank across the desk from Dr. Warner.

"Good news," she said. "The tests have turned up nothing obviously wrong with either one of you."

I stared at her. "You mean we're among the unexplained 10 percent?" I deflated against the back of my chair. That was terrible news. We were no closer to knowing if infertility was really our fate or if there was something we could do about it.

"But since you've failed to conceive for two years," Dr. Warner went on, "there are a few different treatments your insurance will let us try." As she described them, I sensed Frank shutting down beside me, like an engine shuddering from a roar to a sighing hiss. He was already out of there.

We shuffled out of the clinic and returned home, where the bathroom remained a framed-in wooden skeleton and the toilet still sat in the hall, leaning against the wall at a sad angle like a hopeless evicted person. Frank said, "It's like we've stripped away all the skin and fat that concealed the bare bones."

"And we're still a long way from done," I said.

Frank nodded bleakly, because he thought we were talking about a bathroom. On the living room ceiling, a new wet spot emerged and slowly spread into a shape that, if an observer were to squint just right, could be the snickering face of Satan, like on the cover of a supermarket tabloid.

I crouch at the edge of a cliff, the breeze ruffling my hair. Nearby Rosie sniffs the rocks. Far below us, the Vette is a midnight-blue speck where we left it by the side of the road. Beyond it, the Badlands are a naked cellar hole of eroded layers, exposed and broken time. It stretches as far as I can see.

We rumble up out of the moonscape. On the radio, there's still no mention of Marines in the desert. I picture Frank in desert camouflage wading along a sand dune, picture a sniper in a wrapped headdress squinting through a sight. I erase the sniper, leaving nothing but sand blowing and my husband wading along a dune. We rumble up into mountains dense with evergreen trees that are such a deep, towering green they look black.

Tooling through those Black Hills, we come to a stop at the base of Mount Rushmore. I look up at the big heads carved in rock. They look just like they do in the pictures—like big heads carved in rock. I put Rosie back in the Vette and turn northwest into Wyoming.

Winter is in the air. I am determined to get to Yellowstone and over the Rockies within the next day or two, so in the interests of time I stick to the interstate, even though it takes me up through a big, unscenic nothingness, where all I see are rolling, treeless, sagebrush hills, and every now and then a ranch house and outbuildings, and sometimes just a mailbox at the end of a long dirt drive, pointing the way into the distance. A small clutch of antelope floats over a hill. A lone cowboy herds a few cattle along a ridge. Closer in, huge slatted fences run parallel to the interstate, about a hundred yards off in the sage. They run in stretches of a mile or more, about fifteen feet tall and heavily braced. I play a guessing game: Maybe they're meant to keep deer or elk or antelope off the highway. The fences aren't continuous, but maybe they're just meant to block certain patterns of animal movement.

I pass railroad crossing gates, open now, but preceded by signs that read, Road Closed When Flashing, Exit Now, or occasionally Return To Last Exit.

Then it hits me, and my southern-raised mouth drops open. Those slatted fences are in open areas where the wind sweeps down. They're not for holding back animals. They're for holding back snowdrifts. Really, really big snowdrifts.

I peer up through the windshield at the sky. It's clear blue overhead but it's getting a little gray on the northwest horizon. By the end of today I am determined that this interstate will have taken me north almost up to Montana, and a little scenic road will have taken me west over the Bighorn Mountains; I hope by tomorrow to be on my way across the northern Wyoming plain to Yellowstone and the Rockies. I turn on the radio—occasional rain showers in eastern Wyoming tonight, turning to snow in the mountains after midnight.

I heave a sigh of relief. I'll be over the Bighorn Range by 1800, way ahead of the snow. Besides, if I wait till tomorrow to cross over, the snow may have closed my little scenic road. I wonder, Is it cold at night in the Egyptian desert this time of year?

I leave behind the interstate. The snow gate at the base of the scenic road stands open, only a few drops of rain hitting the windshield as the Vette passes through. Before me rise the Bighorns, a creased and folded curtain of evergreen beneath a gray ceiling of clouds. I leave behind the rolling lowlands, steer the Vette up through the switchbacks into uninhabited national forest land, leave behind houses, outbuildings. Somewhere back east there's a whole house full of stuff I left behind, how long ago now? Three weeks? Or is it three years? I try to remember what all that stuff is that's in my house. I can think of a few things I can't replace (the quilt my Quaker grandmother pieced by hand, Opa's hat, Frank's letters to me the summer we fell in love) and a few things I can (the bed, the stereo, the books), but it's strange, I don't miss any of it. Everything I need to get through this world can be carried around in a Corvette. I begin to leave behind the unnecessary layers of my life.

The Quaker testimony of simplicity has led Friends to strip away unnecessary layers in their relationships with others, emphasizing openness and equality, and in their relationship with God, sitting silently together in simple buildings without decoration and without ministers to mediate. Reclining beside me on her bed, Rosie is the living embodiment of the unlayered life. She goes through her days with no more than she can carry, which is to say, with nothing. Her bed, her backpack of toys and bowls and treats, her bag of food—all that is stuff I've added to her life. If she never saw any of those things again, she wouldn't miss them, not even Stinky Pheasant.

The raindrops have thickened to a light drizzle. I pop up the headlights, flick on the wipers, which squeak up from the center like an opening gate, then arc back down, open, closed. Rosie stands, gives me the command to open her window by whining and bobbing her head along the dash. She's trained me well; automatically I hit the electric window control. She hangs out in the drizzle, panting and grinning, but she's still so restless that I realize she's actually giving me the command to pull over and let her out to relieve herself. A couple of switchbacks later, at the next scenic overlook, I do. She jumps out and trots along the guardrail at the edge of the crevasse the road has been following, eagerly sniffing the sharp air.

I get out, too, and look back the way we've come. The road zigzags like a seam stitched into the cliffside of the forested crevasse, which angles down into the forested crevasse that came before, which angles down into the forested crevasse that came before that. The lowlands are no longer in sight. A car appears around the curve below, weaves its way up toward us, swishes past and curves out of sight. Ahead, there are only more forested crevasses, one leading into another into another into another up into the rain. I wish Frank were here to see this.

I shiver and stuff my hands into my pockets, scrunching my neck down into my collar away from the wet. The raindrops start to puff and drift a little. They're turning into flurries.

Rosie's still trotting around sniffing. "Come on, Rosie, do it," I command, but she barely gives me a glance, just shakes the rain off her coat in a silvery mist. I'm not as good a trainer as she is. "All right, if you don't have to go, get back in the car." I hold open her door. "Come on, up and in. Let's get this show on the road."

When we're both strapped back into place, we swish on up after the car that just passed. Every once in a while I catch a glimpse of it rounding a curve above us. Beside me Rosie's crouched like the Sphinx, big triangular ears pricked forward, panting as if she's headed for Canada.

About a dozen switchbacks later the flurries thicken into flakes. Apparently the snow is ahead of schedule. It sugarcoats the trees and quickly starts to accumulate on the ground. I'm still passing signs that announce scenic overlooks, but I have to take their word for it because the only thing those cliffs overlook now is a wall of white.

I consider turning back. But we've come a good third of the way, and besides, the car ahead had local tags and no snow tires, and it's still forging on. It's not like I haven't driven in snow before. I've dragged a trailer behind the Honda through a blizzard, driven the Vette itself through a couple of East Coast snowstorms. Still, I know enough to know that while there's not much that sticks to a smooth, dry road better than a Corvette, everything sticks better than a Vette on a road that's been softened by snow. So on a straight stretch with a healthy expanse of shoulder, I test the brakes with a tap. Like Rosie, the Vette barely gives me a glance, just rolls on. I test the brakes again, give them a good stomp this time. The Vette's heavy swooping nose slows a little, but the lightweight back end keeps on going and starts to come around. I let off the brakes.

Now that I know what I'm working with I don't go any faster than I can stop by coasting. I no longer catch glimpses of the car ahead rounding the curves. Behind me, another set of headlights rises into view, gauzy through the falling snow. It catches up quickly. A big pickup truck. It pulls out to pass and continues on up ahead. I spot it again once, twice, swinging out around the curves, and then it's gone, too.

Rosie bobs her head along the dash again. I crack her window so she can smell the snow. The only thing she likes better than Canada is snow. I realize now, back when I thought she was trying to tell me she had to pee, she was really saying, Hot damn! Snow! She could smell it coming.

She sniffs through the course of one curve, then bumps my shoulder with her nose. I lower her window halfway and she sticks her whole head out into the swirling flakes. She snorts; the snow is really coming down. If it weren't for the tracks of the pickup that just passed, I'd have trouble figuring out where the road is under this new, smooth, white blanket that emerges from the black forest on one side, crosses the open space where the road presumably is, then disappears into the white wall beyond the cliff on the other side.

Rosie pulls her head back in, bearded with snow. Ahead, a glow fades into sight, headlights coming down. The lights twist closer, then whisper past, a snow-covered car. That's good. If traffic coming the other way is still getting through, then the road over the mountains must still be passable. I squint at the pickup's tracks, concentrate on keeping the Vette on course.

Another pair of glowing headlights comes down. It's nice to have company on this lonely road, even if it is going the opposite way. This time as the vehicle passes, I don't take my eyes off the parallel tracks I'm following; they're growing hazy beneath the falling snow. Once the red taillights in the rearview sink away into the dim whiteness behind me, I am alone with the fading tracks that glow in my headlights, and the trees, now ghostly on both sides, and Rosie. When I lift a hand from the wheel to stroke her head, I notice my palm is sweating.

At nine thousand feet the trees thin and the ground levels off into a windy plateau above the treeline. I sigh and relax. It'll be a little easier now. I wiggle my fingers on the wheel to loosen them up. I glance around, but the blowing snow is like a veil and I can't see much, just fewer trees. I refocus on the road.

That's when the dim tracks I'm following do a U-turn.

Beyond the end of the tracks, the snow-covered ground proceeds onward, smooth and virgin into another wall of white. I ease my foot off the accelerator and coast to a stop. The headlights I'd seen coming down weren't vehicles that had made it over the mountains. They were the car and the pickup, both giving up after reaching this point.

I peer through the snow-crusted windshield, through the clear arcs of the squeaky wipers. Without tracks to follow I can't tell for sure where the road is. Rosie sniffs the glass, fogs it with her breath. I look at her. "We're going back down, Rosie."

I ease back onto the accelerator, creep the Vette into a U-turn. It fishtails.

"Maybe not."

I let it coast to a stop again, still on fairly level ground but with the nose now pointed at its own tracks, slanting back down through the trees. They slant down toward nearly thirty miles' worth of steep switchbacks, narrow shoulders, precipitous drops. With no braking power. I leave behind wars. I leave behind moral choices, questions of history, of heaven. I leave behind mothers, fathers, sisters, husband. I am left with this: to stay where I am. Or attempt to go back down.

FINDING GOD IN A SNOWSTORM

Starting date 10/11/01 . . . waning crescent moon . . . pit stop in the Bighorn Mountains = one night

Far below, down where the scenic road begins its climb, down where it now looks as if the mountains above have vanished from sight within a magic cloak of clouds, a gate finally arcs down. Raindrops patter the sign: Road Closed.

High above, Rosie and I squint thoughtfully at the snow-covered road down. Then we squint at each other. Rosie raises her brows.

"You're damn right—no guts, no glory," I say, and floor it.

The Vette rears back, sashays for traction, snow fountaining out behind. The tires grab hold and we leap forward with an open-throated roar. We slalom through one turn, white wave spraying. We hit the next turn and the tires let go, the steering wheel spinning one way, the car the other, gravity gone in this soaring elation, spinning weightless across the snow. The engine dies as the Vette bursts out over the edge in a powdery shower and swandives nose first into the silent abyss. From the cockpit, a faint *"Yeehaw!"* trails softly away, then just the wind remains, and the dancing snow, and the round red taillights, shrinking, shrinking, before finally winking out in the darkness below.

Take two. Rosie and I squint thoughtfully at the snow-covered road down. Then we squint at each other. Rosie raises her brows.

"You're right. I am out of my freaking mind." I yank up the parking brake. "That would be a stupid way to die."

I dig behind the seats for my high-tech sleeping bag, squirm myself into it there in the driver's seat, spread Frank's old green Marine field blanket over both of us, crank up the heat, and fall cozily asleep as snow piles up around the muttering twin tailpipes. In the morning, the snowplow driver finds us both dead of carbon monoxide poisoning.

Take three. Rosie and I squint thoughtfully at the snow-covered road down. Then we squint at each other. Rosie raises her brows.

"You're right. That would be an even stupider way to die. If we're going to camp in the Vette, I should cut the engine."

Rosie whines to get out of the car.

"Except . . ."

She begs to play in the snow.

"Except, hang on." I release the parking brake. "I just want to go a little way back down. Coming up I think we might have passed a building or something, but I was so focused on the road I'm not sure—"

Rosie drops into her alert Sphinx crouch with a frustrated sigh. Going downhill the snowy mountain road is a slope as slippery as the one I slid down after all those tests turned up nothing, grabbing Frank by the ankle as I slid and pulling him down with me, telling him I just wanted to try a few little magic pills.

There's nothing up here but trees. Maybe I dreamed a building. The Vette creeps around a few long, slow curves back through the blowing snow. Suddenly there it is, a dark, squarish blur. A little closer and the blur resolves into solid log walls, a chimney with a question mark of smoke, pale golden windows and two dim neon signs: Open and Miller Lite. It's a rip snortin' miracle. It's a hunting lodge. In the whispery night it sings out soft and low: Come in . . . don't slide over a cliff . . . have a beer instead. High atop these mountains, cloaked in snow, it promises to be the kind of place where one pill makes you larger and one pill makes you small.

When I was twelve, my mother started taking thyroid extract pills. An x-ray had revealed a lump on her thyroid. The doctor told her she'd have to take those pills for the rest of her life. After a year and a half, she went up front for healing at a prayer meeting. Nothing happened. But a week later at the prayer meeting she felt a sudden intense heat in her neck, like a blow dryer switching on and off and on and off. Her whole neck swelled alarmingly. For six weeks her neck was swollen, until one night she woke up with everything she'd ever done wrong parading through her mind, every small cruelty, every lapse in judgment, every selfish act. She started to cry. She begged God's forgiveness. Peace came over her. She went back to bed, and when she woke in the morning, she felt light and new inside. Getting ready for the day, her hand brushed her neck—to her surprise, it was no longer swollen and the lump was gone.

"Oh no, it'll be there," the doctor said when she went to see him. "Those lumps never go away. Trust me, it'll be there." He examined her neck. He examined it again, his fingers digging deeper into her neck. The lump wasn't there. Within a few weeks she had weaned herself off the pills she was supposed to take for the rest of her life. She's never taken them since.

Maybe God reached down and touched her thyroid. Or maybe God designed the brain's chemical processes with more unconscious power over the rest of the body than we yet understand, and one day we'll figure out how to harness that power on a regular basis. Either way, for now it can't be explained with rational science. It's a miracle. Like every baby is a miracle. And every hunting lodge in a storm.

The Vette slides to a stop in front of the lodge. Rosie yelps and scrabbles beside me as if she's been saved. She continues to bark at me from the car as I slog through the snow to the entrance, barking not to be left behind. Back in the summer of 1996, after our nondiagnosis, the first infertility treatment option was pills. Frank didn't see the point of treatment, but it was just pills and it was just me who'd have to take them. All he had to do was continue having sex on a schedule for a few more months.

I stomp the snow off my boots, pull open the door to the lodge, and step into the medical center pharmacy where I pick up my first round of magic pills, artificial hormones that will make my ovaries spit out eggs like an overwound pitching machine, creating more targets for Frank's sperm to swing at. Frank follows me inside. There's another person ahead of us. The man behind the counter asks us to stand further back. "To preserve patient confidentiality," he murmurs.

More people line up behind us. When it's my turn, I step close and quietly ask the murmuring man if there's anything I shouldn't eat or drink while I'm on these pills. He calls over a woman more expert than he, a friendly, helpful woman who announces, as loudly as possible without actually shouting, "WELL, YOU SHOULDN'T DRINK ANYWAY BECAUSE THAT LOWERS YOUR FERTILITY."

Heads turn. Frank backs away.

"AND DID THEY TELL YOU THAT YOU NEED TO HAVE SEX EVERY DAY? YEAH, IT USED TO BE THEY THOUGHT THAT LOWERED SPERM COUNT, SO THEY SAID EVERY OTHER DAY, BUT NOW THEY SAY DO IT EVERY DAY."

What can I say? "Yippee," I say weakly. By this time Frank is halfway to the door.

"AND DID THEY WARN YOU ABOUT MULTIPLE BIRTHS WITH THIS STUFF? AND IRRITABILITY? AND CANCER?"

Behind me I hear the door close. In front of me, there's football on a TV above a bar, a pool table, and two tough, long-haired cowboys. They squint at me through the smoke from their cigarettes, white stubs parked in the corners of their mouths, which leaves their hands free to hoist beer mugs, rope and brand bulls, shoot pool or maybe the occasional stranger.

Hey, I say, know if I can get a room?

One of them points his cue toward a wide doorway. I get the feeling they can tell just by looking at me that I'm opposed to handguns.

My boots leave melting snowprints on the scarred wood floor. I clomp through the doorway into a big room with a high ceiling, a stone mountain of a fireplace, a crowd of empty tables and chairs, and a long front desk. A beefy guy wrapped in an apron leans against the far end. He looks at me like he'd just as soon pluck me and cook me as say hello. A girl stands behind the near end, with a tiny sleeveless midi-top, hip-huggers, and apparently no brain. I'm wearing two sweaters, a coat, and long johns under my jeans. I look at her, at her pale, goose-bumped arms and tummy and cleavage, and I shiver. I ask her if I can get a room for my dog and me.

The cook makes a face like he's decided I'm not even worth cooking. He says my dog can get a room. I can't tell if he's joking, but I figure if Rosie can get a room, I can make her share it with me. The half-naked girl furrows her brow and warns me there's no TV in the room and no telephone, as if I might want to leave and go somewhere else. Are you telling me it's a kennel? I ask. Oh no, she assures me, it's a room.

I'll take it.

I haven't showered in two days; the room has a shower. I'm cold; the room has heat. It also has a broken-down bed, a chipped dresser, and a chair with one leg shorter than the others. It's a beautiful room.

Our room is the first in a long row set apart from the lodge. Only two snow-blanketed cars are parked outside, the Corvette here at this end and a road-weary little compact at the other. Inside, Rosie sniffs the corners, catalogs all the previous guests, their footprints, their dandruff, their gunpowder, their dreams. I reach for the shower faucet and crank on the main water cutoff to our house, still with the skeletal bathroom. I'm on my knees in the kitchen, reaching under the cabinets to crank the water from off to on. Frank's in the same prayerful position in a closet upstairs, next to a pipe he's been working on.

As I crank, water chuckles in through the pipe. Frank would describe it as snickering. Where I hear a happy sound, he hears something darker. Where I see a good chance of a baby with these pills and a negligible risk of cancer, Frank sees a multiplication of risk factors because I and my family have a history of cancer. When I ask him why he has to be so negative, he asks me how he's supposed to feel knowing I might be making him a widower. So I hear water chuckling; he hears it humming with malicious delight as it rushes in, searching eagerly for places from which to leak. That is the nature of water, he would sigh, cheerful malevolence.

Frank's voice drifts down the stairs. "Is it on?"

"Yes!"

A distant whoop. "It's holding! No leaks!"

I whoop, too, and jump to my feet. As I do, a new sound erupts— a splashing sound. I peek around the corner. There's a waterfall in my living room. No, not a waterfall. Niagara. Niagara is cascading from the ceiling register down onto the couch, from there to the floor.

Frank forgot to close off the faucet that still pokes forlornly over the place where the bathtub used to be.

We mop up. Frank says, "What a disaster."

I say, "Look on the bright side—the water hit the couch instead of all that expensive drywall and two-by-fours leaning nearby. And you hate this couch."

Frank shakes his head. "I don't see how you can stay so optimistic. It's unnatural."

"It's because I have vision. I can see what it will become." Upstairs, where Frank sees a dark, gutted hole between two rooms overflowing with tools, power equipment, new fixtures, an enormous antique iron bathtub with clawed feet, and miscellaneous unidentifiable piles of stuff heaped around and on top of the beds, all color-coordinated beneath a uniform coating of dust and debris, I see a finished bathroom tiled in white, a master bedroom, and a nursery. The doctor found nothing wrong with us. The more I think about that, the more I think a miracle is likely. It doesn't even require much of a miracle. I believe these pills will work.

When a freelance job takes me out of town at the beginning of the cycle, I pack the pills. When it takes me out of town in the middle of the cycle, I pack Frank. Far from the grim pressure of our wrecked bathroom, Frank cheers up. "Gotta service my filly," he says in his best Hoss Cartwright. I laugh and tell him he's wonderful.

Then all of a sudden I no longer have vision. None. As I'm tiptoeing across the joists to get to the toilet, I'm crying because I have to tiptoe across the joists to get to the toilet. As I'm taking a bath—which means I'm standing in front of the kitchen sink wearing nothing but socks—I rant, "If our society weren't so uptight, we wouldn't think we have to have fancy bathrooms! We wouldn't have to have any bathrooms at all! All we're doing is hiding something that's just a basic bodily function!"

Frank's standing next to the coffeemaker. He's fully dressed, complete with his backpack of books over one shoulder. He stares. "What's wrong?"

I mumble, "I can't take it anymore," and busy myself with a towel.

He mumbles back, "This is what I was afraid of, that I'd screw it up and let you down."

I nearly throw the towel at him. "Would you listen to yourself? You are so selfish, always assuming it's all about you!"

He glances at me with suspicious bewilderment. I recognize the look. I saw it the day before in a glance from an old friend after I yelled at him while we were working together on a freelance job. I wound up sobbing on his shoulder. "I'm so sorry! It's just that Frank and I are trying to get pregnant and we're having trouble and I'm stuck taking these pills from hell!"

"Clomid?" my friend asked mildly.

I lifted my head, eyes wide. "How'd you know?"

"My wife's on it, too."

It's humiliating, not being in control of myself. Still in that out-of-control, drug-crazed state I yell at Frank, "Only a man would be arrogant enough to assume if a woman's undone like this it must be over a man. Well don't flatter yourself! It's just a side effect of these *goddamn pills!* I'm just *irritable!* And sink baths *suck!*" Then I cry and tell him I'm sorry, and after he hugs me and leaves for class I dream of one day being sane and normal again, and stepping into a shower again, a nice hot steamy one like the one I'm stepping into now. Rosie shoves her head in around the curtain to check on me and lick the water splashing against the side of the tub, her eyes squinting and blinking in the spray.

I poke my head in the door of the lodge, snow blowing in with me, saying, sorry to trouble you but are y'all still serving supper?

The half-naked girl tenderly leads me to a table near the fire, calls to the beefy cook, then wraps all her exposed skin in a fat parka, a six-foot scarf, and earmuffs, waves a cheery well-mittened hand good night and pushes out through the door. She's not as dumb as I had assumed, me the genius who drove a Corvette up a lonely mountain road into a blizzard.

The cook brings me a steamy, heaping plate of ham and broccoli casserole and a big pile of cherry pie, all left over from the meal he had earlier served the staff—that would be the girl and the pool-playing cowboys. A meal as beautiful to me as my room. I dig in, the only sound my fork as it clinks against my plate, the crackling fire, and, from the bar, the occasional ball-click of the cowboys' uninspired pool game.

The cook eyes my appetite. He asks how the dog likes riding in a Corvette all the way from Washington, D.C. Apparently he has checked out my ride and its tags. Loves it, I say. He asks how that Corvette handles in the snow. Lousy, I say. He pulls up a chair. He spent thirty years as a cab driver back east. His hands are big and blunt. They shape the air as he talks. He asks what my husband thinks of me driving all over the country by myself; apparently he has checked out my ring finger, too. He's at sea, I say, with the Marines. What a coincidence! he says. He was a Marine before he drove a cab. He tells me this is the first snow of the season. He tells me I'm lucky it's not next weekend. Next weekend is the start of deer season and every room in the lodge is already booked. He throws out a few jokes, a one-man floor show. He's a single parent, two daughters at the bottom of the mountains. He's gratified by my appetite for his cooking. He's named for a well-known Confederate general.

If this were 1996, I could have sat across this table from him and not really seen him or heard him. In the summer of 1996, I have recovered my vision of the future, but now that vision is all I see. I do not see the tangible present; all I see is the mirage of a baby. Feeling follows action; the more I pursue it, the more I want it, to the exclusion of all else. I want these pills to work. I want one sperm to penetrate one egg in one of my fallopian tubes. I want the cells to divide and grow inside my uterus. I want to push my baby out into the world. I want to hold my baby in my arms. I want to bathe my baby in my finished bathroom. I want to dress my baby in the Peter Rabbit onesie my mother gave me when Frank and I first started trying. I want to ride with my baby through the car wash.

In the summer of 1996 I slog six blocks in rumpled shorts and a t-shirt to the post office, the air so hot and thick even the Capitol dome just up the street looks hazy. I pass a woman bumping a Cadillac stroller over the root humps in the brick sidewalk. She's older than me. She's wearing makeup, her nails are painted, her coordinated pastel mommy outfit has been ironed. She looks like she always gets everything she wants and I sincerely doubt she deserves it.

Sweating in line at the post office, I notice the woman in front of me is pregnant. I doubt she deserves it, either. She's fat, too. I hate myself. Not only am I jealous, I'm petty.

A couple walks in. She's bitching about something. He's holding a baby in a carrier, which dangles from his hand down by the side of his leg. He's got a cigarette in that hand, the ash growing longer and longer above the baby's head. They definitely don't deserve that baby. He's not even supposed to be smoking in here.

I speak through a foggy wall of Plexiglass to the postal clerk, the only person I will speak to all day. I lift the lumpy envelope I'm mailing to my sister and place it in the urban security pass-through. The lumps are the Peter Rabbit onesie and a few other infant clothes. I'm in the final cycle of pills. If the pregnancy test is positive I can always get this stuff back, but if I wait to get rid of it until after a negative test it'll feel too much like cleaning out someone's closet after their funeral.

I slog home to my office, which is also my kitchen, dining room, and bathhouse, glance at the freelance writing project waiting in a stack next to my computer, and instead reread the pamphlets Dr. Warner gave me: "Insights into Infertility," "Pathways to Parenthood," and "Infertility: The Emotional Roller Coaster." Trying to make a baby doesn't leave much creative energy for writing yet another script for yet another video that sells credit insurance or teaches how not to lose a hand in a paper mill.

When Frank comes in the door that night after class, we don't say much. He's afraid of saying the wrong thing to the weepy, snarling, drug-induced she-troll who has possessed his wife, and I no longer even think to ask what's new with him. So at the end of the day the only thing I'm left with is my imaginary baby and me. It's all about me. Me taking those pills.

The door to the lodge eases open. A cold gust of wind blows in more snow and a small woman in a thin jacket.

The cook jumps up, hustles off to the kitchen. The small woman smiles brightly. Do I mind if she joins me? Did I just get in? She's been here two days now, the owner of the road-weary compact. She thinks with all this snow she'll be stuck here a while longer. Don't I find the snow enchanting? We talk about the weather. She arranges her napkin in her lap, just so. She's from Oklahoma. She's on vacation. Soon she's picking at a plate of food like mine. She's been all over Montana and now she's doing Wyoming. This is the first meal she's eaten here at the lodge; she's been eating leftover road food in her room. My, they serve such big portions here, she'll be able to eat this in her room for days. She saves a lot of money this way. She left home three weeks ago for a one-week vacation. After the second week she called her boss. Her boss wants her to come back. She's an office manager. She's not sure she wants to go back. She refolds her napkin on the table, just so. It's too beautiful out here to go back to Oklahoma. But on the phone her son asked her, When are you coming back, Mom? The cook wraps up her leftovers for her. She smiles through me, as if her son is standing behind me, across the room. Her son is fifteen. She wonders, wistfully, if perhaps we'll be snowed in up here a long, long time.

Tires skid on the snow, footsteps bound up the porch steps. The door bangs open, revealing two men and a glimpse of an ice-encrusted rental parked outside. Hallo, hallo! One is pudgy and blond, one thin and mousy-haired. They are both wearing earrings and ugly sandals with socks; they are both German and gay, subtle as a limp-wristed oompah band. Hallo, they wish please to arrange a room for the night! Ho, such snow, they have driven off the road many times almost! Supper? Ach, most definitely, but first beer! They clatter through the doorway into the bar. They can be heard ordering themselves beer. They can be heard ordering the two cowboys beer. I am wincing, waiting for the crack of macho pool cues against queer Kraut skulls. Instead I hear a sudden uproar of laughter, the balls racking up and, crack, the crowded clicks and thumps of the opening break, a two-man game of who-cares pool expanding into a four-man party. They have been in New York City on business, *ja*, and now they are wishing to see America! All of America! In two weeks! The cowboys tell them they have got to see Yellowstone, got to see Old Faithful—*Jawohl*, say the Germans— and then San Francisco, and then they must hurry drive back to New York to catch their plane home. America, hoo! Such a big country! Such a beautiful country! They drink to America! God bless America!

Beyond the windows of the lodge, the snow is still falling. The runaway mother has taken her leftovers back to her room. At a nearby table, the Germans and the cowboys are toasting each other over their heaping plates, the cowboys eating their second supper of the evening. Across the table from me, the cook is back. He tells me stories about his time in the Marine Corps. He tells me stories about his life as a cab driver. He asks me, "What kind of job you got lets you drive around the country for six weeks? Or do you just live off your husband?"

"No," I say, "I have to work for a living."

"Yeah?"

"Yeah, but I work for myself so I can take time off whenever I want. Or at least till the money runs out."

"I hear ya. So what kind of work you do?"

"Uh," I hesitate. What I'm about to say always sounds so vaguely ivory-tower fake to me. I wish I could say horse trainer or mechanic or studio camera operator, but instead I have to admit, "I'm a writer."

"A writer! Hey, me too!" Turns out he's writing the story of his life as a cab driver. "You want to read it?"

Oh no. "Of course I would, sure."

"You want to read it now, tonight?"

"Uh, well, sure." So much for a snowbound evening spent drifting deliciously off to sleep over another mindless romance. "Drop it by my room when you get off work," I tell him as I pull on my coat.

Outside, the night is white. The snow softly drapes the earth. I let Rosie out of the room and send her out for a long snowball pass. She leaps and snaps at it, a creamy explosion around her head. She veers off to plow splay-legged through a drift.

A rock, a bush, a car, even a dog and a woman if they're sitting still, they'd all look the same beneath the snow, like four fingers and a thumb poking up beneath a white blanket. If the material world is like a blanket, what lies beneath it? What pokes up like a finger to shape the material of the blanket into a rock, a bush, a car, a dog, a woman, then after a time subsides flat as an open palm again, leaving the material above flat as well? I'd call it God, the Light. Maybe when we see another person not as an inferior, or a threat, or an annoyance, but as a worthwhile human being, maybe we're seeing past the blanket and recognizing That of God, the Light Within, which from the inside gives us all our different shapes.

When the knock comes at the door, Rosie explodes. Rosie is passionate about knocks. A knock, any knock, is an itch she scratches with all the steely-eyed, heroic abandon of a ham actor in a B-movie. It's one of her greatest pleasures in life. She especially likes it if I hold her by the collar when I open the door, so she can run in place and lunge and bark and snarl and slobber without the burden of being the one responsible for controlling herself.

I take hold of her collar and open the door. At the sight of an actual person out there, Rosie's voice plunges from medium-pitched alarm to deep-voiced blood lust. It's my cook with his life story in his hands. He doesn't run, but he looks ready to, should it become necessary. What he doesn't know is that although my arm is jerking in time with Rosie's lunges, they're not forward lunges. They're up and down. She doesn't really want to get too close to him, she just wants credit for acting like she does.

I reach for the sheaf of hand-written pages he's holding and shout a promise to leave it for him at the front desk in the morning. He hems and haws; he'd been hoping to wait while I read.

Now, intellectually I know letting a stranger into your room is right up there with climbing into the lion's cage dressed as a pork chop. But my gut tells me this guy is harmless, and besides, I can see Rosie's performance has instilled the fear of dog in him. I let him in. But not before I shout that I'm going to let the dog go now and, for effect, add in an ominous tone that he shouldn't make any sudden moves. I don't mention that sudden moves make her duck and run away.

Once we're all settled, he in the chair, I on the bed, Rosie on the floor between us, she ratchets down the barking from a constant roar to the occasional surly woof, just to remind him from time to time that she doesn't like his kind. After a while, as I read and he quietly smokes, she forgets why she's punctuating the silence with woofs and stops bothering to open her mouth when she does, her ferocious bark reduced to a muffled, absent-minded hiccup at the universe: *mmpff.*

He listens to me read silently; he smiles when I laugh out loud, nods when I sigh. Of *course* he needs to be here while I read his story. Life is a lonely enough journey as it is. He's a former Marine (who was so bored with shore duty he kept going AWOL by stowing away on Navy ships—how dumb was *that?* he asked), who drove a cab for a living, who one day went west with his daughters and somehow wound up cooking for strangers on top of a mountain in Wyoming.

I'm a former TV production worker, who writes video scripts for a living, who one day went west with my dog and somehow wound up eating food cooked by a stranger on top of a mountain in Wyoming.

To bridge the chasms that divide us from each other is a small miracle. To feel the arms of the man I love around me again, or to feel a baby growing inside me, now that would be the most intimate of this sort of miracle. But when I was on Clomid, the only thing that grew in me was my desire for a child. I got three tries with the pills—only three. In part because of the cancer risk, in part because if the pills were going to work for me, I'd be pregnant by the third try. After the third month, hot tears leaking from my eyes, I scribbled into my journal, *Why is this happening? Why me?* I prayed it out loud. I heard no answer.

The cook writes like he talks, his voice transcribed into blue ink scrawling across the page, story after story of a cab driver's life. He tells the story of how, when he was driving a cab in Atlanta, a drunk got in, said he wanted to go to Florida, even paid in advance. Next thing you know, he's passed out.

In my journal I wrote, *A month later, Frank and I are at the cottage in Canada. We've been here a couple weeks, walking along the beach, hiking up through the birches, playing Chinese checkers the way Oma and Opa used to by the window overlooking the lake, losing track of time.*

At the Florida line, the drunk is still passed out. Okay, so having no idea where in Florida he's supposed to go, and recalling to mind that the gentleman had mentioned growing up in Savannah, he drove there instead.

Vacation's over, we're locking the shutters on the windows, packing up for the drive home. I look at my calendar for the first time in weeks. I look again, catch my breath.

He gets to Savannah around midnight, circles the streets—everything's dead, shut up for the night. What's he supposed to do now, right? He stops the first person he sees, a random stranger. Guy peers in the back seat and goes, "It's George!"

I'm three days late.

Outside, the snow's still floating down. "Thank you," I say, "thank you," and I mean it. I hand his story back to him. He nods, satisfied.

Rosie and I watch him go, collar up, shoulders hunched, trudging away into the white and solitary night. Soon, even his footprints disappear. Rosie sniffs the cold air. *"Mmpff."*

Semper Gumby

Starting date 10/12/01 . . . waning crescent moon . . . odometer 127,473 . . . route: west across northern Wyoming; to a very short pit stop near Yellowstone = one morning, 112 miles

I stared at the calendar.

"Oh my God," I whispered.

"Do you really think?" Frank sounded stunned.

"I don't know, it could still come." My heart was pounding. "But I'm never late."

He started to smile. Frank, who had been dragged into this, started to smile.

Sun's up. Rosie and I meander past the lodge, snow crunching beneath our feet. Overhead the sky, a sheer blue silk canopy, and the forest, evergreens iced with snow. A blindingly beautiful confection of a day. I anticipate one snowed-in day after another, my imagination piling them on like tiers on a cake. Oh let us eat cake! These days will be like waking up on a cold morning in a bed piled high with comforters and knowing you don't have to get up, you can just burrow in deeper and drift all warm and snuggly and delicious. . . . We meander within sight of the road.

It's plowed.

Poof goes my snowed-in fantasy. I'm back to keeping to a schedule. I'm driving to Yellowstone today and crossing the Rockies. I hustle Rosie to the Vette, load it, bound up the steps to the lodge to grab breakfast. On the TV over the bar, troops are headed overseas, ships churning through the waves.

Frank. He's off his ship, in the desert.

I can't take my eyes off the ships on TV. This is noted by the pony-tailed, cowboy-booted server who's clanking eggs and bacon on the table in front of me, solicitously asking if I want ketchup with that before jerking a thumb at the TV and asking, like he's offering me coffee, "So what do you make of it? Way you're staring, you must have some feelings about it."

"Well . . ." What am I feeling? Scared for Frank. No, proud of Frank. No, sad about the bombing. Vengeful. No, not vengeful anymore. Confused. So many words crowd into my mouth none can get through.

"Whoa!" he laughs. "Stand back! Silence like that, must be some *strong* feelings."

I try to laugh, too, and finally just echo his question back at him. "What do you make of it?"

Unlike me, he's ready with an answer, as if that's just the question he's been waiting for. "I think bin Laden's the wrong guy. There's just no way he could have pulled that off. I mean, come on, bring down the World Trade Center in the middle of New York City and hit the Pentagon, too? We're supposed to believe a bunch of guys living in caves on the other side of the world made that happen? Don't get me wrong, bin Laden's a scumbag, but this is way bigger than him. I'm talking governments. Maybe even our government, looking for an excuse to control the oil. You watch. We're going to wind up in Iraq and Libya and Somalia and all those kind of places, going after who really did it, or *saying* we're going after who really did it. And then who the hell knows where it will end."

I eat my eggs. I rub my lucky locket and hold the man who gave it to me in the Light and repeat to myself, After this exercise in Egypt, it's still possible he may never get off the ship again for the remainder of the deployment. It becomes my silent mantra. He may never get off the ship, he may never get off the ship . . .

When the Vette glides out onto the road's scraped, hard-packed snow, the runaway mother's road-weary compact is still parked outside. In the rearview mirror, the ice cream forest quickly swallows up the lodge and its one remaining guest.

I'm following the Germans. We left at the same time and I let them go first because I figured with front-wheel drive and a plane to catch they'd be the speedy ones. I figured wrong. They creep across the flat plateau above the lodge pointing at every snow-capped peak, every rock, every shrub.

It gets worse when the road starts to twist down the arid western side of the mountain range because now we're passing one savagely beautiful view after another. Why look, Fritz! There's another savagely beautiful view! The snow thins. The road dries out. Still they waddle their way down. They point through the open windows. Sometimes, they even point at the same time, in opposite directions, arms waving out of the car on both sides like vestigial wings. I'm stuck behind a motorized dodo bird. I'd pull out and blast past them except then they'd think I'm an asshole. No, worse, they'd think I'm a typical American asshole, loud, pushy, insisting the whole world move at my speed or get out of my damn way. I can't stand the thought of old Fritzi and Franz, or whatever their names are, going through the rest of their lives thinking I'm an asshole. They were so nice, so jolly, like a couple of oversized elves. I want nice people to think I'm nice, too.

It almost kills me. Finally, *finally*, they pull into a scenic overlook to take pictures of each other standing in front of yet another savagely beautiful view, some snow-capped peak rising out of a chasm. As I pass, I paste a smile on my face and stick my arm out my window and honk. Rosie pushes her head out her window and barks. They wave back enthusiastically, with both arms. Then I give the engine all the gas it wants. The tailpipes roar and the tires squeal. I'm making for Yellowstone.

Driving away from the cottage, Frank and I were giddy with irony. Three months on the pills, we give up, and the next month—ta da! Over the past two-plus years, whenever well-meaning people had told me stories like that, usually about a friend of a friend, trying to cheer me up with optimistic fairy tales, I had always felt patronized and snarly, biting my tongue to keep from snapping, "And that scientifically worthless anecdotal evidence is supposed to help me how?" But that didn't mean I wasn't perfectly happy to become anecdotal evidence myself, thank you God.

By the time we reached the U.S.-Canadian border, we were planning to get a pregnancy-test kit as soon as we got home. Somewhere in the Catskills south of Syracuse we agreed on Audrey for a girl. Flying down the long mountain into Scranton we were still trying to come up with a name we both liked for a boy. Then in Harrisburg, with Three Mile Island's two cooling towers gently steaming in the distance, my back started to ache. The first menstrual cramp hit in York as we passed the giant plaster weight lifter hoisting barbells over his head next to the interstate. By the time we dropped down into the fluorescent tunnel beneath the Baltimore Harbor, the familiar pain was a rhythmic vise from my ribs to my knees. My body was melting. I concentrated on my breathing, trying to hang on till we made it down the Baltimore-Washington Parkway to home, where I could curl up on the floor of my own bathroom, such as it was, and die.

I learned long ago only the Pill or pregnancy can stop this pain. I've had difficult periods since I was a teenager, when the vomiting and diarrhea would strip ten pounds off me in a day; my sisters, too, to a lesser degree. No doctor's ever been able to tell me why, though now that my sisters have been through labor, they tell me that's what this intense pain is like—the transition stage when the pain curve shoots up exponentially as the baby prepares for its final push into the world. But for me, there's no baby at the end to make it all worthwhile.

—◦◉◦—

The Vette grumbles in park by the side of the road. I sit slumped in my seat. Rosie's on her feet, her back against the roof of the car, whining and yelping and demanding to know why we're stopped.

Yellowstone is closed.

Yellowstone. The oldest national park in the world, home to bison, elk, grizzlies, petrified trees, Old Faithful, Mammoth Hot Springs, and other geothermal wonders I won't be seeing, venue for a spectacular route over the Rockies I won't be traveling, gateway to the sublime Idaho wilderness I won't be hiking. The heavy gray cloud cover that moved in as we rushed across the high plains was the front edge of winter. Snow flurries float onto the windshield and melt. Higher up, they're piling up fast and icing over. Today, unless you're riding on snow tires or chains, the park's closed.

I wheel the Vette around to face the way we came, our back to the park and the snow-misted Rockies. Now what? I pull over again, yank out my big book of maps and flip to Wyoming. I'm at that corner of America where Wyoming, Montana, and Idaho come together. Maybe there's some other way over these godforsaken mountains into Idaho. The radio's announcing weather and road conditions. As Rosie gives up hoping this stop will lead to a sniff-and-mark op and lies down with a sigh, my finger traces the bad news across the map.

I'm at a complete loss. My travel plan just blew out the window and now lies buried under several feet of Rocky Mountain snow. I smack the map against the steering wheel. Planning this trip gave me the illusion that I controlled my life. That's why I was on this trip, for God's sake. Not only do I have no control over when I get there, I have no control over where "there" is.

I lay on the bed, too depressed to get up. One day after that long drive from joy to misery, and I had just found out that my friend's wife, who three months ago was on the same pills at the same time, was now three months pregnant. I read the email and cheered, "Yay! The infertiles win one!" Then I burst into tears. Next to their success, my failure felt oddly humiliating. My whole life felt as undone as the bathroom.

Sure, down the hall where Frank could be heard clanking tools against pipes, it looked like progress was being made. The plywood subfloor had finally gone down over the joists, and the DuRock concrete board over the plywood. An impressive maze of electrical conduit lay in place behind the crisp new drywall, and the white, freshly tiled floor and walls gleamed. But it wasn't a bathroom yet. Except for the lonely toilet, it was a barren space, the ceiling and upper walls unpainted, gray, and splotched with white drywall paste. An unfinished hole gaped where the cabinets should have been. Pipes poked out at the air from holes in the floor and wall. Below, mysterious new leaks still silently spread from time to time in the map on the living room ceiling.

Frank sat on the edge of the bed and asked if maybe I'd like to get out and go to church with him. It's an urban church, a lot of single professionals, two-career couples with no children. You have no children, you see other people with no children, especially other people your own age, it makes you feel as if having no children is okay, normal.

"That sounds like a good idea," I said. He squeezed my hand.

But that Sunday morning from across the church I saw one of our fellow two-career couples with no children. I hadn't seen them in a while. Last time I'd seen them, they'd looked like us. Now the she-half of the couple looked hugely, undeniably pregnant. I didn't know her well, and yet I felt like I'd been abandoned by my best friend.

"Oh shit, I'm sorry," Frank muttered when he saw my face. "So much for my good idea."

If God was lighting my way, God needed a higher wattage bulb. And another thing: If God loved me, why would God do this to me? Why couldn't God just let me have a baby like everybody else?

"I'm tired of crying," I said to Frank in the car after church. "I'm buying a puppy."

⟶⫷◉⫸⟵

I needed someplace to put all this primal, uncontrollable emotion that kept spewing up inside me no matter how rational I thought my reasons were for wanting a baby. That afternoon when we opened the newspaper classifieds, I found the perfect vessel to safely contain it all. She'd been born two months earlier, thirty miles away in the Virginia countryside. All black-and-tan German shepherds are born black; the tan comes in as they grow. So far, she was still all black except for a little tan on her face and paws. She had huge paws at the ends of her stubby puppy legs. She had sharp rows of tiny milk teeth. She whimpered puppy breath, fusty, and delicate. She fit in my two hands.

That evening, standing in the middle of some 4-H kid's pack of flea-bitten German shepherds, I paid the kid's mother, rubbed a towel over the puppy's mother, wrapped the puppy in it, and carried her away.

Frank drove; passing headlights flared and faded. I whispered to her in my lap, "It's okay it's okay *sh sh sh*," over and over, but she cried at the dark world rushing by, and the noise of the engine, and the strange smells of the car. I tugged the towel over her head and, surrounded by the scent of her mother, she quieted.

In our bedroom, Frank nested the towel in the borrowed dog crate we'd picked up that afternoon. I placed her at the crate's open door and she wobbled in. It was safely cavelike; it smelled of her mother. I leaned in after her on my hands and knees. I could feel Frank's hand on my back as I stroked the top of her tiny head with my thumb till her eyes closed and her mouth mimed the most contented moments in her short life, those moments when she had suckled with her sisters and brothers at her mother's belly, now suckling the air, soft smacking sounds of happiness.

Later, when she woke up in the night to find herself alone and vulnerable, she instinctively cried out so the pack could find her and protect her. Each time I would stumble out of bed to stroke her back to sleep, until the third night when I finally growled, "Hey! Enough! Cut it out!" and burrowed under my pillow. That night it was Frank who got down next to her crate, and stayed there, and the next time she woke up she heard him breathing a few reassuring inches away and fell back to sleep on her own. He slept on the floor beside her crate the rest of the night, and the next night, and the next, until she finally understood she wasn't alone.

Frank named her Luther's Rose.

Luther's Rose. The symbolic seal Martin Luther designed to express his view of the believer's relationship with God. At the center, a tiny black cross within a red heart, because faith in Christ crucified saves the believer, who believes with the heart. Both cross and heart lie in the center of a white rose, because faith brings joy, consolation, and peace. Behind the rose, a sky-blue background, because of the heavenly joy to come. The sky encircled by a golden ring, because in heaven such bliss is both precious and endless.

My entire family called to get reports on our new arrival. I felt grateful they had guessed I needed to share it with them. I also felt transparently second-rate. I told them about Rosie's milestones as if she were my new baby I'd brought home, except she wasn't; she was a dog. When I analyzed Rosie's entry into our lives, I felt pathetic, like some lonely old lady making goo-goo noises at a beribboned, besweatered Pomeranian named Baby. I wondered if people felt sorry for me, turning to such a naked substitute, *buying* it no less—couldn't have a baby so she bought a dog. Self-pity was one thing. I hated the possibility of other people's pity.

I was sitting in meeting, my eyes closed. The tall windows were open. Outside in the street a car's power steering squealed in the midst of parallel parking and the breeze rustled fallen leaves against the pavement, a cool blue autumn day. I was picturing Rosie curled up in her crate, waiting for Frank and me to meet up at the Lutheran church and come home to her.

During the day we'd move her crate downstairs next to my desk by the sliding-glass door, a space I'd reclaimed along with the rest of the living room now that the drywall and plywood had finally migrated up into the bathroom where they belonged.

Like babies, very young puppies sleep most of the time. But when Rosie woke up and came out of her crate, she pulled me into her timeless world, a world where I left behind past failures and future hopes to enjoy the small, real pleasures of the here and now, where God lived. I'd be lying on the floor doing crunches and she'd poke her head through my legs, scramble up onto my chest to bestow wet nose kisses on my cheek and neck, a snuffling love dispenser. We'd race around the house playing canine football. That 4-H kid, God love him, had created a little miracle. After fifteen minutes or half an hour, she'd fall asleep again in my lap, sighing and suckling the air. I loved that sound. I loved her. She may have been a coping mechanism, but I didn't feel pathetic about settling for a dog when I was alone with Rosie. I didn't feel unloved by the Light.

Buying a puppy had had such a positive effect on my spiritual life, I figured maybe I should do something else I'd been talking about for years—join the meeting. Earlier in the week I'd sat down to write my letter requesting membership. That's the first step—write a brief letter, usually about a page long, describing why you believe membership is right for you and the meeting.

I write for a living; I thought it would be easy. Fifteen pages later, I had to admit way was not opening. For a woman who never particularly liked the role of pastor's wife, I was devoting a peculiar number of pages to explaining why it was okay for a Lutheran pastor's wife to become a Quaker. A lot of people expect pastors' wives to fit a certain stereotype, like, a Lutheran pastor's wife should be Lutheran. Apparently I was one of those people.

By Sunday, I had set aside the membership letter and focused on what was working, just being a meeting attender with a great dog. Rosie was like the Marine Corps motto, *Semper Fidelis,* Latin for forever faithful. The Marines also have a saying, *Semper* Gumby—forever flexible. Because shit happens. Plans change. That was Rosie, too. She was happy to sniff whatever the road brought her way without asking why. She delighted in whatever random stick or carcass she came across, picked it up and played with it as if it were the last, best stick or carcass on earth. Then if something more interesting came along, she'd drop it and bounce on without a backward glance. She made no plans. She required no bathroom. Maybe if I were more like Rosie, with my ears cocked to the reality of the present instead of always listening to the noisy, illusory future, I'd find it easier to hear that still, small voice inside whenever it whispered to me.

Traditional Quakers have the same go-with-the-flow approach to worship as Rosie has to life. There's no liturgy, no sermon. You just sit there in silence. Some people pray. Some meditate. Some nap. Some daydream about their puppies. Sometimes the Spirit reveals a message in your heart. Usually the message is just for you, and inside your heart is where it's supposed to stay. Occasionally it's for the whole meeting, in which case you feel moved to stand up and speak.

As I sat there with my eyes closed, picturing Rosie galumphing around with a stick in her mouth that was bigger than she was, a song came to me and all of a sudden I broke out in a cold sweat, couldn't catch my breath.

I don't know how other Friends know when they're supposed to stand up and speak, but whenever I'm hit with an attack of stage fright, I know. In all my years of sitting in meeting, it's happened to me exactly twice. This was one of them.

My eyes popped open. In order to share a song, I had to sing it. I am not a singer. I stood up, wiped my sweaty palms on my jeans, and opened my mouth. When nervous, I'm not a thinker either—I started with the third line's words and the first line's melody, so halfway through the song I ran out of words, which forced me to stop and start over. This did not boost my confidence. Sung correctly, the song goes like this:

> *Praise God from whom all blessings flow,*
> *Praise Him all creatures here below,*
> *Praise Him above ye heavenly host,*
> *Praise Father, Son, and Holy Ghost.*

It's the doxology, the song most frequently sung by Protestants for the past three hundred years. While the song's doctrine didn't speak to me, in that moment the larger truth of it did. It reminded me to thank God for everything that came my way, because good or bad, everything was an opportunity for growing closer to the Light. "And uh," I mumbled, "that's, uh, the blessing, I guess." And then, mercifully, I sat down.

Just down the road from the park entrance, in the nearly empty parking lot of a strip mall on the edge of Cody, Wyoming, I finally let Rosie out into the flurries. She sniffs a greasy spot of pavement as if it's as exotic and newsworthy as bison spoor.

I sit in the open car door, my elbows on my knees, my breath puffing in small clouds across the map in my cold hands. Okay, so what if I can't rely on a plan? I'm not tied to one either. Maybe all this snow is a good thing. For the past three and a half weeks I've been hurling us up the road like a salmon with a date upstream, huffing and puffing from one destination to the next like the plan is God—gotta get to Chicago, gotta get to Iowa, gotta get to Yellowstone. If the snow hadn't moved in early last night, I'd have blown right past that hunting lodge. I never would have met the cook, the cowboys, the half-naked girl, the runaway mother, the gay Germans, never would have tasted the morning's snowy sweetness. My life's a little richer now for having wasted a few hours there. Rosie trots over, shoves her nose past the map to snort happily in my face, then dodges away to sniff a very provocative stretch of curb.

Snow and ice blanket the roads north into Montana and Idaho. I have no idea what lies to the south, but I have to follow whatever road opens up before me, and the road south is clear and dry. Who knows what random riches this new road might bring? Like the jolly Germans said: America, hoo! Such a big country! Such a beautiful country!

I throw the map over my shoulder into the back, call Rosie to get in, and point the Vette's nose to the south. You've just got to drive the road you're on. The radio trades weather for music and I crank it up, don't care what kind of music it is so long as it's loud enough to hear over the engine. I ride through Cody tapping the steering wheel. Rosie rides with her whole head and shoulders pushing out the window higher than the roof of the car, grinning in the cold, gray wind, eyes on the southern horizon, while off to the right, the Rockies glimmer white in the distance.

IN A BLINK I'LL BE GONE

Starting date 10/12/01 . . . waning crescent moon . . . odometer 127,585 . . . route: south through Wyoming, then west through Utah, Nevada, and California with short pit stops at the Hickison Petroglyphs and Altamont Pass = four days, 1468 miles

The road leads us out from under a bank of clouds that Frank could have named and forecast the weather by; it leads us out into sunshine. Precision-guided bombs have been falling on Afghanistan for five days now as the road winds us south, parallel to the Rockies, through a gorge between a cluster of flat-topped buttes. Rounding a curve, the road throws several cowboys and about fifty head of cattle at us, ambling along the shoulder. I stomp on the brakes and force the Vette to rumble past slowly. Rosie barks at the cattle and horses—keep your distance or else. The horses jingle their harnesses; the cowboys point at Rosie and grin. Afghan mothers and fathers take their children by the hand and flee along dusty roads to refugee camps in Pakistan.

The road finally lets us climb up over the Rockies and the Continental Divide at the southern end of the Wind River Range, in the Shoshone National Forest, which apparently gets its name from the six trees next to the sign, because the rest of the climb to the South Pass is absolutely treeless. The pass tops out at about seventy-five hundred feet, an epic snow-smattered beige steppe, beautifully bleak except for a few distant silhouettes of cattle, and more of those ominously tall snow fences, in places three rows deep. In a video released to the world, bin Laden says when he saw the twin towers fall he praised Allah. I shiver, grateful that for the moment the slats are just empty skeletons.

On the long descent toward the Pacific, the road cruises us through towns that have seen fit to place public stables—each stall in the long metal shed complete with its own miniature paddock—right in the middle of town, the better to keep your ride handy. Back east those long metal sheds would be public self-storage facilities full of the overflow from long-rooted lives. If people were towns, I'd be the one with stables, Frank the one with storage. Rosie and I take a break by a river of green water that snakes its way through grasslands dressed in sage and gold, orange and beige, waving seedheads of fluff and lace and spikes. The wind smells of mint and bay, blowing down from a high stony butte of gray and red.

The road runs on. More terrorist assaults on the United States are expected in the next few days. The road runs through all the gas in the Vette's tank. The vice president urges Americans to be suspicious. At an unpicturesque station in a small town, I'm at the pumps gassing up and Rosie's by the corner of the building chomping on a stick when a loose-limbed man abruptly strides around the corner. Rosie jumps out of her skin and bellows her deep *woof-woof-woof*. The man jumps out of his skin and screams, *"Aaah!"*

I see angry words coming. I see lawsuit. "Come!" I yell at Rosie. "Sorry!" I yell at the man.

But Rosie is already running back to me with her tail between her legs, and the man is already striding on his way again, waving a dismissive, embarrassed hand in my direction. Apparently in Wyoming a barking, charging dog is just a dog doing its job, not a lawsuit waiting to happen, and a man who screams prefers to pretend there are no witnesses.

Some nights the road brings us to the door of pet-friendly motor courts with names like the Pioneer ("Queen size luxury!") and the Tam O'Shanter ("TV in every room!"). Some nights it drops us off in dusty campgrounds. But each night, just like every other night since I brought Rosie home, I stroke her head and listen to the soft smacking sounds she makes as she suckles the air, still a little puppy in a big dog's body. The next morning, if we've been staying in a campground, I have to beat her like a rug, gray poofs rising from her coat, before we get back on the road, which in Utah, curves us back and forth up through folded hills and swoops us down a long pass before suddenly emerging above the broad pale plain where the Mormons finally felt safe enough to stop running from their fellow Americans.

A lot of people came to this continent to escape religious persecution. That didn't stop some of them from doing unto others what had been done unto them, small dogs looking for a smaller dog to kick, like the Quakers of my own Religious Society of Friends hanged by the Puritans. Or later, the Mormons of the Church of Jesus Christ of Latter-day Saints harried all the way from New York to Utah, their leader lynched. Or the latest, a Muslim man murdered in Texas a few days after September 11.

The First Amendment to the Constitution guarantees the freedom of all Americans to worship or not worship God as they please, free from interference by the state, if not their neighbors. That's why the military has chaplains; military life can make it hard to practice a religion. Frank's job is to enable Marines and Sailors to exercise their First Amendment religious rights even when they're stuck on a base somewhere, or out in the field, on a ship or in a fighting hole. Frank's not there to convert; he's there to serve. He gives communion to Lutherans and others who'll receive it, helps lay Catholics or Jews hold services, provides Muslims with a private place to pray, advises pagans and Buddhists, listens to the troubles of Mormons and atheists. He's the only person in the military you *can* tell, because chaplains are the only military personnel who are actually forbidden by regulation from revealing anything that's told to them in pastoral confidence. He's the safety valve. To some, far from home, he's their only friend. He's the one who delivers the news your mother has died. He's the well into which you can whisper your most secret fears.

The road coasts us down onto the plain of the Great Salt Lake, where flat earth melts smoothly into flat water, the transition rimed with white crystals. On the shore, Morton's factories busily process the briny water into great snowy mountains of salt while back in Kentucky soldiers at Fort Campbell prepare for possible deployment. They finalize their wills. Their families try to be brave. The road carries us past the water and I'd like to get closer. I can see a road along the shore, but I can't pick the Vette up from this road and set it down on that one over there. I can only slow down where I am and crane my neck before accelerating toward the setting sun, out into the Great Salt Lake Desert. Fifteen thousand years ago it was all lake. Now, from Salt Lake City to the Nevada line, I-80 is a hundred-mile runway straight across a bleached expanse that stretches away empty as the Arctic, scoured smooth by the wind. I pull over and get out to taste it. It's salt all right.

The road rolls us on and night closes over the desert. Frank would be able to name the stars that crowd down out of the darkness as if lured by the stream of headlights, which twinkle on the road ahead before blazing past like low-flying shooting stars. And the road rolls on. And in the skies over Afghanistan the wrong coordinates are entered into a two-thousand-pound bomb, and so it misses a Taliban airfield by a mile and instead blasts four people to pieces in a Kabul neighborhood. A desolate mother wails for her child, now dead forever. So what that we didn't mean to kill that child.

The road turns and twists us onto Route 50 through Nevada, the loneliest road in America, where a couple of battered trailers, a gas pump, ice, and a one-armed jack huddled together among the rocks and sand are enough to merit a name on the map. American jets drop small yellow packets of food in an effort to feed starving Afghans, and also begin dropping smaller bombs in an effort to blow up fewer innocent people. But some of the bombs are small and yellow, too, and they don't always explode right away when they hit the ground. Instead they lie there waiting to be mistaken for food.

The road I'm on serpentines like an autocross course over a row of rumpled brown mountains, then runs straight as a drag strip across a lakebed ancient and dry, to the next row of autocross mountains, and beyond that to the next lakebed drag strip, and the next mountains, and the next lakebed, and on and on across the middle of Nevada. With no cars in sight, I open it up, a drag race against myself. This much I do control on this journey, how I respond to the road I'm on. At about ninety-five miles an hour, the Vette's L82 kicks out a spurt of torque that presses me into my seat and makes Rosie pant. When the needle pushes a hundred, I drop back to seventy-five because I don't want to die with mustang guts and windshield glass in my teeth, and also I don't want to go deaf—in an old Corvette there isn't much insulation between you and the engine and the road and the wind. As the flood of engine roar drops, the radio resurfaces with the chant of crowds in Europe and Australia protesting the bombing in Afghanistan, though the crowds are much smaller than organizers had hoped.

Maybe that's because all those people they expected to crowd into the streets have had the same thought I have, that protesting on the eve of war is like yelling about the open barn door after the horse has already run off. It feels good, but it doesn't bring the horse back and it doesn't fix the problems that caused the door to be left open in the first place. The time to protest is ten or twenty years earlier, when the problems are still readily fixable through nonviolent means. Or better yet, instead of protesting then, put all that energy into visiting elected representatives and pressuring companies. But it's hard to get people excited that far ahead of time about messy, complicated problems on the other side of the world.

The road rolls us up a mountain scarred with petroglyphs. Rosie and I step out into a quiet, lonely place of juniper and piñon pine. We walk among the rock faces where people worshiped and scratched on the sandstone, back when this was the Garden of Eden, when the lakebeds weren't dry and the mountains weren't bare.

According to the Book of Mormon, America was "a land of promise, which was choice above all other lands, which the Lord God had preserved for a righteous people." I wish I could feel as certain about my country's manifest destiny as the Americans who claimed the whole continent between Canada and Mexico, who told themselves they were reclaiming the promised land for themselves as God's new chosen people.

Standing here, all I feel is tired. I may control my response to the road, but I'm still not clear what that response should be. When I left home, I was running away from hard questions about right and wrong, and if I could, I'd keep running all the way back to some imaginary womblike place and time where those questions no longer mattered. I guess when I fled west, I was hoping I could flee back to the Garden.

But there's no garden here. On relief maps of the United States, this part of the country is depicted in brown. On the ground, it's actually more reddish. It's certainly not garden green. Rosie trots ahead while I stop to examine fertility symbols carved into the rock in the shape of lucky horseshoes, and parallel lines no one knows the meaning of anymore, and in one place a set of initials and a date, 1859, scratched by a surveyor when he passed through.

For thousands of years other people, long gone, have stood exactly where I'm standing and touched this same rock, and more will follow long after I'm gone. Bombs will continue to fall, and still these rocky mountainsides will remain, watching. I whoosh up away from myself, and from a bird's eye view I see clearly that in the life cycle of the planet, I'm just a time-lapse shadow flitting across the surface, puny and lost against the vast backdrop of time. In a blink I'll be gone. I'm thirty-nine. Old age and death are gaining on me. Does anything lie beyond death? Is the soul immortal the way genes are? When I try to imagine everything that is me—my body, my memories, my dreams— gone, it's like trying to wrap my mind around the universe. Now I feel not just tired; I feel infinitely, uneasily small.

It must be comforting to turn away from all that immensity and look instead into a small face that looks like yours and know that part of you, at least, will live on. "You promised no heroic measures, remember?" Frank had said after the Clomid pills had failed and we met with Dr. Warner and I nodded when she suggested laparoscopy. It was a simple outpatient surgical procedure that would relieve my painful menstrual periods for a time, as well as possibly improve my chances of getting pregnant, which made it seem like a practical measure, not a heroic one. And maybe there was nothing heroic about all the measures that eventually followed, either. Maybe it was all just motivated by the fear of dying and being forgotten, of leaving this world without so much as a scratch on a rock to prove I'd been here.

"What if you don't get pregnant?" Frank asked. "What will you say then?"

What would I say then? Hell, I didn't know what to say now. A plane roared low overhead, following the Potomac to National Airport. We were in a park along the river walking Rosie, which meant we were walking and little Rosie was being carried. I watched an empty plastic bottle float by on the current. I tried to be objective about my apparent infertility.

My life was fulfilling as it was, so I didn't need a child to complete me.

I didn't need a child for practical reasons either, to take care of me in my old age; in this society, IRAs, social security, and insurance take care of that.

Since my husband didn't want children anyway, maybe it was for the best.

All very neat and logical and completely unconvincing. I may not have needed a baby, but I still wanted one.

When I started on the pills, I had figured they would probably work; it was easy to say I'd give them a try and let it go if they didn't. But now no matter how objective and intellectual I tried to be about it, I couldn't let go. The wide, gray river carried the bottle onward beneath the Fourteenth Street Bridge till it was just a white speck.

At last I said, "I'm not going to make any more promises to you. All I can tell you is I can't just quit and walk away yet."

Frank let Rosie mouth his hand. "I miss how we used to be. I just want my best friend back."

I wanted to take his hand, reassure him that his best friend was right here beside him where she'd always been. But I felt like I was standing on the other side of the river. I blinked back tears.

He sighed. "Well, do what you have to do."

And so I lay down on a gurney, and while I was unconscious Dr. Warner cut a little hole next to my navel and peered through a laparoscope at my uterus, which looked like Mrs. Potato Head carrying a boulder tucked under each arm, with fallopian tubes for the arms and ovaries for the boulders. She saw that some of the lining of my uterus had begun to grow on the outside, like eyes on Mrs. Potato Head. It's a condition called endometriosis and it's often associated with painful periods. No one knows why the uterine lining grows in the wrong place, but sometimes it does, and there it was. She'd seen worse; there wasn't enough to explain why I wasn't pregnant, but still she cut another hole just above my pubic bone and inserted a laser to burn off the lining, just in case. Then I woke up and Frank took me home and I threw up for thirteen hours.

I remember Frank, on the phone to the duty nurse, slipping ice chips between my lips. I remember him sitting next to the bed, his eyebrows drawn together in worried frustration. I have no memory at all of Rosie sitting next to Frank, her clumsy, oversized paws a month bigger than when we brought her home; her ears were bigger, too, both flopped over in the same direction under their new weight, giving her a windblown look. Frank's the one who remembers her trying to lick my hand where it lay on the sheet.

For reasons nobody knows, fertility seems to increase for up to a year after laparoscopy. I settled in with my growing puppy with the windblown ears to wait and see if that was true for me, too, even though Dr. Warner had said I could move on to stronger drugs right away. Given my advancing age, she said, she was willing to be as aggressive as I wanted to be.

I was thirty-four.

Time is the enemy; time is the healer; time is neither good nor bad, just the road without end, forcing you to move on. I'm nearing my fortieth year now. A thousand years before my mother gave birth to me, someone carved fertility horseshoes into a mountain twelve million years old.

In that fall of waiting, nothing happened. Not in me, not in our bathroom, not in our twelve-foot-wide back yard, which stretched like a trench between wooden privacy fences from the back door to the alley. Some efficient soul had once landscaped it entirely in concrete. Someone else had later added a layer of brick to demarcate a patio next to the house. Some would-be gardener had dumped a pile of dirt and bark chips on top of most of the rest of the concrete, then planted a couple of lonely, undernourished rose bushes in the middle. Our contribution to the concrete concealment process was the mountain of crap piled next to the alley. Sometimes we sat out there in our new patio furniture, which I'd brought home after shopping the neighborhood curbs on trash day, to enjoy the view.

I was curled up on the bench that didn't slant sideways so much now that we'd stacked bricks under it, watching my puppy try to take bites out of a row of pink and white impatiens I'd planted in a hole I'd sledgehammered into the concrete. Rosie's nose kept bumping against the chicken wire I'd erected around the impatiens.

"Kristin?" Frank creaked back in the rocker that had clearly proved it could withstand being left out in all kinds of weather. "I was wondering. Is it possible you're not getting pregnant because I dragged my feet all those years?"

Surprising, grateful tears pricked my eyes. "Oh," I sighed, "I've wondered about that myself." I stopped while the fire engine howled out of the station three blocks away and the huskies two yards over howled back. Why was I unexpectedly, tearfully, grateful? It *was* his fault we'd wasted a decade. If you assumed that whatever was wrong with us meant we had only a very small chance of getting pregnant every month, then we would have been much more likely to hit the target if we'd tried 150 times so far instead of only thirty. But although my sense of fairness obligated me to blame him, blaming is an odious task. The siren faded away. The huskies went back to pacing their patio, nails ticking. That's why I was grateful. Frank had just now relieved me of the burden of blaming him myself.

"You know," I said, "the Pill puts endometriosis on hold. That means it was at the same stage when I went off the Pill at thirty-two as it was when I started taking it ten years before. If endometriosis is why I haven't gotten pregnant now, I would have had the same trouble then."

"Oh," Frank said. "Well, I still feel bad."

Which was why I felt magnanimous and good. It's always easier to be a good person when you have help. Rosie gave up trying to chew the impatiens through the wire and turned to catching and chewing her tail instead.

Several times a day during that fall of waiting, Rosie would spin herself around on her tailbone and growl at her privates while she licked them, then leap up as if she'd been stung and ricochet around the room, her clunky paws scrabbling for traction on the wood floor. She'd ping off the walls, crash into the couch, crash into me, my desk, leave my computer tottering. I envisioned Rosie doing the same thing at seventy pounds instead of thirty.

I'd heard that even though dogs don't develop the capacity to absorb serious training till they are six months old, you can start pretraining them earlier. But the pretraining had such a ridiculous name I hadn't been able to bring myself to sign Rosie up for it till now. I looked up dog schools in the yellow pages. "Do you offer . . ." I winced and forced myself to say it: "Puppy Kindergarten?"

"Do we offer *what?*"

I had to say it again. "Puppy Kindergarten?"

"No," said the voice on the other end of the line. I felt like an idiot till the voice added, "But we do have Puppy Head Start."

The waiting fall turned to winter. A cold, gray stillness hung over the naked trees outside. Inside I was still in bed because if I got up, I'd have to walk into my unfinished bathroom that, although it had a toilet and tub, still had a hole where the showerhead should be, and a bigger hole where the cabinets should be, and a blank space where the sink would eventually go. I was still in bed because if I got up, I'd have to sit at my desk and fail to think of a new way to bring in some money. Freelancing was always feast or famine, and I was starving despite having tried every self-marketing ploy I knew. I was still in bed because if I got up, I'd have to face the fact that my period was starting and there was nothing I could do about any of it beyond what I was already doing.

Something cold and wet bumped against my arm, hanging over the side of the bed. I dragged my gaze away from the window. Rosie cut her eyes at me coyly, jawing her green tennis ball, windblown ears flopping, tail wagging. She rubbed the soggy ball against my bare arm as if she was sure I'd find it irresistible. I grabbed the ball out of her mouth and threw it into the hall, where I knew it was leaving wet spots every time it bounced. I wiped off my hand on the sheet.

A few seconds later she came galloping back and I figured I might as well get up. At least I didn't have cramps. I got up and chased her and her nasty ball around the house.

The knock at the door prompted Rosie to hide.

It was my younger sister Ingrid, her short silky hair golden and coiffed, her makeup perfect, her daughter Annali on her hip. I like showing Ingrid off.

"I have a defective dog," I told her.

She screwed up her face with mock outrage. "Well I certainly hope you can return it."

I knew puppies were genetically programmed to keep quiet unless they were separated from the pack, but I was beginning to wonder if my gutless puppy would ever bark. With each passing month, Rosie passed through another phase of development: from shadowing me to bratty independence, from curiosity to fear of all things new, from sleeping most of the time to just napping, not to mention the endless chewing and drooling when she teethed. But barking eluded her.

Ingrid tried to reassure me. "Oh it'll happen. Annali went through the same phases, including barking. They just lasted longer." And then she left Annali with me for the weekend. Annali was three. She came with a suitcase filled with arty ensembles, enough for several complete costume changes per day. Ingrid had always been artistic; as she grew up her canvas extended from her drawing table to her house and now to her daughter, who couldn't have cared less about clothes. What Annali cared about was dogs.

"I want to pretend I'm your puppy, too," she said.

"Okay. Sit!"

"No, no. You have to name me first."

Back in the days when I pretended to be a dog, I called myself Columbine. I don't know why. I just liked it. "How about Begonia?" I asked.

"Mmm." She made a face. "No."

"What's wrong with Begonia?"

"I don't like it."

I thought for a minute. "How about Puppy Petunia?"

She liked it.

"Puppy Petunia—sit!"

She sat.

We played Going for a Walk, and Fetch, and Tug of War. My favorite trick that I taught her was to lie on her back and, while I scratched her stomach, shake her leg the way dogs do when you hit that nerve.

That night I woke up.

"Mommy," I heard.

I looked around the bedroom, faintly illuminated by the streetlight glowing through the curtains. Annali was standing up in her bed on the floor next to Frank's and mine. She rubbed her face, disoriented. Rosie poked her head out of her crate and Frank elbowed himself up but I was already on my feet.

I tucked Annali back in. She squinted at me. "Who are you?"

"I'm Aunt Kiki," I said. Annali gave me that name, Kiki. She hadn't been able to manage Kristin when she first started to talk two years before.

She closed her eyes. "You sound just like my mommy," she murmured.

"That's because I'm your mommy's sister," I whispered.

Two days later she went home with her parents to Richmond. Back when she was born, on the phone with my sister, I had asked, "Do you just feel this instant love?"

Ingrid had been quiet a long minute. "I'm not sure what I feel," she'd said slowly. "It's tender like love, but it's also a mama-bear feeling, like if someone were to try to hurt her, I could kill them."

I felt that same feeling months later when I saw Annali for the first time. I grabbed her from Ingrid and ran around with her, laughing at her baby giggles, overcome by a fierce, instant connection with this defenseless little person, this sense that I would protect her no matter what or die trying. But you can't defend your child against an anonymous speck in the sky that drops a two-thousand-pound bomb on your house. Or a speck that grows larger and larger until it grows into a plane that crashes in through your child's office window on a sunny Tuesday morning in September.

I have two sisters, a stepsister, and two stepbrothers. I was six when my youngest sister, Erin, was born in 1968. I remember being allowed to hold her on the way home from the hospital in those days before child seats and seat belts. She took up my whole lap. Ingrid was four, earnestly helping me support the floppy newborn head, the two of us pressed tightly together on my side of the Chevy's broad back seat.

Our new sister made the same sounds as those coming from the tiny baby I held on Christmas morning after waiting all fall to conceive one of my own—sweet little grunting sounds. Her name was Lydia Rose, and my baby sister Erin had given birth to her just a few hours earlier. I rocked her. "Isn't she beautiful, Frank?"

Frank nodded, but he was looking at me, not the baby; he was watching me carefully.

I took the train back and forth to help Erin, who lived in Richmond, too, on the other side of town from Ingrid. She and her husband had separated, and we cried ironic tears together, that she had a baby and no husband, and I had a husband and no baby. I slept on the floor of Erin's bedroom, walked Lydia on my shoulder after the night nursings. Once she was asleep I'd take her back to Erin, who would wake up just enough to settle Lydia on her chest, then pass out again, exhausted. By the third week I was exhausted, too. If the day ever came that I had to do it for my own child, I now knew just how hard it would be at my age. I'd hear Lydia start to cry, hear Erin get up.

"Do you need me?" I'd ask groggily from the floor. Just the thought of moving, of getting up, was torturous.

"No, go back to sleep," Erin would murmur.

And gratefully, sometimes I would. Erin, the baby, the little one, the one we always thought we had to take care of, had grown up the tallest and toughest of us all, tackling her single parenthood like it was just another one of her accounting problems to be worked through step by step. When she was laboring at the hospital, she was so stoic the nurses called her Pioneer Woman.

"Erin?" I whispered one night when I did get up to walk Lydia for her. But Erin had fallen as deeply asleep as the soft, warm mound of baby against my shoulder. So that night I just took Lydia to bed with me. I placed her on my chest the way Erin did, her downy head beneath my chin. Every now and then she would wiggle and make those tiny grunting sounds, smelling of sweet milk and powder and new skin. I couldn't sleep at all, though maybe I did; I dreamed I was changing her diaper.

Later, I took Rosie down to Florida and filled in for my mother, caring for Oma so Mom could go up and help Erin with the baby. Opa was gone by then. Oma sat in a rocker next to the sliding-glass door, reading or watching the birds at the feeder among the azaleas and ferns and hibiscus. Framed snapshots sat on the table next to Oma's rocker, most of them old black-and-whites. In one, Oma stands on the edge of Papineau Lake with my mother in her arms. My mother's blond hair is in pigtails; she's about three and looks like Erin did at that age, or maybe it's Ingrid I see in our mother. Oma's wearing a flowered sundress and smiling my mother's smile.

While we were there, Rosie would take her tug toy to Oma instead of me, because Oma was never too busy to set aside whatever she was doing and take hold. "Ooooh!" Oma would exclaim with delight as Rosie tugged back. I watched in amazement as my wild, hyperactive puppy gentled the strength of her tugs to match my frail Oma's.

Nearly a year before, the day Erin found out she was pregnant with Lydia, by chance we were all in Richmond—Oma and Mom, Ingrid, Erin, and I. Oma could still travel then. Erin came down the stairs with a dazed smile on her face and a urine test stick in her hand. As we all gathered round and giggled and hugged, I churned with joy and lonely yearning. For Erin's sake, I tried to keep the yearning stuffed

beneath the joy where no one would notice, and I thought I had suc-
ceeded until I felt Oma's hand take mine.

"I wish the same for you," she whispered in my ear.

Oma, holding my mother on the shore of Papineau Lake, smiling
my mother's smile. I wished the same for me, too. Frank didn't put up
much resistance when I told him I wanted to try the stronger drugs.
He'd seen it coming.

The road is a ribbon, unreeling us through California's High Sierra.
The T-tops are off the Vette and Rosie is up, her nose pointed into the
wind that whips back over the windshield as I swing the car hard
through the curves. A bicyclist waves as we pass. On the radio anti-
American demonstrators are shouting bin Laden's praises in the streets
of Iran, Pakistan, Nigeria, Indonesia, Malaysia, Kenya, while in
Afghanistan more mothers are weeping in the dust over their inability
to protect their dead children, and every day in New York City firemen
carry the dead up out of the hazy, twisted rubble. They hand corpses
and parts of corpses over to the mothers who once rocked these bodies
when they were small and whole, who would have died to protect them
even now if they could have.

Swing left, swing right, the Vette's fiberglass body on its tight steel
frame is built for this, it barely leans.

Other mothers' children are in the Egyptian desert, my husband
somewhere among them, preparing to do whatever has to be done to
protect the rest of America's sons and daughters, because that's what
this feels like, it feels like self-defense and who am I to tell anyone they
can't attempt to defend their children?

Then I can't think about anything beyond the wheel and the stick
shift and pedals; it's just me and the car and the unreeling road pushing us up to ten thousand feet, to gray granite peaks streaked white
with waterfalls and snow, before dropping us down into the deep
aquarium-green of sequoia and hemlock and fir in Yosemite Valley.

I park the Vette and hop the rocks across a boulder-filled stream, water strumming the boulders, firs rustling at the sky, Rosie slowly, cautiously creeping and lurching her way from rock to rock before scrambling up the opposite bank behind me.

The next day the road roars us into the northern end of the Diablo Range. Dry grass-covered hills mound up around us, plain as loaves of brown bread, mile after mile of plain brown hills. Rosie's zoned out. The road curls around a brown hill and there, through the windshield, beyond the Vette's nose, rises a sight that lifts my foot from the accelerator. My mouth drops open.

On both sides of the road, in every direction as far as I can see, three-armed wind turbines stud the hills like hundreds of white-robed mystics in a trance. Some are still, some are slowly turning, turning, turning. I pull over, roll down the windows, silence the engine. At first all I hear is the swish of passing cars. Then, beneath the cars, the wind. Finally, beneath the wind, I hear it, mesmeric and eerie—the turbines, humming.

Rosie's ears swivel. In the slanting golden sunlight of late afternoon, we listen together as the crowded hills *ohmmm* a single, singing chord.

THIS ROAD SUCKS

*Starting date 10/16/01 . . . new moon . . .
odometer 129,053 . . . route: west to San
Francisco, then south to a pit stop in Santa
Cruz = two days, 152 miles*

The Vette coasts down to the water's edge near the base of the Golden Gate Bridge. Overhead, gracefully swooping suspension cables arc away into fog that veils what lies beyond—the Pacific Ocean. After five thousand miles and one complete cycle of the moon, we've arrived on the other side of the continent.

South of San Francisco the moonless night is dark and starlit as we dip and soar through the Santa Cruz Mountains down to the coast. I can't wait to see Uncle Hans.

When my sisters and I were kids, our very coolest uncle was Uncle Hans—"Hansi" to his sister, my mother. He was good-looking. He left his hair long over his ears. He wore flared pants with big stripes. While our parents were into jazz and folk, he dug far-out rock 'n' roll, with shelves of multicolored album spines wrapping the walls around his hi-fi. When we visited Uncle Hansi's swanky bachelor pad in Washington, D.C., Ingrid and I shared a waterbed beneath a mirrored ceiling in a guest room papered in psychedelic posters, dripping with beads, and lit by lava lamps and a black light. We loved that room so much we would have married it.

In addition to being our grooviest male relative, Uncle Hansi was also quite possibly the smartest. He was a nuclear chemist. He worked for the Atomic Energy Commission. Sometimes, he went to the White House.

Then in 1980, Uncle Hansi walked away from the rat race inside the Beltway and moved across the continent to a whole other state of mind. Now, with two partners, he runs a computer chip business out of a garage. He has no children, but around the time he moved west he took in a teenage boy neglected by an abusive family. He was in the process of adopting him when the boy died in a car accident. This is pretty much all I know about his life out here. I've seen very little of my uncle in the twenty years since he disappeared into the sunset.

On a busy street, I pull up to a modest two-story clapboard house, half-hidden by an enormous weeping willow. I park the Vette in the drive, next to a newish Toyota Corolla, a 1970s-era faded red pickup with an extra-long bed, a white Dodge Dart, a beat-up panel van, and a hatchback that's missing a few tires.

I knock at the door. When it opens, a squat black hound shoots out, fat as a stuffed sausage and baying for Rosie, who wags her tail uncertainly and circles on tiptoes to face him, but then he spots a passing cyclist and charges past Rosie to the street, still baying. The door opens wider and someone charges out after him, shouting, "Saber! Cut it out! *Saber!*"

It's Uncle Hans. He crabs his way back to me, dragging Saber by the collar. "Kristin! Boy, every time I see you I can't get over how much you look like Barb."

"Yeah, funny how that works with mothers and daughters." I can't get over how much Hans looks like Opa now. He pushes Saber inside and straightens to give me a hug and a kiss. His face has always been Oma's, but now that he's reached the age my grandfather was when I knew him, I recognize the slightly stooped march that leads me inside, the way he half-turns and points one way then another in moments of excitement.

I recognize other things, too, the modern art on the walls, the mod Swedish recliner, the shiny, lacquered coffee table that's actually an inkblot-shaped slice from some exotic tree—they all hail from his D.C. bachelor-pad days. But the house itself has the humble, haphazard air of a college-town group house. A good-looking young guy, thin as a whippet with bed-head hair, is kicked back on the sheet-covered couch watching TV. A tall, thirtyish rocker dude bounces on his toes toward me from the kitchen, his long dark hair tied back. A woman my age follows behind him, as effervescent and tan as a beach-volleyball player. Her name's Sharol—Hans is introducing them all—and she presses her palms together to greet me with a prayerful bow, saying, "Wow, this is so beautiful!" Her rocker boyfriend, Chris, shakes my hand. "Hey, cool." And Scott waves from the couch. "So which engine you got in that Vette?"

They're all Hans's housemates—Rosie weaving in and out between them and ducking away from their hands—though Scott's just here temporarily on the couch while he's fixing up a house he's going to rent down the street. And the other bedroom upstairs is rented to Jesse, whom Hans tells me is studying to become a massage therapist, but who's out at a music gig tonight. Oh, and there's also a keyboardist who has temporarily taken up residence in the attic under the eaves, accessed through a Munchkin-sized door in the bathroom. He knows not to come out when he hears the bathroom fan go on, and his keyboard practice serenades you while you shower.

"So hey," says Chris, "if you're hungry, I threw some stuff together, it's like a gumbo stew watchamacallit sorta deal—what's in it, I don't know."

I don't know what's in it either, but it's really good.

At dawn, heavy trucks start rumbling in and out of a gravel lot across the street. I lie in my sleeping bag on the floor of Uncle Hans's tiny home office and stare at the ceiling. If I had x-ray vision, I'd see a guy sleeping up there under the eaves. This is a long way from Uncle Hans's former life. I can't decide if it's an improvement. Though Hans seems happy with this new life of his, it doesn't seem like a destination to me, more like a way station on the road to somewhere else.

That was what got to me about trying to make a baby. I always felt like I was on the way and never quite getting there, so focused on the "there" of a possible future event that meanwhile the "here" of my life was passing me by. "That's why I'm looking forward to this whole final round of treatment," I told Frank shortly before it started. "I can finally see the light at the end of the tunnel."

"Huh," he grunted. He was crouched in an awkward position, painting tar onto the brick half of our living room floor. The bathroom was almost done; the sink was installed, only the cabinets were left to build. So we had torn up the living room floor. The back half was mildewy brick, the front half dark, unhappy parquet. Frank had discovered the bricks had been laid directly on the dirt, so he was sealing them with tar before laying a new layer of brick on top. I had sanded the parquet and discovered it didn't look much better sanded.

"Within five months," I said as I painted the parquet, "one way or another, my fate will pretty much be settled. We'll be able to get back to a normal sex life. I'll be able to focus on my life as it is, not as it might be. I just want to take a deep breath, get through these last months, and move on."

I was pretty sure I could move on because when Ingrid had called me earlier in the month with the news that she was pregnant again, I was thrilled for her and didn't even remotely feel like crying afterward. My own proof that I wasn't pregnant failed to distress me that month; I was no longer melting. Even the fact that the laparoscopy had worn off and I was once again having to curl up on the comforting coolness of the bathroom tiles didn't distress me. I had clearly achieved a new level of unruffled fatalism and could take anything life threw at me.

"Maybe I'm kidding myself," I said to Frank that day as I slapped down the paint that halfway hid the inadequacies of our living room floor, "but I think I'm in the process of letting go of this baby thing, preparing to get on with my life."

I find a phone jack in Hans's dining room and plug in my laptop. Still no email from Frank. Hans and I go for a walk through a woodsy field, our dogs' tails whipping above the tall grass like banners for us to follow. At a restaurant on the water we drink wine as a flock of sailboats race against the setting sun. Afterward we meet up with some of his house-mates at a palate-challenging Asian restaurant, Hans's treat. He's brought them here before; they order tongue-twisters with confidence while Chris uses rocker terminology to blissfully describe the symphony Hans took Sharol and him to hear last weekend. Me, I puzzle over my menu as I puzzle over Hans and his life.

Perched on the cliffs among gnarled pines and redwoods, with Silicon Valley breathing down its neck, Santa Cruz is a shabby hippie town gone rich, the kind of place where you really do see Deadhead stickers on Cadillacs. When Hans came here, he abandoned his wide ties and leisure suits for baggy shorts, cotton t-shirts emblazoned with slogans, and plaid flannel shirts. He wears Birkenstocks year round. He looks like a poster boy for the counterculture. He votes Republican. On the other hand, he exulted when O.J. Simpson was acquitted, possibly the only white man in America besides the ones on O.J.'s legal team to spontaneously react that way, saying that would show those dirty cops. I can't figure him out.

Back at the house, Hans sits in his Swedish recliner like a rock, watching TV while late-night waves of youthful energy wash in and out the front door, churning around him and pounding up and down the stairs. He's watching the heaviest day of airstrikes yet, carried out by fifty carrier-based fighter jets, ten long-range bombers, and an AC-130 gunship. Explosions rock Kabul, the Afghan capital, and farther south, the Taliban stronghold of Kandahar.

The two most common sounds in this house are the conservative FOX News Channel and classical music—Hans listens to more Bach than Rolling Stones these days. Even when Hans is out of the house and his housemates control the remote and the CD player, both play on, habits they've picked up from him.

"Hold it like a dart," the nurse said. Her name was Joan.

Frank hesitated. "You're sure I'm not going to hit a bone?"

"Positive." Nurse Joan was a cheerful mother of four grown boys, unflappable as a tank, the kind of woman who could say "vaginal fluids" in mixed company without blushing.

Frank took a deep breath. Then he sank an inch and a half of needle into the big muscle of my upper buttock. He was surprised it slid in so easily. It didn't feel easy to me, but I just clenched my teeth because I was a stoic fatalist and could take anything.

Nurse Joan congratulated us. "You'll start the real thing next week." Our lesson in how to mix and inject hormones was over.

On our way out of the medical center Frank kept asking me if it still hurt where he'd stuck me, and I kept assuring him it didn't. Walking into the parking garage, he hooked my arm through his. "Having to go through it with you like this," he said, "is making me feel especially close to you."

When we got home, Rosie bounded to us with her usual joyous yips, spinning and leaping, wacking the wall with her tail. Frank said, his voice muffled by her licks as he knelt and she jumped in his arms, "It touches me the way her world revolves around us." He watched her bound away to find a toy so she could celebrate our return from the dead with a game. "Seeing how much she's come to mean to me has made me realize how much a child would mean to me."

In 1997, the supply of injectable hormones required for a single treatment cycle cost one thousand dollars. Blood tests, sonograms, and artificial insemination cost an additional two thousand. We paid one hundred dollars of that. Insurance paid the rest. We would get three tries, one every other month, before the insurance company would pull the plug. Each try started with the injections.

To make my ovaries produce a lot of eggs at once, for seven consecutive evenings Frank and I trooped into our almost-but-not-quite-finished bathroom, where I mixed up—and bent over the sink while he nervously injected me with—urofollitropin, a preparation of follicle-stimulating hormone derived from the urine of post-menopausal women. On the eighth evening, to stimulate ovulation Frank shot me up with chorionic gonadotropin, derived from the urine of pregnant women. I felt like I'd performed the usual female ritual of going to the ladies' room with a herd of other women, but this time had come out possibly pregnant.

During those eight days of shots and nervous tension I had three sonograms and four blood tests and sex once when the doctor told us to, so Frank's sperm would be the right vintage on artificial-insemination day.

I sat in the silent, empty waiting area outside the medical center's fertility clinic with a cup of sperm in a nondescript paper bag balanced primly on my knees.

To ensure I wasn't late, Frank had conscientiously started the sample-production process seventy minutes before I was due at the clinic, and then proceeded to get the job done in under ten. The half-life of unprocessed sperm in a cup is about an hour, which meant the sperm balanced on my knees would take their last gasp at 8:30 A.M. The clinic opened at 8:30.

I watched the clock and tried not to hyperventilate or think about how nasty I'd been to Frank when he'd emerged so quickly with the sample cup, beaming with success. "Way to go," I'd said in a voice dripping with sarcasm. "This is going to ruin everything." I couldn't blame my reaction on the drugs this time, because unlike Clomid, these natural hormones hadn't poisoned my emotions. It was just me, the worst part of me. That part of me had watched my words shrivel and darken his face like crumpled paper at the edge of a fire and then tossed off only an unconvincing "Sorry" as I left.

A technician appeared at 8:34. I wasn't sure how prompt sperm were about expiring, but I could see three thousand dollars circling the drain. While the wretched sperm were whisked away for a wash and a centrifuge, I dejectedly hoisted myself up into the stirrups.

Nurse Joan bustled in carrying a big syringe with a long tube on the end of it. "I must tell you," she boomed, "this specimen Frank provided—" She raised the syringe and I imagined his sperm in there twitching like dying fish on a beach. Her voice hushed with awe. "Is *wonderful!*"

There was no time to celebrate. Nurse Joan stepped between my legs. "Now this is what we call baby by turkey baster!"

The next day, Frank and I had sex again, doctor's orders. To support a possible pregnancy, I also began inserting little wax bullets of progesterone to melt inside me, which required me to find something to do in a prone position for fifteen to thirty minutes twice a day. So I read a book a friend had recommended. The book, *The Gospel According to Jesus* by Stephen Mitchell, attempts to chisel the New Testament down to its most ancient, slender core, the Gospel verses this particular scholar believes were most likely to have come from the mouth of the actual historical Jesus himself. In none of those verses did Jesus claim to be divine.

Beneath my feet, the rock of faith suddenly felt like air. To wonder if you're levitating over nothingness when you thought you were standing on solid ground is both exhilarating and terrifying.

I think I first started wondering about whether Jesus was really God incarnate back while Frank was in seminary. Frank clearly didn't share my niggling doubts, and I knew that for him our shared faith was the foundation of our relationship—he often said how glad he was that we were connected in that way. So beyond asking a few questions, I never said anything to him about it.

There wasn't any scientific proof Jesus was divine. Then again there wasn't any scientific proof he wasn't. Since it was a matter of faith either way, and given the dire consequences my Protestant Christian religion predicted if I didn't put my faith in Jesus as my divine Savior, I made the sensible choice to believe in his divinity.

But the exhilarating, terrifying sense of discovery I felt while reading *The Gospel According to Jesus* intrigued me. My curiosity was piqued. In between attempts to make a baby, I read on. When I finished that book, I checked out Frank's wall of theological books. I found a copy of the Koran.

Just as before, I said nothing to Frank.

Frank said nothing to me about what he was thinking either. I could tell, though, that once the injection phase was over, his truce with the idea of a baby was over, too. I was tempted to blame it on that verbal slap I'd given him when he handed me the sample, but then I found myself comparing the way he tensed up when a baby cried on the Metro to the sympathetic, patient way he sat and listened to a homeless woman who'd shown up for church. Maybe he really was meant to nurture adults, not children, and that was why he was once again dreading the possibility of a baby. I parked that line of thought. The re-emergence of his original feelings was a setback, but it was a setback I could handle because, after all, I now claimed to be a fatalist.

Fatalism required me to play by new rules. They went like this. I'd say, contrary to everything I hoped, "I am not pregnant. Barren as a desert. Not pregnant. No way."

And Frank would say, contrary to everything he hoped, "Of *course* you're pregnant. Completely knocked up."

Sometimes we'd laugh at ourselves while we performed this ridiculous exercise. And yet my pessimistic words put the brakes on both my hopes and Frank's fears, while Frank's optimistic words saved him from disengagement and me from depression.

These rules were diametrically opposed to the ones I learned in my born-again youth. Back then, our rawboned engineer-turned-preacher taught the power of positive thinking. He quoted Jesus, King James version of course, because that's the language in which God wrote the Bible: "Like it says in Matthew chapter seven, verse seven, 'Ask, and it shall be given you; seek, and ye shall find; knock, and it shall be opened unto you.' And now y'all flip over to Matthew nine, starting at verse twenty-eight, 'The blind men came to him: and Jesus saith unto them, Believe ye that I am able to do this? They said unto him, Yea, Lord. Then he touched their eyes, saying: According to your faith be it unto you. And their eyes were opened.' "

I don't discount the untapped power of the mind, or faith, or whatever you want to call it; it had a hand in my mother's healing. But in my born-again days I explicitly asked God to heal me of my painful periods. I regularly went up to the front of the church for prayer and the laying on of hands, and afterward I'd visualize myself healed and thank God in advance. I had faith it would happen. I believed.

At the end of the month, when the cramps and nausea descended on me again anyway, my built-up hopes made the failure that much more crushing. The message was clear: My faith wasn't good enough, my best efforts inadequate. There was no way to salvage anything good out of a set of rules that reduced miracles to an engineering equation—a clear request plus faith equals healing. It was a recipe for discouragement.

These days when I looked beneath the limiting facts of each of those Bible verses, I found a broader, much more helpful underlying truth. "Ask and it will be given." Jesus didn't say what "it" was. The truth is he just promised an answer, not what the answer would be. Then he opened the blind men's eyes, both literally, to the world, and figuratively, to the light of the underlying Truth.

So I was seeking an answer to whether or not I was meant to have a baby and waiting for my eyes to be opened—to my fate, to some lesson to be learned, to a more peaceful walk in the Light, anything. Meanwhile, I relied on the common sense God gave me to hope for the best and expect the worst.

When my body gave me an answer to my immediate fate right on schedule, before a pregnancy test was even necessary, I said flatly, "Ha ha ha. I was right. I'm *not* pregnant." That made Frank laugh a little, which made me laugh a little, and I felt a little less crummy.

I quit reading the Koran about halfway through. As with the Bible it was hard to get past the anachronistic misogyny, but I got the gist of the book. The Koran included a lot of the same Truths as the Bible, the same guidelines for life: do unto others as you would have them do unto you, honor your parents, repay evil with kindness, place no limits on forgiveness, let God do the judging. They'd just been picked up like Dorothy's house, spun around in a tornado, and set down in another culture in another part of the world.

The basic difference I saw between Islam and Christianity was in how you got to heaven—near as I could tell, Muslims believed you did good deeds to get to heaven, while Christians believed you got to heaven by the grace of God, who, as Jesus, had taken the punishment for your sins and sacrificed himself to save you from being separated from God forever. Roman Catholics and some of the more fundamentalist Protestants believed that in addition to believing in Jesus, to get to heaven you also had to do good deeds, while other Protestants, including Lutherans, believed Christians only did good deeds to show God how much they appreciated what God had already done for them.

I had long ago decided I couldn't believe God would condemn people to eternal separation from God just because they believed in the wrong religion. If I were God, I could never do such an intolerant thing, and God's love had to be exponentially bigger than mine. What had drawn me to Frank's Lutheranism was its built-in ambiguity—the idea that we were all saved by the unconditional love of Jesus, who was God, and that only if people actively rejected Jesus would they be separated from God. Even if people appeared to reject Jesus, only God knew what was really in their hearts, so who were we to say who was saved and who was not?

But now I had to ask myself, why would God come up with an exclusive system for getting to heaven, like faith in Jesus, if that meant God then had to go to all the trouble of making exceptions for most of the rest of the world? And another thing: Why would God play favorites if God was the perfect parent?

I felt a little unnerved just thinking like that, as if I might be struck by lightning. Working beside Frank as we installed an organizer in our bedroom closet, a complete system of tidy racks and shelves, all straight lines and square corners, I longed to reach out to him for comfort. I held a shelf and watched the concentration on his face as he measured where to drill the supports. I longed to talk to him about it the way I talked to him about everything else; he had never made me feel stupid for anything I'd said or wondered. I especially wanted to share this with him because his years of seminary study had equipped him with both a broad knowledge of the world's religions and the analytical tools for sorting through these kinds of questions.

"Okay, you can take the shelf away," he said. "Can you hand me the drill?"

I'd seen him patiently work through the big questions with other doubters, but I wasn't just any doubter. I handed him the drill. I was his life partner, and just as I had joined with him expecting one day to share our children, he had joined with me expecting to share our faith for all our days. Frank believed in a God who loved him enough to die for him. That faith was his reason for being. It had given him hope back when bad luck left him sick and without the military career he'd expected. It had guided every choice he'd made in his life, including his choice to marry me.

No matter how much I wanted to talk about it with him, I didn't dare.

"It's weird how this baby thing takes over your life," I said while I was still waiting to see if I was pregnant.

My spiritual friends, arranged around the living room on the old couch and wingback off of which I had frantically vacuumed sawdust an hour before, nodded sympathetically. It was my turn to host. The refreshments were artfully arranged on the new bricks I had stacked into the shape of a coffee table until Frank had time to lay them on top of the old bricks, which were now hidden under a rumpled sheet of black plastic in addition to a waterproof coating of tar.

I rambled on, "The daily shots, the sonograms, the suppositories. It's like when you stare at an object long enough without blinking and your peripheral vision fades away—the baby thing becomes the only thing you can see in front of you. I forget to even look around for the Light anymore. I don't feel abandoned by God, like I did last fall. I just don't have the time or energy to seek the Light beyond what I have time to read while I'm lying down."

I stared off into space. "I can see now why couples break up over this, especially if they're not both equally obsessed. I heard about a woman who left her husband because he turned out to be completely infertile and didn't like the idea of using a sperm donor and she was desperate for a biological child of her own. There must have been more to it than that, but still, I'm glad I know Frank's not the cause. I don't think I'd be able to help thinking that, with a different partner, I could have a baby and my life would be what it's supposed to be."

My spiritual friends listened without judgment.

My other friends were not so circumspect when I mentioned the same thing.

"Kristin!" one exclaimed. "I can't believe you could say that!"

"What happened to 'for better or for worse'?" exclaimed another.

I protested, "All I'm saying is how mind-bending it is—"

"It's not as if Frank would be infertile on purpose," the first pointed out.

I ducked my head, properly shamed. "You're right. I'm just saying I'm glad we don't have to deal with all that because it's *not* Frank's fault."

I told Frank about it later, laughing at myself. Frank didn't find it so amusing. But he didn't make me feel stupid for saying it.

I carry a bowl of breakfast cereal and my laptop into Hans's dining room and plug in again. Still no word from Frank.

Uncle Hans passes through with Rosie and fat Saber at his heels. A few minutes ago he was sitting on the edge of his bed, feeding them treats and giving insulin to the diabetic cat. Now he offers me a green power drink and nutritional supplements, a colorful assortment of tablets and capsules in a neat little cellophane packet, a full day's supply of vitamins and minerals in every one. I decline, explaining that as the daughter of his sister, who is also into health food and supplements, I had made a solemn vow that when I grew up I would eat and drink all the crap I wanted and would take no supplements.

Hans pauses on his way into the kitchen and gives me a puckish smile. "Good for you."

A minute later Chris and Sharol come out of the kitchen with their hands full of supplements and power drinks. "Hey," says Chris. "Shalom," says Sharol. They go out on the patio for a smoke. Upstairs, the bathroom door opens and closes repeatedly as more people begin to stir.

Like the dog and the cat, who arrived as unlucky strays, Hans's wealth of housemates started with one and grew from there. One was hit by a car and needed some place to recover. Then there was a friend who was born with a gene that led to mental illness. The mother of another gave her son his first toke of marijuana when he was three. They've all been unlucky at one time or another, at an age when they're vulnerable, in a town that's one of America's most expensive places to live, though like Hans, many people who live here aren't rich. His housemates could move somewhere else, start over somewhere cheaper, but they're from here. This is home; Santa Cruz is what they know.

A sinewy guy with stringy blond hair and dark half-moons under his eyes stumbles out of the kitchen and drops into a chair at the other end of the table. He crackles open a packet of supplements and chugs a glassful of green.

"I'm Kristin," I say.

"Jesse," he gasps, bobbing his head and extending a long-fingered hand.

"The massage therapist?"

He smiles at the table, a green crescent on his upper lip. "One day."

"Hans says you're really good."

"People tell me that."

"If you're taking clients, I have about five thousand miles I need worked out of my back."

"Sure, sure." He frowns unselfconsciously at the ceiling, all his thoughts on his face, then nods and smiles. "Mmm, yeah, I think I have some time late this afternoon." He just got in from his job driving a fish truck. He's on his way to his other job, where he's an aide to people with brain injuries. He dreams of becoming a concert promoter. He has a bad back himself. He talks gently, in spurts. I want to feed him something fattening and tuck him in for a nice long nap. But when he says, "Well, gotta run," all I do is say, "Take it easy."

The empty packet that held the supplements Hans gave him lies on the table. The boy Hans almost adopted, if he were alive, would be in his mid-thirties now, ten years older than Jesse, about Chris's age. If his almost-son had lived, I wonder if Hans would have opened his house and his heart the way he has. He's always been extraordinarily generous. But I feel more than generosity in this house. I feel love.

Yesterday evening, while Hans and I were drinking wine and arguing politics, I somehow mentioned his lost son. His usually sunny voice changed, all the political gusto gone. "Terrible," was all he said about that time, very softly, "it was terrible . . ." And then he fell silent.

It's easy, even exhilarating, to be a fatalist if you happen to like where you're going. But what if you don't like where the universe's random twists and turns are taking you? How do you continue on when it sucks, when unexpected events take you willy-nilly over a cliff?

I bolted straight up in bed. "We forgot the shot!"

"Huh?" Frank lifted his head and squinted at me, hair rumpled. He dropped back on the pillow. "Yell when you get the hormone mixed."

I stumbled into the bathroom, which now had unpainted cabinets to go with its unpainted walls.

We'd had no time for nervous energy during the second try. Frank had accepted a call as a part-time pastor at his church, neighbors who'd been in our new bathroom were starting to offer him money to build cabinets for them, too, whole walls of cabinets, and finals were approaching. I'd started temping because freelance work was still pretty slim; I joined the herd of commuters trotting down into the Metro each morning, dressed in my pantyhose with running shoes and late-eighties officewear left over from the last time I'd worked in an office, carrying a backpack with a sandwich and books on religion and uncomfortable heels. Rosie had started obedience school. She had also, at long last, started barking. Busy-ness: an excellent technique for convincing myself I really had achieved a fatalistic state.

"Frank," I called from the bathroom. A little louder, "Frank!"

Frank staggered in, stuck the needle in me and staggered out. He'd barely opened one eye. I followed him back to bed.

Training Rosie kept us busy. All three of us spent an hour a week with the trainer, a woman who had first raised dogs, then used the same techniques to raise her children and could now claim none of them ever drank from the toilet. After the weekly hour with her, Rosie and I had to spend an hour a day practicing what we had supposedly learned. The trainer gave Frank a pass on the daily practice.

"Dogs are chauvinists," she said. "A man's deep voice sounds like an authoritative bark to them, so they listen. Women's voices sound more like a playful bark, or worse, a whimper, so women have to work a lot harder to get any respect at all. Of course, this isn't just true with dogs."

After I set aside the Koran, I read everything ever written by a Vietnamese monk named Thich Nhat Hanh. I read Joseph Campbell's *The Power of Myth*. Riding the subway I stared out at the underground darkness, a book in my lap, and tried to reconcile two contradictory things about both men. Hanh was a devoted Buddhist, yet wrote as if all religions were equally valid. Campbell had abandoned the Catholicism of his youth, yet still found value in its rituals and stories.

On a Sunday morning, I watched Frank dress for church. More than ever, I wanted to talk to him about my doubt—it was a heavy weight hanging between us that only I could see and feel. But after so many ups and downs trying to have a baby, we were finally sliding hand in wobbly hand along the same tightrope. I couldn't bring myself to toss an unexpected weight at him that I knew would send both of us flailing into the air.

I watched him button up his black clerical shirt with the white collar, the uniform that represented the faith that gave his life meaning, that used to give my life meaning, too. And I said nothing.

When Rosie wasn't training, she stayed busy practicing her barking. I stayed busy obsessing about how to make her stop barking. I obsessed about that instead of obsessing about getting pregnant.

"Correct her in a way she understands," said the trainer. "Have you ever seen a mother dog correct a puppy? She dominates it. She bites it firmly on the scruff of the neck, shoves it to the ground, and growls."

I was imagining all the fur I'd be spitting out and wondering which one of us this was supposed to punish when the trainer added, "Of course, *you* would shove her down with your hand."

The trainer was right. When I did that, Rosie understood exactly how I felt about excessive barking. It didn't always stop the barking, but she knew exactly how I felt about it. She was a barking overachiever. She didn't just bark at knocks on the door. She barked at the mail when it slithered through the slot to the floor. She barked at me when I was on the phone. She barked at the air in front of her face whenever the aliens sent her messages from outer space. Worst of all, she barked on the other side of the bedroom door while Frank was trying to produce his sample.

I bounded into the clinic twenty minutes late with Rosie's fine neck fur still stuck to my hands, hurled the cup in its nondescript bag at the technician, took my seat in the waiting area, which was packed this time, and waited for them to work me in. While I waited, I had plenty of time to watch woman after woman shuttle in and out that door—in for the consult, out for the drugs, in for the blood work, out for the sonogram, in for the artificial insemination, out for the long wait at home. It was clear I was just another widget on the assembly line, and I resented it.

A vague cloud of unfocused anger still hovered around me when my turn finally came to shuttle in for the artificial insemination, which because of a "mucous plug"—proclaimed by Nurse Joan without a trace of a blush—hurt like hell and left me bleeding.

I shuttled out for the long wait at home.

The next morning, far away in Florida, as Oma sat on the edge of her bed and my mother hooked her bra, an artery in Oma's brain burst. Her face went blank. She lurched sideways, but her daughter was there to catch her before she fell off the bed.

Mom laid her back on the pillow. Oma's eyes stared up at a corner of the ceiling as her brain flooded with blood and began to go dark. Mom called me while the paramedics were taking Oma out to the ambulance. Mom was on the cordless, searching the house for Oma's living will, her voice quivering. She asked me to call Ingrid and Erin. She'd already called Hansi and their older brother.

Along with Opa, Oma lived with us in Florida during most of our growing-up years. My Oma was a tall, substantial woman with a soft, forgiving voice and an accent like music. Every child in the neighborhood called her Oma. Evenings she'd unlace her orthopedic shoes, roll up her stretch-knit slacks, and dangle her feet in the tub, providing a tiny baby voice for both gnarled old feet so my sisters and I could pretend they were our children.

When my parents divorced and my mother put on her old nursing uniform and went back to work, Oma was the one waiting for us when we arrived home from school. Sometimes I found her sitting alone, listening to Bach with tears on her face. I always felt safe to be myself with Oma, whether I was happy or sad or out of sorts. I confided in her, and she told me things about her childhood she never told anyone else. That was my Oma, who loved a good joke and covered her mouth when she laughed herself to tears, who held you when you cried, and whispered, "*Ja,* just let it out," because she'd suffered from depression for years and knew what it meant to be sad.

We were loading the car to drive to Florida for Oma's funeral when Frank locked the keys in the car with Rosie inside. To my surprise he yelled at me as if it were my fault. I yelled back. After he finally unlocked the car with a wire through a window that was slightly open, he continued to overreact to everything, inexplicably, outrageously. For the first hour of the drive I continued to yell back as I cried with grief and indignation.

Rosie laid low in the back seat till Frank eventually stopped yelling, and I seethed through my tears. Then she pushed her head between the seats and rested her muzzle on the parking brake. I stroked her head. I pulled my hand away whenever Frank stroked her, to make sure we didn't accidentally touch. How could he do this to me right now? How could he let me down like this? The seething boiled up inside me again: "You are such an asshole! My grandmother just died and you're yelling at me for things that have nothing to do with me!"

He yelled back, "She was my grandmother, too!"

All at once I understood. He hadn't spoken to anyone in his family in six years. My family was his family now, but in times of crisis, he still fell back into the patterns he had learned from his first family, and now the ghost of his father glared at me from the driver's seat of our car. I glared back. I wondered if Frank had ever had the nerve to glare back at his father when he was a child, because I was sure that's what I was witnessing—an unconscious reenactment of his father's anger, something he had witnessed thousands of times.

The miles rolled by in silence, wearing away my anger. By the time my anger was finally gone, many miles lay behind us.

"Frank?"

"What?"

"If I'm pregnant and it's a girl, I'd like to name her after Oma."

"Elisabeth?"

"Yeah."

He reached over and took my hand. "I'd like that," he said softly. He gave me a long, beseeching look. "I'm sorry."

I wasn't pregnant. The world's redemptive cycle of death and birth revolved on without me, a merry-go-round of children waving and laughing in sentimental slow motion that I wasn't allowed to climb onto. "No, no, Kristin," the world laughed with a wag of its finger, "*you* can't join in. We have no good reason. We just don't want you."

I went out in my back yard, ripped up the two emaciated rose bushes, shoveled all the dirt and bark chips into a mound on the patio, and took a sledgehammer to the concrete. My body threw itself into the hammer. I rose and fell. I was the blows as the concrete cracked, broke apart, then shattered, cracked, broke apart, then shattered, over and over and over again until 250 square feet of concrete lay in pieces all around me. It took me two days. I piled all the pieces onto the mountain of construction debris by the alley.

"Wow," said Frank, standing beside me. The back yard looked like a ravaged moonscape. "You should feel proud of yourself. Are you?"

I leaned on the sledgehammer and shook my head. "Just really, really sore."

Jesse has the hands of an empathic baker. He works the cross-country miles out of my back and neck. Earlier today I scored an oil change for the Vette from Scott, the guy who can fix anything, another sublime meal from Chris, the improv gourmand, and now a massage from Jesse. This has turned out to be an excellent day. Out in the living room Saber starts barking, which sets off Rosie's barking, their voices fading away as they charge out the flap in the back door to run up and down the fence, barking their happy heads off. An excellent day for Rosie, too.

Lying on my stomach on the massage table, my face in the donut-shaped head support, I mumble to the floor, "Visiting Uncle Hans with all you guys here, I really feel like I'm visiting his family."

Jesse laughs. "Hansi's crew. It does have certain things about it that are like a family." His hands pause. "He doesn't always show it, but I think he kind of likes having everybody around." The kneading resumes, then another pause. "Even when it gets crazy sometimes."

After Oma's funeral, after the second try with the injections failed, I met my father for lunch. I told him I was glad for Oma that she had her faith. And I was glad for me. It helped me know she was peaceful and ready for death, even looking forward to it.

"But people like me," I said to my father at a greasy spoon near his office, "won't be much comfort for those we leave behind. Too much doubt. If I go now, nobody will be able to comfort themselves with the thought that, well, at least she was ready, at least *she* was sure what lay on the other side."

We were sitting at the counter, Dad in his suit, me in my outdated officewear. Dad loves these kinds of places. He had tucked his tie in his shirt and pushed up the sleeves of his jacket to eat a big juicy hamburger.

"Oh, I think doubters have the potential to leave the people around them with some comfort," he said as he chewed. "We all face coming to closure on various issues and stages as we move through life, and if we learn how to do it and apply that to the final stage, that's comforting to others."

It was a comforting thought to me.

There's no comfort, though, when someone dies young, before they've had a chance to live out the fullness of their days. The comfort has to come from somewhere else.

We gave the shots a third and final try. I didn't need a pregnancy test that month either.

Once the cramps eased to the point I could get up off the bathroom floor, Frank and I walked past the Capitol, down past the Washington Monument through the Fourth of July crowds, to our favorite spot near the fireworks battery. We lay side by side on our backs on the warm pavement in the dusk and waited for night to fall.

Frank was relieved it was over. Me, I thought I had let it go, this desire for a child, but I now realized I had only hidden it beneath the hope of a new round of stronger drugs. There was no hope now. The only thing we hadn't tried was in vitro fertilization, something we could not afford and Frank refused to consider. I wasn't going to have children. My life would continue as it was. I would just have to get back to liking it as it was.

As the sky blackened into night, thundering bursts began to bloom against the darkness. Heaven rained sparkling tracers, floating ash, charred bits of cardboard. Far below, tears oozed out of my eyes, down past my temples, into my ears and hair.

A few evenings later, Frank and I were making supper and then he was kissing me. We made love against the kitchen counter, and it was wonderful and spontaneous and such a relief to have this part of our lives back. And then afterward I cried again, because God's sense of justice is not ours. From a weightless, timeless perspective, is anything here on this puny planet inherently good or bad? Does anything mortal matter in any way except how it affects our relationship with whatever eternal force underlies the universe? "It's our free will that matters," Frank said. "If we had no choice in how we respond to God, then our response wouldn't be love. If you try to force someone to love you, it's not love."

About a month later I found a half-finished roll of film in my camera. I had no idea what was on it; I hadn't taken any pictures in a long time. Standing at the counter in the photomat, I flipped through the snapshots of long-forgotten parties and construction stages to the last shot on the roll, and there they were in a dim and shadowy photograph, Oma and Rosie, still playing tug.

I sit at Hans's dining room table, checking my email. As ever, nothing from Frank, just an email from the neighborhood back home in D.C. Behind me, Rosie and Saber growl and play tug-of-war with Stinky Pheasant. Around the corner in the living room, Uncle Hans's young housemates discuss the pros and cons of fighting terrorists in caves. On my screen, I read that at an upcoming party, the neighbors plan to whack the hell out of an Osama bin Laden piñata.

I feel a flash of unease. It reminds me of images of mobs burning our presidents in effigy. Shouldn't we strive *not* to give in to that part of ourselves? I peer around the corner at the television, where America's leaders are promising to rebuild Afghanistan even as they're dropping bombs on it. I squint at the fuzzy black-and-white images of things blowing up on the other side of the world. I feel no satisfaction. Somewhere along the way to Santa Cruz, that burning need to see something destroyed over there has flickered and gone out.

Uncle Hans and I take Rosie and Saber for one last walk together through the grassy woods. We're arguing politics when I ask him, "So what do you think of all this?" I ask him from out of the blue, but he has no trouble following.

"I think bombing's a bad idea," he says, "but I don't have any better ones."

Sometimes, like now, he sounds very middle-of-the-road. "Sometimes you sound like a right-wing reactionary," I tell him, "and sometimes you sound like a complete libertarian. What are you registered as?"

He gives me that rascal's smile again. "Republican. I'd be independent but independents can't vote in the primaries."

My uncle is a practical man.

As I pack the Vette to leave, he wanders around growling about one of his housemates, "Where is he? He was supposed to unload the groceries from the car and pack them away. Now it's all melting." There's a sign on the kitchen counter, a piece of cardboard folded into a tent, the words written in Magic Marker: *The dishwasher will accept your dirty dishes now.* Next to the sign, the sink is full of dirty dishes. In his practicality, Uncle Hans has long since figured out what has slowly been dawning on me—you do what you can and what will be will be. His house *is* a way station, and the way is good.

With Rosie beside me, I back the Vette into the street. I know now I'll never be a stoic fatalist. I hope one day I can at least be practical, but I'm not quite there yet. Yesterday when we were alone in the car, I referred to Hans's life as a ministry, and he looked at me as if I were a nut.

Maybe it's because offering someone a little good luck when bad luck strikes has always just been one of those things he does automatically, like leaving big tips when he goes out to eat, and distrusting the police, and smiling and bobbing his head when he listens to Bach.

Maybe it's because the word "ministry," with its religious overtones, presumes you're exercising some kind of divinely inspired power to change someone's luck. Hans knows he doesn't have that kind of power. All those years ago, the boy he was trying to adopt died while driving Hans's car, which he would not have been doing if he had not been lucky enough to meet the one gentle man in the world who wanted to be his father.

JESUS LIKES ME

Starting date 10/19/01 . . . waxing crescent moon . . . odometer 129,205 . . . route: south along the Pacific Coast Highway to pit stops near Morro Bay and in Los Angeles = two days, 477 miles

Fog rushes up the cliffsides and curves over the Pacific Coast Highway like a breaking wave, so that we shoot through a pipeline of clear air. When the fog lifts, container ships dot the horizon, steaming from China. More and more often now, time recedes into the road's white noise the way it did that night in Iowa when I watched tractor lights moving through darkened fields. Heading south, I live in the moment with Rosie, sniffing the salty wind as it blasts across the open top of the Vette.

We pull over to marvel at the broken edge of the continent, the sheer walls of rock that plunge hundreds of feet down to the water and the waves that slam back up. We hike a cliffside of sage trembling in the breeze, stare at crowds of elephant seals flopping immensely on a beach. At twilight we pull into a nearly empty campground in the hills and fall asleep in a narrow canyon to the wind-sigh of towering pines.

At dawn I follow Rosie up out of the pines. We clatter up a chilly, stony path through smaller, stunted trees that give way to hardy wind-hewn shrubs at the rocky top, where we sit down to watch the rising sun paint the scrubby hills in swathes of pink and gold. As I watch the light creep across the rumpled folds of land, as I absorb the peace that radiates from this daily miracle, I feel closer to the mystical side of life, the instinctive, emotional, irrational pagan, deep inside, who sees God in the rocks and the trees and the sun and prostrates herself in awe. Quakerism is an odd mix of airy-fairy mysticism and practical social action. We Friends depend on the mysterious work of the Inner Light to guide us in everything, from our meetings for worship to our daily lives. We trust that God will speak to us, directly, inaudibly from within our consciences as well as through the mouths and writings of other people.

There are risks to this approach. One early Friend thought he heard the Light tell him to go stand on a London street corner wearing a platter of hot coals like a hat. Passing parents probably pointed him out as an object lesson to their children: See that man over there? The one with his brain on fire? That's what happens when you think too much.

Once during meeting a young guy in the row behind me apparently thought he heard that still, small voice tell him to stand up and speak at length about some recent challenges at work. Meeting for worship is not a public forum where anything goes, but messages often include secular anecdotes to demonstrate a spiritual question or truth, so I listened with my eyes closed for a while, trying to stay centered and just absorb whatever the moral or spiritual point of the message was, obscure though it might be. Messages are usually pretty short, and as the minutes dragged on I got a little restless. I looked out the window, counted cracks in the wall, pondered a smear of dirt on the toe of my shoe. He'd been rambling for a while about how the stress of a personality conflict with his supervisor had been affecting other parts of his life when he sighed and said, "It's gotten so bad it's even inhibiting me sexually."

Whatever he said after that, I didn't hear it. I was concentrating on limiting my reaction to staring pop-eyed at my knees. A minute later a weighty Friend, a woman with some seasoning, spoke up firmly from the row in front of me: "Our Friend needs to come to the point." Our Friend dutifully stammered through two more sentences trying to come to one, and sat down.

Fortunately, if we don't hear the Light correctly the first time, it's usually willing to repeat itself.

The sun's up. It's getting hot. Back down among the cool, dim pines, surrounded by the gentle twitterings of mystic Mother Nature, I'm packing the tent into the car. Rosie is nearby, bronco bucking after something small in the leaves. All of a sudden, with no warning, I'm slammed from behind so hard I stagger, my breath knocked out of me with a gasping grunt.

I whirl around, fists up, but there's no one there, just a pine cone, hard and solid and green and about the size of my palm, rolling away. My back feels knifed, my chest vised in a muscle spasm—can't get a breath. I get down on my hands and knees, then flop over on my back. Rosie pads over to sniff me curiously. As I writhe around trying to force air into my lungs, I blink at the cone-studded branches spiraling a hundred feet above me. This goddamn pine tree just tried to kill me. I reach back over my shoulder, feel beneath my t-shirt for the painful spot where the heavy, unripe pine cone had plummeted down and hit me next to my spine. My fingers come back bloody.

Once I can draw a breath again I shove Rosie in the Vette and screech the hell out of there. Nature may be mystical, and I may like the way the mystical side of life takes me deeper, but I don't entirely trust it.

Whole rivers of car-rushing freeways sweep you into Los Angeles at an amphetamine-fueled speed. Exotic fashion-forward sports cars pass you on the shoulder even when you're already roaring along twenty miles over the speed limit, even when all the passing lanes to the left are clear, just to make a point. Pristinely chromed, dramatically finned classics in sherbet colors, unspattered by mud or snow, unchipped by gravel, go out of their way to cruise along beside you to make a different, but equally nasty, point. All the drivers of these automotive freaks wear very tiny, very hip sunglasses, even at night, as if they're blind. Nose jobs, chin tucks, silicone, and steroids stare you down from movie billboards as you scream by, so unnaturally, mathematically perfect they're scary. I've never in my life seen so many billboards advertising movies. A ceiling of solid gray clouds hangs low overhead, makes me feel like I have to duck. The clouds trap the mist that rolls in off the ocean to thicken the yellow haze of ozone and carbon monoxide and all the other poisons that circulate through this mean, self-absorbed, self-important town. I don't care for L.A.

It's strange that I don't, because I like cities. I love New York, city of my birth. Urban environments are the rational, intellectual side of life incarnate, the aspect of myself that I trust even as I feel limited by it. I trust logic the way I trust my senses; I can feel the concrete beneath my feet. I treasure this life more than the next one, assuming there is a next one, because I subscribe to the supply-and-demand theory of the value of life. Eternal life goes on forever—if you assume oversupply drives prices down, then it must not be worth much. Mortal life, on the other hand, is short—if undersupply drives prices up, then it must be priceless, and I'm determined to get my money's worth out of this, my life on earth. This is my father's influence on me. He never had much patience with the mystic side of Quakerism; he's an atheist, a rationalist, with his faith in the material world that he can see and smell and hear and touch.

But L.A., materially successful, spiritually blind, meaningless L.A., turns that faith into materialism and worships the thing.

Maybe it's my Quaker background that makes me so self-righteously disdainful of people whose lives are all about being seen at the right parties.

Friends were early pioneers in abolition, women's rights, fair dealings with Native Americans, humane treatment of prisoners and the mentally ill, and war victim relief. Thanks to their refusal to swear oaths, for which they went to prison, participants in official proceedings now have the option to swear *or* affirm the truth of their words.

You can even thank Friends for fixed retail pricing; they believed it was more honest and just to offer the same deal to everyone, regardless of a person's ability to haggle. When other shopkeepers started losing customers to Quakers, they started setting fixed prices, too.

Quakerism's practical side, its tradition of social action, is based on the idea that since there is That of God in everyone, humanity is perfectible, that paradise is possible here on earth.

L.A. is not paradise. I'm tempted to keep right on going and shake the dust of this skin-deep town's face powder from my feet as quickly as possible. But there are a couple of friends here I'm hoping to see and Rosie's ready to get off the road. A block off Hollywood's Walk of Fame, I check us into the Celebrity Hotel, the only place I can find that allows dogs. Well, there's another hotel in Beverly Hills, but the rooms are three hundred dollars a night and Rosie would have had to cough up half that much again for the privilege of shedding there.

The Celebrity Hotel has an awning and carpeted steps out front and fancy chairs in the halls, but the guests sit on those carpeted front steps while they nibble complimentary danishes from plastic wrappers and sip coffee from Styrofoam cups, and the fancy chairs are decorated with the odd stain and cigarette burn. In our room, Fred Astaire and Ginger Rogers dance across the wall over the bed, flat, monochromatic, and big as life. Rosie is more impressed with something I can't see in the corner behind the toilet.

I turn on the TV and throw myself across the bed beneath Fred and Ginger. I point the remote—a game show, a sitcom, a shoot 'em up. They're all derivative. Inane. Stupid even. I hate TV. A television program nearly broke up my marriage. But it wasn't the fault of some derivative, inane, stupid game show, sitcom, or shoot 'em up. It was a highly literate documentary on PBS.

It happened around the time we sat down for our final debriefing with Dr. Warner. She expressed her sympathies. She summarized her findings, summarized options. There weren't many—in vitro fertilization or adoption. I got a little weepy.

"Sorry," I said, "but I guess you see a lot of this."

Dr. Warner smiled sadly. "That's why the box of tissues is on your side of the desk." Frank handed me one while she added, "Of course, you're the kind of couple who might call me up next month to tell me you're pregnant."

In between blowing my nose I asked, "Is it possible the sperm or eggs are having chemical trouble that would prevent the sperm from fertilizing the egg?"

"There's no way to check the egg, but the sperm can sometimes have a problem where they don't recognize the egg or can't penetrate it. That was one of those tests you underwent, Pastor, when you first came here . . ." She flipped through our records while she described the test, in which the man's sperm are placed in a petri dish with the egg of a hamster so they can prove they know how to get inside an egg, any egg. She flipped through our records a second time. "Well that's odd. For some reason I don't see your assay results in here, your hamster-egg test." She flipped through again.

They hadn't run the test.

Dr. Warner mumbled she didn't know how they had overlooked that. If we still wanted to have it done, we'd have to go to a lab out in Maryland. And if that proved to be our problem, the only solution was in vitro fertilization, which wasn't covered by our insurance, cost nearly eleven thousand dollars, had an overall success rate of 25 percent, and wasn't performed by this particular medical center in any case.

Frank refused to take the test.

A couple nights later, Frank turned on the TV just to have something to watch while he punched holes in the margins of his class notes and organized them into big three-ring binders. I was in and out of the room during the beginning of the program, packing away laundry, but pretty soon we were both watching how Jesus, the man, was transformed into Christ, the Son of God, in the first hundred years after his death, Frank sitting still in his circle of paper and me on the couch wiggling the tug toy for Rosie.

Watching it confirmed all my increasingly lonely, heavy doubts about whether or not Jesus was God incarnate. Maybe the time had come to tell Frank the truth. Maybe I owed it to him. Several times I opened my mouth to share the burden of uncertainty I was feeling, but Frank was sitting right next to my feet and I knew he must be thinking this program was full of baloney. I shut my mouth. What good would it do to tell him anyway? It wasn't like he'd be able to talk me into believing again. I might feel lighter, but he'd be stuck with this burden he couldn't do anything about. It would be selfish to tell him.

At last the credits rolled. Frank resumed punching holes into his notes and said, "I can think of a lot of people I wish could see that." *Kachunk.* "That was great." *Kachunk, kachunk.*

I stared at him in amazement. "Really?" I'd had no idea I wasn't alone in my struggle after all. Why did his evolutions always have to be so subterranean? "Me too! I've been having trouble believing Jesus was God for a while now. I mean, he was probably exceptionally in tune with God, but not actually God incarnate. And this documentary just brought it all"—I noticed the hole punch had gone quiet—"home."

There was a long silence. "Do you really mean that?" A prestorm stillness hovered in Frank's voice, his face.

My stomach sank. If I could have sucked those words back into my mouth, I would have. "You . . . you didn't get that out of it?"

"No!" He caught himself. He said more softly, "To me it confirmed that Jesus Christ is the Son of God and that they and the Holy Spirit are all one and the same."

Oh shit.

He pushed himself to his feet. He walked toward the kitchen. He came back. "Are you telling me you don't believe that anymore? Don't you believe that?"

I wanted to lie. I couldn't. I couldn't say anything. I sat on the couch and didn't look up at him.

"Come on, Kristin, either you believe or you don't. You can't be a little bit pregnant."

"That's not true." I tossed the tug toy across the room, Rosie skittering after it. "I've been a little bit pregnant for years."

"Answer the question!" he erupted.

"I can't!" I jumped up and away from the couch. "I don't know what the answer is! I don't know that he is God, I don't know that he isn't." I stopped to face him from across the room. "I guess I don't think it matters either way."

"My God, Kristin." He looked as if someone he loved had just died. "This is going to have serious consequences for our relationship."

"What?" I gasped. I nearly choked on a hysterical bubble of laughter, a sudden feeling of unreality, like skidding across ice in your car. It was happening so fast I felt myself slowing down in response. My voice went flat. "I find that response extremely disturbing and distressing."

"I'm disturbed and distressed, too! God, Kristin, I can't believe this! I allowed myself to get serious with you because I trusted that we believed the same thing! And now you tell me we don't? That I've been trusting a lie?" He stormed out of the room.

I sat on the couch telling myself to breathe. I should have kept my mouth shut. If only I'd kept my mouth shut. With Rosie clicking behind me, I found him in the kitchen, leaning against the counter in the dark, arms crossed, pale face outlined by the streetlight outside.

I asked, very tentatively, "Is it because you think I'm going to hell?"

"No. I'm not God, I can't know that."

I folded my arms, too, and leaned against the doorjamb. Rosie trotted away and returned. I looked down. She had a toy in her mouth and she was looking from me to Frank to me.

His voice shot raw and hard across the kitchen. "The idea that God Almighty loved me enough that God would humble God's self to become a human being named Jesus and suffer and die for me, out of love for me, who is so unworthy . . . that's, like you know, the foundation of *everything* for me—my career, my spiritual life and, I thought, my marriage."

Rosie dropped the toy and clicked quickly away again.

"If we don't share that, we share nothing."

I felt overwhelmed and blank. I heard myself say, "How can you say that, after all we've been through together?" I heard the clicking return, but I couldn't look—I was trying to read Frank's face in the darkness.

"If you don't believe in Jesus as Savior, then you're rejecting me and all I stand and work for." His face was too shadowed to see, but his voice had become pleading. "You're saying I'm wasting my time."

"Oh I am not," I snapped, suddenly exasperated. "I don't think you're wasting your time any more than I think a Buddhist monk is wasting his time. What you're both pursuing is very worthwhile. You're just pursuing it in different ways. As am I."

He turned his face away. I tried to soften my voice. "Look, all I know is, even as I struggle with the divinity of Jesus, even as I lean away from that teaching, my spiritual life has become richer, more meaningful, more reflective of who I am. Truer."

The clicking had continued away and back and away the whole time I was talking. When Frank didn't answer, I finally looked down. Four toys lay on the floor between us, and here came Rosie, more slowly now, with another toy she hoped might tempt us. I leaned down to pet her, to console her the way I wanted to be consoled, but she ducked away. She just wanted to play.

"How long have you felt this way?"

I didn't look up. "Years."

"It makes me feel like you're not the person I thought you were. It's as if you told me you're having an affair." He walked past me to the front door, picked up his keys, and went out.

I couldn't believe this was happening. I couldn't move. And yet I was moving, mechanically taking Rosie out back to pee in the dirt, stroking her to sleep in her crate, crawling into the bed. It was my spirit that was too heavy to move. Telling him was every bit as bad as I had feared. It was worse. Not only had I weighed him down with a burden he couldn't do anything about, it hadn't lightened my load at all.

I lay there, wide awake. I wanted to feel wronged, persecuted for my non-Lutheran faith. But if I were Frank, I'd see it the same way he did. The bed felt very wide and lonely.

That night, when he came back, he slept curled up on our short, two-seater couch. When he passed me in the hall in the morning, he walked like a man carrying big buckets of rocks.

In the days that followed, as I sat at my computer, as I rode the Metro to work, as I swept up dog fur from the corners, I kept seeing Frank's face, that moment in the living room when he looked as if someone had died. Sunlight felt cold and dim.

When I looked back, I could see I'd been headed for this spiritual destination all my life, easing myself into the place where I was now, where I could almost feel comfortable uncrowning Jesus. It was still hard. It was like walking out of a warm, cozy house where I had lived, mostly easily, for more than twenty years. It was like opening the door and stepping out into pitch darkness with no way of knowing if I was stepping out into thin air.

Of all the people in the world, why did *I* have to fall in love with a pastor? I wanted to tell him, "Yes, I believe Jesus is God," but I couldn't bring myself to do it, and he'd know I was lying anyway. There was nothing I could do to end this sadness, this waiting. He said it would have serious consequences. I was waiting for him to leave me. I wanted him to get it over with.

All the great religions come layered with doctrines that make intellectual conjectures about why we're here. Directly or indirectly they all claim they're right and everyone else is wrong. The newer they are the more strenuously they make the claim. That smacks of human nature to me. Seeing the world as us versus them is a human weakness.

But underneath the conflicting layers of doctrinal debate there's another layer. When I peer closely, I see the same things underlying all of them—simple, generalized Truths about love, and compassion, and doing unto others. Those Truths have the whiff of God about them.

It's a vague, mushy faith I've settled into. But it is a faith.

"Why can't you believe? What happened?"

I looked up from my desk. Frank would never leave me—what had I been thinking? The faithful bulldog in him was one of the qualities I loved best. I was the one who always had one foot out the door.

He jingled his keys at the other end of the living room, dressed in his black suit and his white collar, ready to head out on his regular round of visits to the congregation's elderly shut-ins.

I knew I couldn't give him what he wanted and it made me tired.

"Is it because you can't have a baby? Are you mad at God?"

I shook my head. "You know, we find God through whatever God brings our way. My experience of God hasn't given me the proof I need to believe Jesus is more than an exceptional role model. At the same time I can't prove he's not God either."

"It's a question of faith, not proof."

"I know. I guess I'll find out for sure when I die. Until then, I don't expect to find any clear, definitive answers, but the answer's not the point. The search for the answer is." I sighed. "Look. You were right. This does have serious consequences. You have to decide. Either you love me and that's enough even if we don't share the same faith. Or else loving me isn't enough and maybe we should go our separate ways."

He sat on the arm of the couch and stared at the floor.

"If you can't just love me as I am, then I want to know because I don't want to stay in a relationship like that. The days since we saw that program have been horrible."

"I'm not going to divorce you."

"I know. You have too high a misery tolerance. But if it continues to be this ongoing wedge between us, *my* misery tolerance isn't that high."

He pushed himself up off the couch. At the door he paused a moment. Then he opened it and went out.

For me, Christianity is a way, not a doctrine. Christian monks and nuns who model their lives most closely on Jesus' humility, charity, generosity, gentleness, and integrity look pretty much like the monk and nun equivalents of other mainstream religious ways. They're all on different roads leading to the same mystical center, because mystical experience is very much the same across religions, from the singing in tongues of born-again Christians, to the trancelike dancing of Muslim dervishes, to the intense stillness of Zen Buddhists, to the gentle still-ness of Quakers.

I happen to be most comfortable with the Christian way of seeking, but that's an accident of birth. If I'd been born in a Hindu or Muslim land, I doubt the Christian Gospel would appeal to me. That means my salvation would have depended on the random event of my birth, or worse, the preordination of a hard-ass God I'm not interested in get-ting close to. Heaven by lottery is not something I care to believe in. That would be a waste of faith.

Frank came in from cutting wood in the back yard, a project for a client. He opened a beer in the kitchen and watched me wash down the walls in the front hall, preparing to paint. He smelled of sawdust, resiny and fresh, and of sweat and beer. My father had smelled like that every weekend when I was a kid. He'd come in from a woodworking project in the carport, open a beer, and fall asleep on the floor in front of a baseball game, stretched out big as Gulliver while my Lilliputian sisters and I clambered around him. It was a comforting smell.

I had to tell Frank about my doubts. I'd realized that now. Sooner or later, I had to tell him. I probably should have told him a lot sooner, as soon as I'd realized the doubts weren't going to go away. It wasn't fair to keep a secret like that from him for so long, knowing how much our shared faith meant to him. I had been lying by omission.

"How can you take Communion?" He sounded baffled and disapproving both.

"Because it symbolizes good things to me."

He sipped his beer. I finished the long wall, moved to the short one around the door.

"Unless you believe Jesus is actually embodied in the elements, I can't in good conscience give you communion from now on."

He went back out to his sawhorses on the patio.

He was right about that, too. It did seem hypocritical to mouth the creeds and take the Host when I didn't buy the doctrine. Yet on a symbolic level it meant something to me, the idea of being nourished and strengthened by the living presence of God. The familiarity of the ritual comforted me. Still, I knew I'd never take Communion again.

A couple days after that Frank patted me on the shoulder at last and joked, "I still love you, even if you are going to hell."

"I appreciate what you're really saying," I said. I felt relieved, but the weight was still there.

"When we see each other in heaven, I'm going to say I told you so."

I laughed, despite the weight. "Nothing would make me happier."

His smile faded. "I feel like I have no one to share that whole part of my life with anymore."

"You can still share it with me."

"It's not the same."

"Okay, so we're not on the same road, we're on parallel roads. We can at least reach out and hold hands, can't we? Encourage each other?"

He took my hand. He kissed it and patted it and looked off into the distance. Some of the weight fell away.

We paid a couple of guys with a truck to come haul away the mountain of debris at the back of the yard.

Frank still refused to take the hamster-egg test.

"What's the point?" he growled. "There's no way we could afford the solution anyway." I followed him around with my arguments until finally, backed into a corner on the brick he'd just laid in the living room, he roared, "Okay! I'll take the test! Now will you please just leave me alone?"

The egg of a hamster proved to be no match for Frank's sperm. They nailed it.

"Oh God, that is good news." Frank closed the front door behind him with a happy swat of his hand. "That is such good news. Really, really good news. I'm glad to hear it. That is just good news."

He was so effusive I was puzzled. It reminded me of a time back in college when he spent three solid days bulldogging his way through an insidiously tricky math calculation for a celestial navigation class. When he finally solved it, he said over and over again, "It works. It really works. It works. It really works. . . ."

Remembering that, I peered across the kitchen at him still grinning by the front door. I frowned and started cranking open a can of tuna fish; ever since I gave up trying to be the perfect wife, I had turned out to be a less-than-inspired cook. "Well, I figured you'd want to know as soon as you got home."

"Definitely." He reached for the refrigerator. In our small kitchen, I had to step aside so he could open it. "This calls for celebrating. Where's my barbecue sauce?"

He closed the fridge, sauce in hand, and reached for a bag of chips. I stepped aside the other way. "I didn't expect you to be quite so . . . happy about it." Personally, I hadn't been all that thrilled with the news; we still had no idea what was wrong. "Why are you so relieved?"

He crunched chips and barbecue sauce with enthusiasm. "Because now you won't leave me." He said it as if it was like, so obvious.

I put down the tuna fish and gaped like one. "What are you talking about? Why would I have left you?"

The next dripping chip paused on its way up. "You said you would. If it turned out I was the cause, you said you would consider leaving me."

"When on earth did I say something like that?"

So then he reminded me of that time several months before when I had told my friends I was glad he wasn't the cause of our infertility because if he were, I would be faced with choosing between having Frank or having children.

I had completely forgotten. But he hadn't.

"Give me a break. The only reason I told you about that was because I realized my friends were right to jump all over me for it. I was never serious about it, anyway."

"Maybe not 100 percent serious, but you weren't joking either."

"I was speculating. Come on."

He said quietly, "We both know how much having a baby means to you."

We eyed each other across the gulf between us. In that moment, on the other side of that two-foot space I saw a man who undertook a test for the woman he loved even though he believed it might mean he could lose her. No wonder he didn't want to take that test. No wonder. The gulf filled with tears and disappeared as I wrapped my arms around him.

"Oh Frank," I whispered, and his arms wrapped around me. "I love you."

His mouth moved against my ear. "Thank you."

While Fred and Ginger look on and Rosie tries to wedge herself behind the toilet, I check my email. Nothing. In a moment of squirrel-like panic, I check my cell phone to make sure I haven't missed any messages telling me to stay put wherever I am.

I need to get out, so I put Rosie in the Vette and head over to my friends. Their apartment is artfully decorated in flea market chic. With the TV on in the background, we sit around on vintage furniture playing poker, smoking English cigarettes, drinking microbrew beers and expounding on how to balance the two sides of life, the mystical and the rational.

"So where's Rosie?" asks Kyle.

"She's outside in the Vette. It's like her den, she feels safe there."

Kyle insists I bring her in. He's a burly, blond southern boy, and his landlady is a wrinkled, lipsticked, henna-haired, no-pets fascist—in Rosie he sees a golden opportunity to buck the system. Under cover of darkness we sneak her in the back way. Kyle pets her vigorously. "That's it! Get your fur all over the place! Shed for freedom!" He takes a swig of his beer. "Just don't bark."

Kyle writes movie scripts. He knows the system, can dissect its non-sensical doctrines one minute and cheerfully, mulishly work it the next, calculating how to turn its catch-22s to his advantage and make a break for himself. If being seen at the right parties is what it takes, he'll be seen at the right parties. Listening to Kyle, I wonder if maybe I didn't take this town's silly facade a little too seriously.

Osama bin Laden's face flashes on the TV. Kyle points with his hand of cards. "Our boys better lock that one up, or he'll do it again."

"Amen," I say, because while I no longer want revenge, when I think of those people at the windows, I have to admit I really don't have a problem with the judicious use of force to prevent another September 11. I realize now: I'm a Quaker . . . but I'm not a very good one. Sadness seeps into my bones.

Around midnight, as the Vette growls down Sunset Strip, the sadness hangs my hands from the wheel. I slow the Vette to arc it cautiously around a middle-aged woman in jeans and a jean jacket who's stumping unsteadily along in the lane closest to the curb, talking to someone who's not there, saying, "Hello? What the hell do you mean by that?" and waving a cigarette and a latte, which is sloshing onto the street.

I want to believe in the Quaker ideal that humanity is perfectible, that paradise is possible here on earth. I'm all for the good works that result from such a belief, even if I don't ever have much to do with those works in a formal way beyond writing a check. But I can't and don't believe in it. I don't believe in the fantasy of a world that doesn't need police. I've seen no evidence that over time the balance between good and evil has shifted for the better. Human beings and the world we inhabit all seem as brutally ugly and sturdily beautiful as we've ever been.

My judgment that I'm not a very good Quaker is incorrect—I'm a *terrible* Quaker. For generations the majority of Friends didn't smoke or drink or curse or play cards, much less justify the use of violence. I can't even say for sure I believe Jesus is God, and though I have a lot of company on that subject among Friends now, Quakerism was originally Christian, its faith firmly based on Jesus Christ. If I don't believe in Jesus and I turn away from pacifism, what's left? Why still call myself a Quaker?

From the moment we're born, we spend our lives trying to figure out who we are, where we fit in this world. When I peer inside at my inner resource, at the Light Within, trying to figure out who I am, I'm trying to figure out God. Birth was the first step on the path toward becoming who I really am. The last step will be my death. Meanwhile, every time I think I know everything there is to know about myself I prove myself wrong. Back when I first tried to write that letter requesting membership in the Religious Society of Friends, I defined myself as a Lutheran pastor's wife, and I wrote fifteen pages about it and still couldn't finish the letter. By the time Frank passed the hamster-egg test, I'd had a year to get used to my expanding definition of myself. Once we faced down my crisis of faith together, I figured, hell, if I could be agnostic on the divinity of Jesus and still be a Lutheran pastor's wife, adding the label of Quaker was no big deal. I sat down again to try and write that membership letter. One page. Took less than an hour. I was sure of who I was and where I belonged.

Now, three and a half years after I officially joined the Religious Society of Friends, as my definition of myself continues to evolve, I'm no longer so sure.

The two men sitting silently on the dark steps of the Celebrity Hotel look like the kind of men who've been wheeling for a deal all their lives, their faces lined, their dress shirts untucked and unbuttoned to reveal tank tops and gold chains. Their silence seems ominous. I grip Rosie's leash a little tighter and start up toward them. They stand to let us pass. They bow their heads slightly.

"Evening, miss," says one.

"Beautiful dog," says the other.

Their eyes are tired and sad, but their smiles are easy. I smile back. They lower themselves to the steps behind me, and now in the lonely night their silence just seems companionable.

As we pass the front desk, the night clerk rouses himself. "Calling it a night already?"

"Yep."

"Sleep well. You too, pooch."

This is the part of L.A. I should have been taking seriously, the part below the concrete surface, the mystic, irrational part you find everywhere but you can't quite put your finger on, where human need causes us to call out into the lonely darkness: Hello? As I lead Rosie along the hall toward our room, the little stains and cigarette burns transform before my eyes, more homey now than homely.

A ROLL OF THE DICE

Starting date 10/21/01 . . . waxing crescent moon . . . odometer 129,682 . . . route: north-east through the Mojave Desert to a pit stop in Las Vegas = one day, 306 miles

Cruising east, the Mojave Desert rolls like a sandy ocean. Just before I left L.A., I checked my email one last time, and there was Frank. He has left the desert and is back on the ship and back online. I felt very cool and nonchalant about it all until I got to the end of his email and realized I had no idea what I had just read. I read it again.

By the time we arrived at our site way out in the desert, we had eaten about a pound of dust and gotten pretty well knocked around in the truck. Combat Engineer Battalion had a backhoe and dug us a slit trench, and over it they placed a box with toilet seats. A hilltop machine-gun nest overlooked it for security. While they could not actually see any detail of your activities, they could watch you do your thing. None of us objected to it being there. The last thing you want to do is

```
catch an enemy bullet while you're
sitting there with your pants down.
That is not how you want to be
remembered.
```

The vast desert afternoon fades toward evening. I pop up the headlights. As the sky ahead deepens to a midnight blue, a strange red glow from behind highlights the tips of Rosie's ears and glints off the dashboard. I glance at the rearview mirror and gasp. The setting sun has set the sky on fire.

I pull over. The mountains of clouds that had brooded over L.A. are now lit from below. Standing by the side of the highway looking back the way we've come, Rosie, the Vette, and I are tiny black cutouts against a sky of orange embers and molten wines that slowly, silently seethe toward the night.

```
I got up about an hour before sun-
rise and shuffled toward the slit
trench. After passing the machine-
gun nest, getting challenged, and
giving the password, I sat down fac-
ing east and saw the most glorious
sight. In the blackness just over
the pastel strip along the horizon
was a waning crescent moon, a day or
two away from burning itself up in
the sun. A few degrees away was
Venus. For a Muslim, it would look
like a sign from God.
```

Where is my sign? Am I a pacifist or am I not? We drive on with the radiant western sky at our backs and it hits me: We've turned for home.

From now on we'll be driving away from sunsets instead of toward them. The melancholy of the night before settles back over me.

It used to be that Quaker meetings disowned Friends who did things like marry outside the society or take up arms. That rarely if ever happens now. If I leave the Religious Society of Friends, it will be because I've disowned myself.

From out of the endless desert darkness, Las Vegas emerges as a distant glow that finally explodes around us like a firecracker, glittering and neon and outrageous. Driving into town, cartoon casinos loom larger than life. In our room in a motor court tucked in along the strip, one of those fast-talking, high-pressure, sixty-second spots bursts on the TV screen. I've been seeing this particular ad on CNN for weeks now. It's the kind of ad that used to hawk the incredible Ginsu knife set that never needed sharpening and came with complimentary orange peeler and apple corer. Only now it's selling flags. Plastic flags. Flags that let you show your colors. Just hook the base over the car window, roll it up (It's that easy!), and drive down the street with your very own Old Glory snapping smartly above the roof of your car, making a patriotic statement everywhere you go.

Rosie and I walk the strip among gaggles of businessmen, bridesmaids, and families with toddlers, out taking in the sights at midnight. We walk past the panhandlers and operators lounging around fountains that erupt like volcanos, if volcanos erupted every fifteen minutes to music, pluming several stories into the air. Rosie prances with her head up, her nose twitching. We cross paths with a woman handing out flyers; she's wearing red-white-and-blue braces on her teeth. Overhead, electronic billboards sparkle with animated waving flags and "God Bless America! We Sell Propane!"

It's the same thing I've been seeing all over America, only more so. Here as everywhere, I see a lot of those TV flags snapping smartly, as advertised, above the roofs of cars, making patriotic statements up and down the strip. A fifty-thousand-dollar SUV goes by sporting one of those shiny new flags. I can't help it. I think: Hypocritical beneficiary of our country's riches who couldn't be bothered to fly one before. I look around at the electronic billboards: Cynical commercial exploitation by shallow moneygrubbers. Earlier on this trip, when I saw shiny new flags flying over everything from minimansions to trailer parks, I thought: Unthinking people caught up in mass emotionalism. I sure don't want to leave Quakerism for this.

We walk along sidewalks blasted by loudspeakers that shout the sales pitches of invisible sideshow barkers. A lagoon in front of the Treasure Island Casino booms with a life-size naval battle. Through Harrah's open doors people come and go, and while a few are putting their money down and playing the odds, most of the rows and rows of gaudy green tables and flashy slot machines stand empty. People are staying home for the same reason those patriotic slogans are flashing and throbbing on every block and those SUVs are flying flags. It feels like a party with more no-shows than guests.

We peer in the open door of an all-night wedding chapel. No one's at the altar.

```
I have two good pictures of you and
Rosie where I can see them as I sit
at my little desk here in our state-
room. You still wearing that locket?
My ring line is almost gone, but
everyone knows I am married. I talk
about you.
```

I press my fingers to the locket beneath my shirt. His ring he had to leave behind for safety reasons. Rosie and I back away from the empty chapel of love and walk on. With three-in-five chances of success, the odds a married couple in America can avoid divorce are better than even. The odds a couple will avoid experiencing infertility are much better, more than five in six. For the unlucky 15 percent who are dealt the infertility card, the odds still aren't bad among those who ante up and seek treatment, with two out of three likely to draw a small card and catch a baby.

"Well, now it's really all over," Frank said. "Don't let the molding move."

I held the crown molding tightly up against the living room ceiling, over the conduit that would run electricity out to the garage we were building for Frank's workshop. He carefully hammered the molding in place. I let go. "We could still try in vitro fertilization."

He rubbed his thumb against his first two fingers. Money. "Hand me a couple more nails, will you?"

I jumped down off the high, teetering stool I'd been standing on. "Some insurance companies actually cover IVF." I reached up to hand him the nails. "I just have to find out about limits on pre-existing conditions."

He hammered a couple more nails. He looked down at me from the ladder. "Kristin." He looked almost like he had after he ran the Marine Corps Marathon. "Do us both a favor and take some time to sort out your feelings. Take a year. See a counselor."

He'd been begging me to do this for a long time. "Okay," I said glumly. "But not for a whole year. I'm only getting older."

It's estimated that among fertile couples who don't practice birth control, the monthly odds that a sperm will fertilize an egg and that the resulting embryo will successfully implant are only one in four. The odds that a fertilized egg will not spontaneously abort sometime before reaching the stage when a baby can survive apart from her mother are somewhere between one in three and one in two; most are gone before their mothers even know they're there. Of all the potential lives that nature offers up, God lets most drift away.

As I tried to sort out my feelings, I could honestly say we had tried almost everything we could try. I could also say that so far the cost hadn't reached what I would consider a selfishly extravagant level, which was important to me in my Quaker practice. I could even say we had a good and satisfying life. So why did I still feel no peace about being childless?

If I could figure out the answer to that, maybe way would open and I could come to clearness about what was the right thing to do—give up or push on. I felt like I was standing at a gated crossroads with the sun in my eyes. Even when I squinted into the glare, I couldn't see clearly which road was the right road for me to take. The gates across both roads were in motion, but I couldn't make out which one was opening and which was closing.

"So, any children?" a client asked me as we sat around during a break in a meeting, just making conversation.

"No," I said, trying not to wince.

"Well, get going, you don't know what you're missing!"

I managed to give him a bland smile. And I thought, You have no idea, you jolly asshole.

"Hey, have you thought about adoption?"

My smart-ass friend Dave said this over the phone with such sincerity I thought he was just being, well, a smart-ass.

I gasped. "Adoption? Why no, Dave, that hadn't occurred to me! Gee, thanks for the tip!"

"Jesus, I'm just trying to be helpful." He sounded hurt.

"You were serious?"

"Well. Yeah."

"Oh, and you didn't think we could figure that one out for ourselves."

"Okay, I take it back. Let's see what else I can come up with to insult you."

That was why I felt free to unload on Dave. He could take it almost as well as he could dish it out. I suggested, "How about, 'Sorry to hear you couldn't get pregnant, but, hey, at least you got to have fun trying!' "

"Aw man, I wish I'd thought of that one."

"You did. A year and a half ago. You want to kill your sex life? Spend a few years trying to have a baby."

"I'm a shithead."

"You meant well." With a few nosy exceptions who were clearly just fishing for dirt, most people meant well; they just didn't think through the insulting, hurtful implications of what they were saying.

Why don't you adopt?

Whenever people without adopted children ask me, "Why don't you adopt?" I always want to ask, "Why don't you?" The question implies it's the same thing as giving birth, and it's not. Most people are never forced to examine why they have children. If adopting a child and giving birth to one were the same thing, it wouldn't matter which baby you took home from the hospital. But it does matter, though it's hard to find the words to explain why. As a teenager, planning my life, I daydreamed of having one of each—an adopted child of my own and a biological child of my own. On some level I knew the experiences were different, and I was hungry to experience both.

Why don't you adopt?

I know this: A child's origins make no difference when it comes to shaping and nurturing that child. Your biological child needs the same care as your adopted child. Being a parent is about action, not genes.

Maybe the difference lies in the tangled desires, conscious and subconscious, that drive adoption and pregnancy. Had I adopted, I would have had the satisfaction of knowing I'd made the world a more loving place, whereas if I'd conceived, I would have had the comfort of seeing my parents and my husband in my child's smallest gestures.

Maybe the difference lies in the initial process of how that child would have entered my life. My adopted child wouldn't have entered my life easily or by accident. I would have made a deliberate decision to seek out and curl my life protectively around another. I would have set aside my pride and privacy while strangers judged my worthiness to become a parent. I could have changed my mind at any time, even sent the child back, but I would have kept her because I wanted that specific child in all her miraculous uniqueness, not the general idea of a child or a recreation of myself.

My biological child would have come together inside me in an ancient dance of cells that divide and swirl through a choreography so intricate and subtle most of it is still a mystery to medical science. As miraculous as infertility treatment has become, when those specialists look through their microscopes, all they see are dim shadows on the cave wall. At the time when Frank and I were undergoing treatment, the only thing the specialists could tell me about my eggs was whether or not I had any, whether each one was mature enough for fertilization, and whether its quality was good or poor. About Frank's sperm they could tell us quantity, vigor, shape, and whether or not the sperm could recognize and penetrate an egg.

With my biological child, I would have watched in amazement as my body, all on its own, transformed itself into a vessel capable of nourishing another life. I would have felt my child moving inside me. I would have had to let my child go by hauling myself up mountains of pain.

But whether I had biological children or adopted children, I don't believe I would have loved them any differently.

Why don't you adopt?

I've never been asked that question by an adoptive parent. They know how personal and complicated that decision is. Frank and I talked about adoption now and then over the years. While I sorted through my feelings in the fall of 1997, having exhausted all our other options, we talked about it seriously.

217

We talked about adopting locally, especially about welcoming an older child into our lives, or a baby with a disability. We talked about gearing up to adopt a baby from China like my cousin Mary was preparing to do, and I do mean gear up—that fall she was already well into her preparations and still had two years to go in a fourteen-thousand-dollar process, not counting what she was spending on her aging house to get it to pass the adoption agency inspection.

But by then Frank knew there were limits to his emotional energy. He knew he occasionally felt wistful at the thought of children; he knew the rest of the time he felt only dread. The fact was, he just didn't feel called to have children, biological, or adopted. His work fulfilled any need he felt to nurture.

I would have adopted if Frank had wanted to. I might even have been able to bring him around, and in the end I'm sure the child who called him Daddy would have convinced him. But there were limits to my emotional energy, too. I had fought so long and so hard to make a biological baby with him, I didn't have it in me to open a whole new front.

I said goodbye to Dave and hung up the phone. Had we thought about adopting? The short answer was, yes, we thought about adopting. We chose not to.

While I continued trying to sort out my feelings, Frank's bishop encouraged him to look into the Navy chaplaincy. The new garage was finished, Frank's tools and power equipment all in one place at last. He liked cutting and shaping wood, he liked serving his inner-city church and he would soon be finished with school. But the Marines were his first love.

He'd looked into the chaplaincy about ten years earlier; at the time, they had said even though he wasn't sick anymore, his medical discharge disqualified him.

The Navy's chaplain recruiter assured him things had changed. The recruiter was right—things had changed. This time they said he was too old.

My friend Sandra stopped by to see how the kitchen cabinets were coming. I was painting them in lieu of replacing them or the thirty-year-old appliances. I wiped my hands on my paint-smeared clothes and let her in.

Sandra and I had known each other since high school and had been roommates in college. She was the maid of honor at my wedding. As we talked, her two small children hung on her legs and I got a strange feeling. Not envy that it had been so easy for her to have children. Just an intense awareness of how different our lives were now, hers and mine, because she had children and I didn't. I had this constant sense she'd gone somewhere I couldn't follow.

I tried to sort out my feelings about motherhood and babies while my spiritual friends listened, and although I presumed the Light was listening, too, my spiritual friends were the only ones I heard offering any guidance. One of them suggested a workshop on centering prayer.

I'd never been very successful at mastering any spiritual discipline that didn't involve some sort of action, like reading, writing, or talking out loud. But I went anyway. Centering prayer seemed to involve sitting down, telling yourself you consented to the presence and activity of the Unnameable—which I promptly named God—within, and then holding still and not thinking about anything in particular for longer and longer periods of time, trusting that the Unnameable was busy doing whatever work needed doing inside you. This was supposed to be such a passive exercise that if you found yourself thinking about one particular thing for too long, you weren't supposed to refocus yourself by using the phrase, "I consent to the presence and activity of the Unnameable within." You were supposed to pick a simple word or image or even just a deep breath to represent that phrase and refocus yourself.

I figured even I could do that. To represent the phrase "I consent to the presence and activity of the Unnameable within," I picked a simple, short word. I picked "Oma."

I began practicing centering prayer. I had to tell myself "Oma" about twice a minute. I did this for fifteen minutes once a week.

With her due date approaching, Ingrid asked Erin, "Do you think Kristin would be willing to help during the birth?"

Triangulation being our communication method of choice, Erin asked me, "Ingrid was wondering if you'd be willing to help during the birth."

"Sure, I love hanging out with Annali."

"Actually, since I've got Lydia, I'll be taking care of Annali. Ingrid was hoping you'd be willing to help coach. When Annali was born, Duane had to keep leaving Ingrid alone to go find a nurse and they think it will just be better with two coaches. But we all know it's a lot to ask with everything you've been through—"

"Are you kidding? I'd be *thrilled!*"

Erin told Ingrid, "She'd be *thrilled.*" And then she added, "Told you."

I continued practicing centering prayer. I was up to four or five times a week. For me, this was the spiritual equivalent of sitting down and eating a record-setting thirty-seven lemon meringue pies. But I was still telling myself "Oma" every couple minutes.

Then one day I stood up from my fifteen minutes of centering prayer and realized I'd only told myself "Oma" twice.

Duane and I were squeezing Ingrid's hands hard and holding her knees up when the head emerged, enormous and elongated and alien. The mouth opened a little, already trying to breathe. Then Ingrid pushed again, a long, swallowed roar, and slowly the shoulders emerged, then quickly slithering, the torso and legs, the long white umbilical cord.

Luke's life had begun, one of more than three hundred thousand that began that day on earth.

Tears ached in my throat as the doctor laid him on Ingrid's stomach. Duane placed his hand on his new son, and I saw tears spilling down that stoic man's cheeks and then my cheeks were wet, too. When it was my turn to hold this profoundly plain and ordinary miracle, I loved him so much it seemed like it should be enough.

I queried the Light: I have so many beautiful children in my life, why do I still want a baby so badly? Is in vitro fertilization an exit to a selfish dead end or a new road to an even more fulfilling future? Why does it feel okay to spend borrowed money on a new bathroom, or a new garage, or tuition, but not on this?

Maybe it was because there was no guarantee of winding up with anything tangible in the end. In vitro fertilization would be a gamble.

The procedure called in vitro fertilization, or IVF, is a final Hail Mary roll of the dice. In the late nineties, depending on the age of the mother and the specific cause of a couple's infertility, the odds they would win their bet in any one treatment cycle ranged from less than one in four to slightly better than one in three. Like any crapshoot, the players never had the advantage, though the more embryos they implanted, the greater the chance they'd buck the odds. Of course, the chances also increased that they'd hit a really big payoff and take home more than one baby. The chances they'd experience complications went up, too.

At meeting, an elderly Friend who knew a little about what I was wrestling with asked me how it was going.

"It's frustrating. I want a baby as much as ever, but I just don't know if pushing on is the right thing to do. The desire for a baby is so murky and primal it's hard to analyze with the higher brain's rational tools."

She watched me thoughtfully. She tilted her head. "Moral and ethical considerations are meant to provide guidance, not answers."

On the phone that night, my mother said, "Honey, if God has planted such a strong desire in your heart, there must be a reason."

It was almost the same thing I'd said to myself three years earlier.

That night, I sat next to Frank on the bed. "I don't know why I want a baby. I just know I do." I told him if I didn't feel sure I had done absolutely everything I could, I would never be able to move on; I would look back with regret and wonder if I'd missed my chance. I would have no peace.

So rather than spend money we didn't have on a counselor, I'd prefer to spend that nonexistent money on the one thing we hadn't tried—in vitro fertilization.

Frank didn't take it well. But he took it.

The odds a marriage will survive infertility have not been calculated. But whatever the odds, they probably improve if one of you stubbornly refuses to leave.

Above our heads on the Vegas Strip, Wayne Newton gazes down at Rosie and me from his billboard. He's wearing a big honking grin. He looks crisp and casual and tan. Wayne Newton, the billboard says across the top. Beneath that: Stardust. An American flag is pasted across part of his name, and they've added, God Bless America!

I gaze up at Wayne. He gazes back. Why the flag and the slogan? I wonder. Did he do it for money? Out of a sense of connection with his fellow Americans? A little of both? He seems harmless enough. What would it hurt to give him the benefit of the doubt? If I presume the worst, I'm more likely to treat him badly. Besides, as I learned when I was trying to have a baby, I'm not always sure of my own motives; how can I presume to know someone else's?

Before Rosie and I came out here on the strip, while the TV was hawking shiny new flags, I got another email from Frank describing a "letter" they'd received on the ship. It was a crayon drawing from a little girl with seventy cents enclosed, addressed to any Marine or Sailor. Maybe people are flying the flag for the same reason. Maybe they're just trying to help the only way they know how.

The more I think about it, the more neutral patriotism seems. Like religion, it can be used for good or ill, but all by itself it's not likely to cause a war. America, love it or leave it . . . Make love not war . . . Reduce patriotism and pacifism to slogans and they're both too simplistic to fix a very complicated, very broken world. No matter how hard we try to avoid it, millennia after millennia we humans have continually resorted to war for a complex mix of reasons: Because our economic interests are at risk; because we don't want someone else to have the power to hurt us or tell us what to do; because we feel morally or ethically obligated to fight—what we used to call fighting for our honor and now call things like "peacekeeping" and "liberating oppressed people." When all three come together at once, our moral stand lining up with our economic and power interests, which we perceive as being threatened in some way, the result is often war.

Our enemies go to war for reasons as tangled, and as understandable, as ours. I know this. I've always known, intellectually, that trying to see the other guy's side of it is one of the first steps nations have to take in order to prevent war. But until September 11, I had never admitted how hard that first step is, not just for nations, but for individuals too. And until I looked up at Wayne, prepared to dismiss his flag and his slogan, I had never admitted how often I should have been taking that step in my own life.

Outside a home-décor liquidator, a four-foot statue of a fireman stands at the ready, hose in hand, a beatific expression on his face. Someone has wrapped him in a flag, the way firemen wrap blankets around the people they rescue. When I find myself standing in front of it for several long minutes trying to decide if it's too cheesy to be moving, I realize it's time to leave Las Vegas.

HOWDY, NEIGHBOR

Starting date 10/22/01 . . . first quarter moon . . . odometer 129,988 . . .
route: east across Hoover Dam into Arizona, then north into Colorado
with pit stops at the Grand Canyon, the Navajo Nation, and Mesa Verde
= three days, 679 miles

I found insurance that would cover one round of IVF. We followed the tall, angular back of the infertility clinic's therapist into a closet-sized office so stuffed with books and files we had to stand up till the door was closed, then slow dance our way around and into chairs that sat us knee to knee. In such a setting, a setting so intimate you hope you didn't have anything even slightly garlicky for lunch, it's easy to get right to the point.

"We're trying to decide ahead of time how many embryos to put back," I told her. "We're having a little trouble coming to agreement."

The therapist asked how many we each would want to transfer from petri dishes back into my uterus.

"Four," I said.

"One," said Frank.

"Hmm," the therapist said. She pointed out one wouldn't give us much chance of success.

"That's why I want to put back four. That gives us the best odds."

"I can't handle more than one baby, definitely not more than two. Three, forget it. I will not be a good father and they will hate me the way I hate my father. And look ahead. How will we pay for college for more than one child just as I'm entering retirement?"

The therapist proposed that perhaps one solution would be to put back four, and in the unlikely event all four implanted, reduce to one.

I shook my head. "I could see reducing from four to three. I mean, I know with four you run the risk of losing all of them. But reducing more than that would seem like an abortion of convenience to me." I thought about those nights spent walking Lydia. "Taking care of three babies would just about kill me, but I know my family would be there for me."

"It *would* kill me." Frank's face was grim. "And there are also medical risks with even three," he added with an unspoken "so there." Then his voice softened. "But you're wrong, it *could* kill you. If it were up to me, there is no way I would risk you for a possible baby. You're real. A baby is still just a fantasy."

In the silence that followed, I felt annoyed and touched at the same time. I grumbled something about maternal death being a highly unlikely outcome.

The therapist suggested perhaps it would be helpful to compare, on a scale of one to ten, how strongly each of us felt about reducing the number of implanted embryos, should it come to that.

Frank didn't even hesitate. "Ten." He absolutely could not handle more than one, possibly two, babies.

I shifted in my chair. I squinted up at the corner of the room. I bit my lip. "Six," I finally admitted. I'd always been one of those people who supported other women's right to choose while piously believing I would never make such a choice. And yet when push came to shove, when I held in my hands four potential lives huddled together as elliptical and fragile as tiny frogs, I was more practical than principled. Idealism was too neat and square a box to contain fully the tangled mess of questions—Which life would I sacrifice? Should all four lives be put at risk, or never even given a chance to exist in the first place? Do the needs of a life already four decades down the road trump the needs of a life that hasn't yet started? How do you balance the survival of each individual with the survival of a larger group?

Huddled together with our brothers and sisters, we humans are pack animals. Ultimately, I had to admit my commitment to the rights of one individual only rated a six.

"Does that change things?" asked the therapist.

It did. After a long minute spent sitting in silence we agreed between ourselves to put back three and reduce to two if necessary. Neither one of us was very happy, which I suppose was a sign of success.

As the Vette grumbles eastward out of Vegas, I'm not very happy about squinting into the morning sun. The sky is obnoxiously bright. I can't avoid the fact that driving east means my escapist trip is more than halfway over. Since I'm now roaring along wondering if I can honestly call myself a Quaker, I'm not particularly happy about where this trip looks like it's going to end up.

Meanwhile back home, someone is mailing letters laced with anthrax to Congress. People are starting to die. A stranger at a gas station looks at my D.C. tags and says cheerfully, "Bet you're glad you're not there right now!"

Rosie's big mouth spares me the trouble of telling him to mind his own business. I'm slumped against the back of the Vette with my hand on the pump, watching my life savings pour into my gas tank. We're off blowing up terrorists overseas when we've got plenty of homegrown ones right here. People are so discouraging. That story about those Quaker legislators who resigned back in colonial Pennsylvania during an Indian war rather than impose their pacifist beliefs on their fellow colonists? You know why they were faced with an Indian war in the first place? Because the son of William Penn, the Friend who founded Pennsylvania, got greedy.

Penn Junior started chiseling away at the treaties his father had arranged with the colony's native inhabitants, taking advantage of every loophole to cheat his native neighbors out of the lands where they'd lived since time began for them. For instance, one treaty measured a particular parcel of land sold to the Europeans as the distance a man could walk in a day, about thirty miles. Penn Jr. hired the two fastest men in the colony to go out and run as far as they could in a day, which added up to about sixty miles, and then he claimed the extra land.

After repeated injustices like that—and after repeated peaceful appeals failed to win them any justice—the native Pennsylvanians, who were not a particularly warlike people, finally resorted to violence for the same reasons human beings have always resorted to violence. And Friends had no one to blame but one of their own.

It's discouraging. Human nature is a disease from which no one's immune.

Frank and I were tested and screened for sexually transmitted diseases that spring of 1998—blood group, Rh factor, and various antibodies. Then the back wall of the back bedroom was suddenly streaming with rainwater. The leak was located and fixed. The plaster wall was ruined. We gutted the whole room because I had wanted to move the closet anyway.

Meanwhile, somewhere a phone was being dialed.

My uterus was mapped, the sonogram wand moving inside me. A mock embryo transfer was performed. The doctor, a ruddy energetic fireplug named Nash, declared my uterus looked good and smooth. On the screen next to the exam table, it looked like the gray, cratered surface of the moon.

Meanwhile, somewhere a phone was ringing.

Insurance forms were filed, and since the insurance I had ferreted out paid only for the procedure, three thousand dollars was borrowed, drugs and syringes purchased. Cabinets were desired in the upstairs hall, wood was bought. Frank was buried under class work, both of us under sudden avalanches of freelance jobs on top of regular jobs. The gutted back bedroom was ignored.

The phone—it was ringing inside our house. Frank answered. It was the Navy. The chaplain corps had a shortage of "baby baptizers," Episcopalian and Lutheran ministers like Frank. All of a sudden, at age thirty-nine, he was no longer too old to join the Navy. All of a sudden we had a deadline—in four months he would be gone, and would continue to be gone more often than he was home for years to come.

The hormone injections began.

The gas pump clicks off and I hoist myself back into the Vette through the window because this morning the twenty-three-year-old lock in the driver's door woke up feeling balky. I pretend not to notice the stares of the drivers at the other pumps, people I don't know and will never see again. They drive boring cars anyway.

I'm not the only one who's out of sorts about the way things are going.

```
There has been constant re-evaluation
at the highest levels of planning. We
were told that the most immediate ops
have been canceled (again). Who's on
first, what's on second, I don't know
is on third . . . stand by to stand by
. . . Semper Gumby. We say we are at
the tip of the spear, but so far we
have only been stabbing at air.
```

So have we all. Approaching Hoover Dam, I pass a mobile electronic sign parked by the road: Passenger Cars Only Hoover Dam. Then I pass another one: Cars with Trailers All Trucks Exit Now. I watch the car ahead of me pull its trailer right on past the exit, headed for the dam. Red alert sounds in my head. No way I'm crossing Hoover Dam the same time as *that* thing. I drop back. I wonder if I am witnessing something. I wonder if I should grab my cell phone and dial 911.

It turns off onto a side road.

Suspicion. Hysteria. According to the radio, I am not alone in this. It's a not-so-brave new world.

Then I see a checkpoint up ahead. Of course. What did I think, they were doing it on the honor system? The state trooper has stopped the car ahead of me, but sends it on as I approach. Me, I don't even have to stop—he waves me through. The car behind me, it has to stop. I'm a little insulted. I can't even get stopped and searched in this country; I can't even get looked at sideways. I miss my husband. I miss my friends. I miss my Quaker meeting back home.

Arizona passes by the windows, a lot of sand and dirt and scattered beige tufts, a couple of twisted little Dr. Seuss trees, and every once in a while the far-off silvery glint of an old dented mobile home. A white-and-red frame building sits all by itself next to the road. Santa Land, says the sign. It's dusty and closed looking, as if Santa went fishing and never came back.

As the sun drops, Rosie and I sit alone at the edge of the Grand Canyon. It gapes before us, shadows lengthening below into blackness. It swallows me whole. Lying in our tent we both hear the pack of coyotes that stops outside to lap from Rosie's water bowl. We stare in that direction as if we can see through the tent wall, Rosie's head up, ears pointed forward. Neither one of us makes a sound. They're not our kind. When we hear them again, yipping and barking in the distance, Rosie lowers her head to her paws, breathes in deep and releases a long sigh. I am swallowed by an even deeper loneliness.

Everybody needs a pack to travel with as they move through this life. On his ship, Frank is surrounded by Marines and Sailors. I don't know if he's still in the Mediterranean, or is moving through the Suez Canal, or is in the Red Sea or the Indian Ocean by now, but wherever he is, I know he is with his community. Wherever he goes, he's always home.

I left Frank sleeping in the bed, went into the bathroom, and took off my t-shirt. I washed my hands. I swabbed alcohol on the rubber stopper in the tiny glass bottle of Lupron. I unwrapped a syringe and pulled back the plunger to twenty units. I uncapped the needle, stuck it through the rubber stopper, and pushed the plunger all the way in, air bubbling into the bottle. I turned the bottle and syringe upside down. I slowly pulled back the plunger to twenty units again, the clear liquid following the plunger down into the syringe. I unstuck the syringe. I swabbed a spot on my lower abdomen and pinched up a roll of skin. Rosie trotted in, eager to greet me for the morning.

"Go away," I said sternly. She ducked her head. "Go away." She slunk out. I pushed the door shut with my foot.

I held the syringe over the pinch of skin for a moment, then quickly slid it all the way into the subcutaneous tissue. I pushed in the plunger. I pulled the needle out and dropped it into the empty plastic Coke bottle Frank had donated as a sharps container. Then I cheered up Rosie by taking her to the park.

I did this every morning for eleven days until my ovaries shut down.

I rode the Metro downtown to the clinic for a baseline sonogram and blood work. Dora's slim black hands moved like shadows across the chalky skin of my inner arms. Dora had no trouble getting blood out of my small, rolling veins. Dora's hands were the hands of God. I loved Dora.

I added two more shots to my day. In addition to Lupron, I started injecting Fertinex morning and evening, this to restart my ovaries. Not just restart them, kick them into overdrive. I was at three shots a day now; I started running out of places to stick. Sometimes I'd hit invisible capillaries. They leaked little bruises, blue and yellow speckles across my stomach and thighs. Every other day or so I went in for a sonogram and more blood work. Bruises mottled my inner arms. On the screen, the moon began to sprout follicles.

"Excellent, excellent," Dr. Nash murmured, "ah excellent," as he pointed the sonogram wand inside me and measured the big follicles. Twenty-eight of them.

Frank and I both started on the antibiotic doxycycline. It's hard to stomach. Frank's stomach was empty the first time he took it, except for coffee, and two hours later he threw it up.

Rosie tiptoed around me as I shoveled up broken plaster from the tarp on the back bedroom floor and tipped it into the chute Frank had constructed. I had told him he had to get all our projects wrapped up before he left. The broken plaster debris slid down to where he waited on the patio, wearing a dust mask, holding a large tub in place to catch the plaster debris. A rattling, thumping roar, a crunchy thud. A cloud of dust rose up around him.

The night before, I'd said, "I know the insurance only pays for us to try the procedure once. I know I kind of implied I was willing to stop after that. But the more I think about it, the more I feel like, given the odds, I need to give it two or three tries."

Frank had looked stunned, his voice disbelieving. "You said one. One try."

"But what about the fact that just because it doesn't work the first time doesn't mean it won't work at all? If it's going to work for you, they say it will in two or three tries."

His face flushed. "But we agreed. You promised."

"I didn't promise, I just—"

"How can you break a promise like that?"

Inside me a little voice said, Yeah! Aren't Quakers supposed to practice integrity? "But," I insisted, "the situation's different now. If they discover we have a fertilization problem that can't be gotten around, I'm ready to let it go. But if we do wind up with embryos and it fails, I have to try a full IVF cycle one more time."

He started to walk away from me.

"Can't we talk about it?"

He held up an index finger, his face furious and wounded, and mouthed it: one.

Rosie watched me dump another rumbling shovelful of rubble down the chute at Frank. We both watched him stand up with the loaded tub in his arms and stagger with it to the back of the yard.

Aside from that incident, I was as happy as Frank was miserable. Washington, D.C., is glorious in the springtime. I held smart-alecky conversations with myself while I sat at my computer next to the sunny sliding-glass door, cranking out one pedestrian freelance writing project after another. I hummed as I hurried from the Metro to the clinic so Dora could take my blood, then on to a mindless temping job. In late spring the trees were fresh as limes, the medians and traffic circles frothing with National Park Service flowers. I dodged and chased Rosie across the new grass in the park. On calm blue days the Potomac mirrored the cloud-puffed sky, the fuzzy green shore, the Memorial Bridge stretching between Arlington and the Lincoln Memorial. The glassy river combined the clean white yin of the arches with the wavery white yang of their reflections—the illusion of perfect circles. I had no time to practice centering prayer anymore, but I was taking action. I was doing everything possible. All was right with the world.

In the late spring, the nights were still cool and glowed softly with the pinkish gold of sodium-vapor streetlights. Rosie and I burst in the door from her last outing before bed, and Frank slammed down a small plastic case on the kitchen counter. "I can't find my drill bits!" he shouted. "What did you do with my drill bits?"

"I haven't touched your drill bits," I said. "That's not them?"

"No! Those are my small screwdrivers!" Rosie circled him, tail wagging, eager to greet him after not seeing him for five minutes. "Hi Rosie girl," he said gently, a quick distracted pat. Then he went back to slamming his tools around, looking for a different small plastic case.

I watched him for a minute. "I'm going up for my shot."

In my perfect world he would have said, "Wait for me, honey. You shouldn't have to be alone while you do that. I'll keep you company."

But he never kept me company while I stuck needles into my thighs and stomach. Never went to appointments with me unless his presence was mandatory. Never discussed the subject unless it was to express how unhappy he was about it. He was so afraid of becoming his father he was becoming his father.

Frank had told me early on in our relationship that my family's indirect method of meeting each other's needs through manipulation and mind reading wouldn't work with him.

"You have to be direct with me," he'd said.

So the next morning I told him, "I need you to be supportive these days."

I continued to tell him that every couple days, and for half a day or so afterward he'd pat me on the back and say, "Well, I guess I better tell you I love you." He tried. But the closer we came to the possibility of a child, the more he was possessed by the demons of his own childhood, and that was the best he could do. It was starting to get to me. Not only that, my job, all my jobs, were starting to get to me. The lack of time for practicing centering prayer was starting to get to me. I set a goal, a very modest goal I thought, of sitting down for two minutes each day to pray.

I set the bar too high. That week I sat down for my allotted two minutes of prayer exactly once.

My mother and sisters are helping me move into my new dorm. Rosie is there, too, and the noise and commotion scare her, so she shrinks to the size of a two-month-old puppy. I pick her up to comfort her and she turns into a mixed-race baby. He's mine, but it's not clear if I adopted him or birthed him. I carry him all around with my family. Then we discover we have put my stuff in the wrong dorm room. We gather everything up to transfer it to the right room, but when we get there and I put down what's in my arms, I realize I no longer have my sweet baby. I must have let him slip from my hands at some point and not noticed because my hands were full of other things. I search the room in a panic, then run back the way I came, retracing my steps, my mother and sisters running behind me. Unlike other times when I'm in a hurry and I feel like I'm running through molasses, this time I feel a surge of power in my legs. My feet move faster and faster.

Before I could find my baby, I woke up.

It was midafternoon when the medical coordinator called to tell me that based on the morning's blood work, tonight was the night Frank should give me the shot that would trigger my ovaries to finish ripening up. It occurred to me that Frank and I had not had sex in a month. His sperm had to be pretty old and feeble by now.

"Should he ejaculate tonight so he'll have fresh ones for fertilization the day after tomorrow?" By now, even I could say things like ejaculate without blushing.

"No, no," the coordinator said, "it's too late for that. No sex for two days before the eggs are retrieved and fertilized. If the first sample's no good the day after tomorrow, we'll just have him do another a couple of hours later."

I laughed. It was not a humorous laugh. It was a horrified laugh. Frank had already spent the whole day predicting doom for his attempts to perform on egg-retrieval-and-fertilization day. "There is no way that would happen. Are you sure it's too late?"

"Yes, it's too late."

"They're really old."

"It'll be okay."

"Not if the first sample sucks it won't be."

She sighed. "I'll check with the doctor."

While I was on hold, Frank came in from the garage. "It's the clinic," I said.

"What do they want?" he asked, suspicious.

I held up my hand—someone was picking up the phone on the other end. "Kristin?" It was Dr. Nash.

"I'm here."

"Go ahead, but do it right away. Where's Frank?"

"He's right here, too."

Frank looked as though I'd just pulled him naked from behind a shower curtain. "No!" he mouthed at me. "Don't tell them that!"

"Well, what are you doing on the phone?" Dr. Nash laughed. "Get off the phone!"

I laughed. I got off the phone. I explained to Frank what was going on, tried to make the fact that we had to have sex right that very minute seem oh-so-lighthearted and merry. He didn't laugh. "This isn't a good time. I'm too stressed out."

"We have to do this, Frank. Please?"

He didn't answer.

"Will you please do this for me?"

He shrugged and walked back out to the garage. I thought he was closing up so he could come back in, but when I peered out the sliding-glass door, I could see him puttering around out there. I had never felt so alone. Not just alone. Abandoned. I don't remember crossing the yard between the house and the garage.

"What are you doing." It was a demand, not a question.

He looked over his shoulder at me standing in the garage door. "Sorting." He resumed poking through a pile of nuts, bolts, screws, and nails, dropping them one by one into rows of tiny drawers.

"No. I mean what kind of game are you playing."

"I'm not playing any game. I'm serious."

Tears were on my cheeks but they felt more like condensation on steel than sadness or rage. I heard this unbending part of me say, "And so am I. I have never felt so betrayed in my life. If the tables were turned, I would never, never do this to you. I never have. Now you want to go back in the military and I'm even supporting you on that. I have sacrificed so much for you over the past thirteen years, and it's finally time for you to sacrifice for me. If you do not do your best to support me on this, I will leave you."

That shocked us both. And yet I knew it was true. I would. I was breathing hard. He stood still, his hands filled with small bits of metal. Then he turned away and threw the handful of nails on the floor. "I can't believe you would hang a sword like that over my head!"

"Wait a minute, wait!" And the words continued to flow out of me as effortlessly as the tears slipping down my cheeks. "I'm not saying this to scare you, or bully you into doing what I want. I'm not saying it just to get sperm out of you. I'm saying I will leave you because I just realized I can't live with someone who would betray me like this, who could be this cruel, this selfish, as to stand there and say no to me when I need you most, in the final steps of pursuing *my* dream. I could never do this to you, so the fact that you're doing it to me makes me wonder if you don't love me as much as I love you. And I don't want to spend the rest of my life with somebody who doesn't return my love. I deserve better than that."

He picked up the nails he'd thrown down. He threw them, one by one by one, into their small drawers. He threw them hard. Then he walked past me into the house. I stood there for a few minutes, wiping my eyes.

He was upstairs taking a shower. When he got out, he lay down on the bed and I lay down beside him. I waited. I couldn't think of anything else to do.

Eventually he said, "Ever since we've been together, there have been times when I was afraid maybe you just loved me because it was convenient. Or because you had to." I watched his profile. "That's how my father made me feel." He was squinting at the ceiling as if he could see through it to the sky. "Sometimes I was afraid I loved you more than you loved me. But when you said you were afraid of the same thing . . ." He turned his head to look at me. "I know how I feel about you, and the fact that you could, like you know, feel the same way as I have from time to time must mean you love me as much as I love you."

It's easy to make love with someone who loves you as much as you love him.

Afterward, whenever I started to get up, his arm tightened around me to keep me by his side.

With Rosie beside me in the Vette, after having figured out the complex but necessary new procedure for coaxing the driver's door to unlock on a reliable basis, I leave the Grand Canyon behind.

We pass through the Painted Desert, which looks like a striped hand-woven blanket, and enter the Navajo Nation, a stark and subtle land of pink sand and gray and tan rocks, rose-colored buttes, creamy grasses, silvery green dots of sage. An old man and woman float by, he in brand-new-looking jeans, boots, and cowboy hat, she in a long full dark skirt and scarf unspecked by dirt, their dried apple faces as eroded and furrowed as the land. They're both standing at the end of a long dusty driveway to nowhere. They look past the Vette, watching and waiting for someone who isn't me to come down the highway.

Further on, an Open flag snaps smartly above a folding table, a smoking grill, four small women, and a child. A hand-lettered sign on a piece of cardboard announces, Food. I pull in. The women seem surprised I've stopped. From their practiced hands I buy roasted mutton and peppers wrapped in fry bread with half a plain boiled potato on the side, plus a Styrofoam cup of crushed ice drenched in root beer syrup, for $3.50. We're all too shy to speak with one another.

Sitting in the parked Vette, I share my lunch with Rosie and look past the women and their grill to a small, distant cluster of dusty cinderblock houses that anchors the emptiness. Tacked up on the side of one is a huge American flag. I stop chewing for a moment. I have to assume they know their own history. And yet they've chosen to fly an American flag.

After a moment I start chewing again. I respect the deliberateness of that choice in a way I haven't respected others.

Up the road in Colorado, the NPR station switches to local news. The announcer's Midwestern voice is clipped and nasal. "I guess we've had some worries about anthrax here. But looks like the government's got all that under control. They've got drugs that, even if you do get anthrax, will put it into admission."

That's the word he uses, "admission."

"So you don't have to worry about that. And looks like we had an accident just outside of town. Looks like a car went through a stop sign and hit another vehicle, killed two of our local teens. 'Course our condolences go out to the families."

In journalism school, they teach would-be broadcasters to be conversational on the air. If you listen to the buffed and polished national announcers long enough, you start to believe they really are conversational.

"Looks like our weather is going to be nice today. Moonrise this afternoon around three, then it's gonna set about an hour after midnight. And a full moon for Halloween, so watch out for those vampires."

But this. *This* is conversational.

"So uh, I just want to tell you people out there, everyone take care of each other and love your brother. And uh, I am going to say goodbye now. We'll go back to our regularly scheduled programming."

I listen with a big grin on my face. Alone in my car, listening to the radio, I finally feel like I'm part of a community again, a real community of real people.

As I check us into a motel for the night, the no-nonsense woman behind the desk, who wears her gray-streaked hair like a watch cap and her earrings like a female duty she could do without, interrupts her unsmiling recitation of the rules and regulations about pets to look at my D.C. driver's license for a long moment. Then she says brusquely, "Every time I see one of these I worry about those poor people in Washington."

"Me too," I say, and we talk about it for a while. I pick up my key. "Well, take it easy."

"Stay safe." She peers past me at the Vette outside. "Least you got your dog to look out for you."

The next day, after climbing around the cliff dwellings of Mesa Verde, where a thousand years ago a small community of people perched together like birds found comfort, I slip back into the Vette where Rosie waits. She greets me with a cold-nosed snuffle in my ear, reading my scent like a laser scan of my palm or pupil. Last night when I entered my password and checked my email I read:

```
Really have nothing to say. Just
want to enjoy the illusion of some
kind of contact with you.
```

It's afternoon here. Circling the Mediterranean somewhere in the watery night, Frank is asleep and dreaming in his rack, surrounded by the even breathing of his fellow officers. I lean over, Rosie's body my pillow, and close my eyes. Behind my lids I see a photograph from the days right after September 11—a man and a German shepherd, both pale gray with ash, both curled together asleep on the pavement at Manhattan's ground zero, both too exhausted to go on searching.

I turn my face into Rosie's chameleon fur, smell the way it absorbs and blends with the scents around her. I smell gasoline and my perfume and dog bed and grass. Frank's skin, the first time I pressed my face to the hair of his chest, surprised me with night-blooming sweetness, the way some flowers do at dusk. Rosie's personal scent I only find deep down in the fine black fluffy undercoat next to her skin, corn-chip salty and woody and comforting. We are a pack of two.

I left Frank asleep in the bed and took Rosie to the park, where I threw her ball for her to chase in the early evening light. After we'd been there a few minutes, her mutt friend Rollie raced into the park, half black Lab, half unknown, and she chased after him.

Rollie's owner strode over. We'd been exercising our dogs together for a year and a half and I'd never seen Beth do anything but stride. Even when she was moving slowly she strode, her great mass of dark hair swinging. "Hey doll!" she yelled.

"Hey Beth," I yelled back, "your hair looks great."

"It should. Just had the roots done." And she laughed her husky belly laugh. She exuded the confidence of someone who had always been popular, even in high school, and with good reason. Beth always left you feeling better than you felt before she showed up.

"Hey," I said, "I understand Frank asked you the other day if you could possibly look after Rosie sometime this weekend."

"Yeah that's cool. I checked with Doug and we'll be around."

"Well, it turns out we won't need you to do that after all, but thanks." I hesitated. "I think he told you why we thought we'd need help?" I had been surprised when Frank said he'd told her we were undergoing infertility treatment. We'd heard enough insensitive comments to learn to give out that information on a need-to-know basis only. She was nodding. "Because we weren't sure when the retrieval procedure would be scheduled? And it's way the heck out in Maryland. But we've just been told to do the shot that triggers everything late tonight, so that means the procedure will happen around noon day after tomorrow, and we can handle Rosie before and after. So that's why we don't need the help after all. But I appreciate it."

"Sure, anytime. Good luck."

"We'll see."

"Hey, you can always try again."

"Only if we can save enough money again."

"Yeah, they definitely want their money up front. You ever notice how they never really tell you everything that's coming? Probably because they know then nobody would do it, and they'd all be driving Caprices instead of new Land Rovers."

I frowned. "That sounds like the voice of experience."

And she said, "We're about a month behind you."

I stared at her. I liked Beth, but I'd never thought I had much in common with her beyond dogs and wisecracks. All of a sudden we were comparing diagnoses, drug reactions, psycho-spousal relations, injection strategies. On the subject of shots, she pointed to a bruise peeking out below the hem of her shorts and said, "I think I hit a major artery this morning."

I tugged up the hems of my shorts to show off the bruises on both my thighs. "Look! Me too!"

She pulled down her waistband. "And your stomach?"

"Oh yeah." I showed her.

She pushed up her sleeves. "Arms?"

"Ditto."

"We're the pod people!" she crowed. "We're everywhere!"

Twilight had fallen. We called our dogs. We hugged before we left.

ALIEN NATION

*Starting date 10/25/01 . . . waxing quarter
moon . . . odometer 130,667 . . . route: southeast through Colorado and New Mexico to a
pit stop in Roswell = two days, 526 miles*

The Vette blasts into New Mexico, the landscape alien and dry. We bear down on Albuquerque and roll into a sunburned suburb landscaped in cactus and pastel rock. "Stay with my mother," my friend Ellery had emailed me. "I'll let her know you're coming—she loves being the hostess. Just leave her a message so she'll know when to expect you." I left her a message this morning.

She didn't get it. Savannah stands in her front door and frowns up at me. She's a small black woman with the ten-foot-tall command of an elderly matriarch and the face of a much younger movie star. "When I didn't hear from you, I thought you'd changed your mind."

I'm so intimidated I can hardly speak. I've never met her before. I stammer my apologies, wishing Rosie would stop rudely woofing from the Vette. "That's okay, we can stay in a motel, it's no problem." I edge away from the door.

"Oh no no no." Savannah dismisses that option by walking away from the door faster than I do, leaving the door wide open as she disappears around a corner inside. I follow her hesitantly. Behind me Rosie's woofs grow more concerned.

Savannah turns to me in the hall. "What's your friend's name?"

"You mean Rosie?"

She repeats it like a fine wine. "Rooosie." Then she sighs. "My

German shepherd's name was Joy. A few months ago I woke up and found her dead on the floor next to my bed. She usually liked to sleep in the yard, but she had a dog door. I guess inside next to me was where she wanted to die."

Savannah's house is the kind of place you savor layer by layer, rooms that inundate the senses then resolve into individually carved chairs the color of tannin, curtains like smoke, hand-painted vases, perfumed candles, spice-painted walls crowded with paintings, flocks of pillows nubby with color. She confesses with a conspiratorial smile, "I like too many things."

She's put in a full day at her executive office, and now she cares for her invalid mother in the room next to mine, which is made up and ready as if guests drop in all the time. Then she whips up shrimp creole and serves it with the wine I handed her as a hostess gift. As we're saying goodnight, she asks, "How long will you stay?"

"Oh, only overnight. We'll be out of your hair tomorrow."

"Well, you can't leave till you've seen Sante Fe."

She marches to her own drummer. I meekly fall in, let her whisk me away in the morning to the stucco fantasy of Sante Fe, a whirlwind guided tour. Over brunch in a tiled courtyard ringed by galleries of wrought-iron, she points her fork at me. "I am in awe of you, you know."

I blink at her dumbly. She? In awe of *me*?

"I would never have the nerve to drive across the country alone. That would scare me to death."

Savannah's not the first woman to tell me they'd be afraid to do what I'm doing. Maybe I'm just stupid, but to me it feels like a completely natural thing to do. Driving alone, driving fast, driving through snowstorms, that's not what scares me. It's that business of putting your life, or the life of someone you love, at the disposal of leaders who may throw that life away without solving anything and there's nothing you can do about it. Five weeks into this road trip, that still scares the hell out of me.

Back at Savannah's house, she heads to the office and I lie down, thinking I'll just nap for a minute before getting back on the road. Instead I drop into a deep pit of sleep. My cell phone drags me up. I throw pillows around hunting for it and by the time it's in my hand I have only a split second to decide whether or not to answer. It's a 900 number. A sex line, how weird. I don't answer.

I'm starting up the Vette before I notice I have a message. I dial my voicemail, put the phone to my ear, and there's Frank's voice, calling me from a phone on a ship somewhere on the other side of the world. "Oh no!" I wail, "I can't believe it!" and I punch the car's padded door. Ow, ow, ow, I shake my hand. It's padded, but not padded enough. Rosie leans across me to sniff my hand. They don't get access to those phones very often and when they do, an overseas call is not cheap and Frank is. He's never called before.

I had him. I had him right there in my hand, and I let him slip away.

I replay his message, one minute and seven seconds of him nattering on about how someone had given him a leftover prepaid phone card that only had about a minute left on it, so Frank just thought he'd call, and now that he'd had a chance to listen to my voice on the outgoing message, he'd just talk till the card ran out and let me listen to his.

I do. Over and over again.

The small downtown clinic was closed on weekends. Frank gave me the triggering shot on a Friday night, so Saturday I had to drive out to an innocuous four-story medical office building in suburban Maryland that housed ophthalmology offices and the exam rooms of internists and podiatrists and dermatologists and, on the second floor, the main infertility clinic and its lab. A new nurse tried and failed to get blood out of me. Another nurse came in. I watched her dig around under my skin. By now, both sleeves were rolled up.

It seemed in keeping with the way the rest of my body felt. Ordinarily ovaries are two to three inches long. Mine were now much larger, bursting with follicles. They felt swollen, as if they were big as basketballs, all my insides so tender everything felt like it would burst if I didn't sit down gently. My breasts were so tender that if I could have worn a jog bra twenty-four hours a day, I would have, even in the shower. My thighs and stomach and arms were bruised. The top of my right buttock ached from the triggering shot.

The second nurse finally struck blood. I watched her fill eight fat tubes. My eggs, if I had any eggs, would nest in my blood after they left my body.

When my grandparents were born—at home in their mothers' beds—human beings were just beginning to defy gravity and fly. People gathered in darkened theaters to watch a flickering pasteboard rocket blast off from the earth and hit the burlesque moon in the eye.

When my parents were born—in hospitals by then—humans were turning the power of flight into blitzkrieg. Peopled huddled in their homes around their radios, and mistook a science fiction broadcast for real news that Martians had invaded the earth.

By the time I was born, half a century after my grandparents, humans had begun to leave gravity behind and fly into space. Families gathered around televisions to watch a man walk on the moon and a robotic rover roll across Mars.

As I looked at the phases of my ovaries on the sonogram screen, I wondered, If all this science gives me a baby, what will my baby grow up to see?

UFO Crash Site.

That's what the sign says. It stands just off the highway just outside of Roswell, flat stony fields all around. The Vette's hot engine ticks in the cool air. The occasional car swishes by, the occasional truck. The flying saucer crashed thataway—that's what the sign says—on the ranch of an upstanding local citizen back in 1947 with the bodies of dead aliens and everything, but then a government conspiracy hushed it up.

Rosie stares across the fields, bored. Alien spoor is nothing compared to whatever was behind the toilet in L.A.

Downtown, a giant inflatable green alien in a space suit greets passersby from the roof of the Honda dealership. The window of the boot shop features a cartoon alien decked out in cowboy boots and a ten-gallon hat. Diners and hardware stores alternate with alien museums and alien knickknack emporiums. One sign proclaims Indian Jewelry, Mexican Imports, Alien Gifts.

Strolling with Rosie after dark, I spot a huge bonfire across an athletic field, a crowd of bustling silhouettes. I wonder if this is some sort of weird ritual conducted by true believers, perhaps one-time abductees trying to get the attention of their former abductors in outer space. We approach cautiously, Rosie sniffing the charbroiled air. A group of well-muscled guys in crew cuts overtakes us and runs toward the fire, none of them looking like people who might have otherworldly mind-control devices implanted in the backs of their necks. And then I realize they're true believers of a different sort: The New Mexico Military Institute is across the street. It's homecoming weekend.

Rosie and I change directions. We stroll around the campus through pools of light. The dark shrubs are squared off, the neatly shorn lawns grooved by a century of lined-up marching drills, the dorms and classrooms built like a defensible castle, complete with watchtowers and crenelated ramparts. Not so long ago this sort of world felt alien to me. But Frank assured me I'd get used to it, and sure enough, after four years of doing my grocery shopping within earshot of booming artillery and crackling rifle fire, and driving through guarded gates and past tanks to meet Frank for lunch, it has grown to feel familiar. I've even grown to like it. The military men I used to imagine were all baby killers, I like them, too. Most of them are like the Quakers I know, decent people trying to do the right thing.

But even though this world has become familiar, it still doesn't feel entirely comfortable. A passing trio of uniformed young people offers me a respectful, "Good evening, ma'am," as they pass, and I think, If they only knew where I go to church on Sunday. I think, They might not respect me if they knew I'm one of those people who won't stand up and fight for what I believe in. They assume because I'm here on this campus I'm one of them but I'm not; I'm not a true believer.

The truth is, they probably don't give a flying fig what I believe. If they think of me at all now that they've passed me, it's probably Rosie they're thinking about.

Rosie and I sit on a bench to watch the dimly lit changing of the guard. It occurs to me that I've grown to feel the same edge of discomfort among Friends. Greeting acquaintances after the rise of meeting, more than once I've thought, If they only knew where my husband goes to work each day. I don't know why I think that. The ones who do know don't seem to care, or at most are a little curious. I guess the edge is my own discomfort with the fact that I'm not a true believer anywhere anymore. Now that I think about it, I felt out of place long before September 11 caused me to question my Quaker beliefs. Like Oma and Opa in America, grammatically correct in English but forever marked by a foreign accent, maybe I've always felt like the outsider and always will. When Oma and Opa went back home to Germany, they discovered their American way of life had left them out of step there, too.

Rosie and I climb in the Vette and tool down the road to get some supper. I pull in at a fast-food franchise where the sign promises, Aliens Welcome!

Exactly thirty-six hours after the triggering shot, Frank drove me back to the main clinic. He sat next to the gurney as a nurse anesthetist inserted an IV in my arm. I was wearing a blue hospital gown, papery blue booties, and a papery blue big-hair cap. I made a joke about the cap. I wondered if they would find any eggs. Just because I had follicles didn't mean there would be eggs in them—that could be the reason I hadn't been able to get pregnant. Frank sat next to me till they wheeled the gurney away.

In the procedure room, I climbed up on the table. I lay back and put my legs in the stirrups. In a minute I would be lying there, unconscious, in a room full of strangers with my legs spread, handing off vulnerable little bits of my life to technicians. Then someone cranked up the sedative and that's all I remember.

Voices. I was moving. I was back on the gurney, being wheeled into a curtained cubicle. Someone, a nurse, was saying to me, "Twenty-three, twenty-three eggs," and I started to cry. And Frank's voice whispered, "Why are you crying?" The nurse peered in, thinking I was crying from the pain that's the inevitable result when a six-inch needle penetrates the vaginal wall a couple dozen times, but that wasn't it.

I whispered, "Twenty-three eggs. Not zero."

"Oh," Frank said softly, "those are *happy* tears."

The nurse closed the curtain and went away.

I was waking up more and starting to feel a little nauseated. The nurse said something about tachycardia and cranked up whatever was dripping into my arm. The nausea went away. My teeth chattered a little. The woman in the next cubicle was telling someone she had five follicles. They discussed the size of the follicles. I felt bad for her. Frank and I exchanged looks. He felt bad for her, too.

"I hope she didn't hear me saying twenty-three," I whispered.

A half-hour later, Frank helped me walk out of there. We were in a hurry because now it was Frank's turn.

"We have a room here at the clinic if you like," a nurse said.

"We already arranged for him to go home and come back," I explained.

Frank kept me moving toward the door.

"Well, we'll be here," she said.

Sample cups are enormous. Frank peered inside. "I hate these things."

I lay on the couch with Rosie, drifting. "They don't want you to miss," I murmured.

"A cup this size always makes the sample look abnormally small." He added the medium they'd given him to the sample in the cup and put the cup in the bag. "See you later." He touched my hand and left me drifting on the couch. I was too drifty to notice how long he was gone. He was gone a long time.

Including sample production time and travel both ways, Frank got back to the medical office building in less than an hour. In that hour the parking lot had emptied.

He grabbed the bag off the passenger seat, jogged to the front entrance, and yanked at the double glass doors. They didn't open. He yanked again. They were locked. He pounded on the glass till his hand was sore. No one appeared. He dialed the intercom phone next to the door, first the clinic, then the lab. No answer. He dialed every office in the building, but no one answered anywhere, not even at the number labeled "security." He ran around back, tried all the doors there, but they were locked, too. He ran around to the front again to pound on the glass doors some more.

Frank looked at the bag. He looked at his watch. He considered leaving the bag on the doorstep with a note: *Please give them a good home.* He thought of me, drifting on the couch, still bleeding a little, and he stepped back, squinted up at the second floor to calculate which anonymous glass panel might be the window of the lab, picked up some pebbles from the landscaping, and threw them with all his might.

A few moments later a woman in a lab coat pushed open the glass doors. "I heard a noise and looked out and saw you standing there with your little bag," she said, as if this were perfectly normal. "Come on in, we've been waiting for you."

Sometime after that, Frank's sperm were added to the petri dishes containing my eggs. Then they were left to find one another in the serum sea of my blood.

Three days later Frank drove us back to the main clinic. I was on steroids now, but if there were no viable embryos in those petri dishes, I soon wouldn't be. A nurse handed me another blue gown. She handed Frank scrubs.

"What're these for?" His voice was sharp.

"Father needs to be there for the start," winked the nurse.

Father made faces as he put on the scrubs.

When Dr. Nash came into our cubicle with the embryo report, an unsmiling Frank worked him hard on the numbers—number of embryos (eleven) and cell divisions (four divided once and quit, four were at seven or eight cells and still going, the rest somewhere in between) and quality (three of the bigger embryos were very good, the rest fair to poor).

Frank kept firing off the questions, and Dr. Nash worked to keep up—taking all the factors of our situation into consideration, including my age (young compared to many) and the embryos we had to work with (very good), we had a 30 to 35 percent chance of pregnancy, excellent odds for IVF, and if we did become pregnant a 25 percent chance of twins with less than a 5 percent chance of triplets—after which Dr. Nash caught his breath and asked, quickly, before Frank could drill him anymore, "So how many do you want to put back?"

"We agreed on three," I said, and Frank nodded. I could tell his mind had moved on to something else. I had no idea what that something might be, but I didn't press him on it. Whatever it was, it seemed to be lightening his mood.

In the procedure room Frank was more interested in what they were doing than in holding my hand. He watched them pass the catheters containing our embryos through the small window between the procedure room and the lab. He quizzed Dr. Nash on how and where they were implanting the embryos in my uterus (upper back side) and why (based on the map they made earlier, they would stick better there). Then he wanted to know, "So have you ever put a rubber glove over your head and blown it up?"

I was about to give Frank a look: What kind of goofball question is that? But before I could Dr. Nash said, "Why, yes."

The Frank I fell in love with was back.

The recovery area was hushed, like a library. I lay on my back inside our curtained cubicle. The gurney was tilted at such a steep backward angle I was practically on my head. So I was just lying there, feeling a little crampy and concentrating on thinking sticky thoughts like Dr. Nash had ordered as I was rolled out of the procedure room, when Frank asked a passing nurse if she had an extra rubber glove.

"Uh, sure?" she said uncertainly. She didn't stick around to find out why he wanted it.

He pulled it over his head, below his nose. "Now if you ever try this yourself," his exposed lips instructed me, "be sure you cover your ears so your eardrums don't burst." And pressing his hands against the latex over his ears, he breathed out hard through his nose.

The fingers popped up on top of his head. He looked like a chicken. Then the whole glove filled up, giving his head a light-bulb shape that made him look like an alien chicken. After that he let go and the glove shot off his head, through the crack in the curtain, and across the recovery area.

I clapped my hands over my mouth and shook so hard with stifled laughter I was afraid I might shake the embryos loose. He ducked out to retrieve the glove. He blew it up and shot it off his head again for the uncertain nurse when she passed back through. She laughed so hard she insisted he had to demonstrate it for the couple in the curtained cubicle next to us.

"Please!" they called. "We're dying to know what's going on over there!"

The nurse pulled back the curtain to reveal a man wearing scrubs like Frank's, and a woman tilted practically on her head like I was, except she was on her stomach because her embryos were implanted on the front of her uterus. And so Frank blew up the glove and shot it off his head for a third time. The man roared. The woman shrieked with delight. "Party favors!"

I lay there upside down on my back, deliriously in love with my husband.

In the car, he tilted the passenger seat back for me, as far as it would go.

"Oops, bump!" he said merrily. "Sorry, I'll drive more gently." And he did, pointing out, "Pothole! Better go wide around that one," even though it surely made no difference whatsoever.

He settled me under the covers for my twenty-four hours of bed rest. "Can I get you anything? Cigarettes? A cocktail?"

I laughed. "You are in rare form, and you were so grumpy this morning. What happened?"

"Nash gave us great news!"

"It was pretty good."

"Yeah, the odds are all in my favor. Nineteen in twenty chances of no triplets, and three in four chances of no twins!"

He looked so pleased with himself I laughed again. What a relief it was to laugh. I felt like I hadn't laughed in years, and now here I was, happy, optimistic, in love. I wanted to add to our joy, to his joy, and I said, "And don't forget two in three chances of no pregnancy at all."

His smile widened at first, and then it faded and he just looked at me. And I looked at him. And we shrugged.

Frank peered in the bathroom door. "You've been in here a long time. You okay?"

"I don't want to flush."

"Why?"

"What if I'm flushing our embryos away?"

"I don't think it works that way."

"I know. I know it's stupid."

"It's not stupid. It's just not accurate. Here, I'll flush it for you. I'll even carry you back to bed."

"I can walk," I said, hugging his neck.

He set me down on the bed and sat beside me. I watched him stroke Rosie, curled up next to my feet, listened to her sigh and suckle the air. I folded my hands over my stomach. "They're in there, aren't they."

He nodded.

"I can't hope. I shouldn't hope."

He shook his head.

"Well, for the time being at least, I'm pregnant."

He put his hand on mine, resting one atop the other on the covers over my belly, over our potential babies.

Back with Rosie in the Roswell motel room, fast-food wrappers littering the floor, I curl up with my computer and Frank's email. Rosie curls up with Stinky Pheasant, *whee-ee, whee-ee*. On the TV news, the six-time Pan-American karate champion is demonstrating various methods even your average granny can use to take down a hijacker. Outside the window, whooping voices jog by in celebration of homecoming. Rosie looks up and growls.

> We are getting care packages from people we do not know. Part of the patriotic fervor back in the States. We have no idea what is going on. One of the motors on the antenna that feeds us Direct to Sailor programming

```
has burned out, so we get no news.
There is no word on when it will be
repaired. All   for   now.   Enjoy
Roswell. Bring me back a space rock.
```

The most popular items you can put in a care package: prepaid phone cards, wet wipes, Pop-Tarts, batteries.

In the morning, from the Roswell post office I send Frank a care package of my own: one inflatable green alien, one pink-and-green alien party banner, two green alien Gumbys, and a flying saucer of candy.

DEATH AND TEXAS

Starting date 10/27/01 . . . waxing quarter moon . . . odometer 131,193 . . . route: east across Texas to a pit stop in Houston, then east to Louisiana = two days, 1148 miles

Before crossing Texas, I pull over next to an oil field to consult my guidebooks on America's scenic drives. The first book doesn't even have a listing for Texas. The second advises the reader to hop on the nearest interstate and get across as fast as possible. I look beyond the prehistoric oil wells to the rocky, scrubby plain that stretches all the way to the edge of the endless sky. The wind smells of rotten eggs and burned rye seeds. The nearest oil well pump creaks up and down. I head for the interstate.

The plain breaks up and drops down into cattle and cotton country. The cotton harvest is on, fluffy white bales of it by the side of the road, mile after mile as afternoon passes into night. The Vette rumbles into Houston at 1:00 A.M.

My poet friends and their dogs are waiting for us. The last time I saw Gary he'd shaved his head on a dare. It's grown out now, into a peroxided crew cut. They've just cleaned themselves up from a Halloween party. Gary went as a dead fly, complete with an oversized fly swatter smashed against his back. His new girlfriend, Landon, went as a murdered unknown starlet. There's fake blood smeared all over the bathroom. Poets.

We sit around the table in Gary and Landon's shotgun rental in a neighborhood of squat bungalows and sleepy, overarching trees. We finish off the beans and tortillas and salsa Rosie and I started somewhere in West Texas. Outside, Rosie and the other dogs race around the dirt yard and bark at the moon.

Gary and Landon live much more lightly on the planet than I do. They drive one little gas-stingy car. They're vegetarian. And they have no more idea of how to respond to September 11 than Uncle Hans did, or my Quaker relatives. Gary, who usually builds great baroque towers of words in the air, just shrugs. Landon gives it some thought. She has an open face, an idealist's face, and the voice of a grand dame who's seen it all. "Learn to live without oil," she says dryly, at last, with poetic simplicity. She munches the chips and salsa. "So what does your husband do in the military?"

"He's the combat chaplain for a battalion of Marines."

"Oh, a chaplain." She nods. "I think that's the coolest thing you can be in the military."

"Except as an antimilitary pastor I know once pointed out, it's just helping the military to do what it does, which is kill people."

"True," she concedes.

Because, I mean, what's wrong with this picture? A Christian pastor, follower of a religion that calls its God the Prince of Peace . . .

Who signed up for a job that requires him to stand ready to go unarmed and defenseless into harm's way . . .

To support people whose mission it is to kill and destroy . . .

So those of us at home can live in peace.

And yet . . . and yet . . .

Landon points a salsa-ed chip at me. "But soldiers are people, too."

Exactly. I still have my doubts about what Frank and his Marines are being sent over there to do, and I will always think a big military just makes the easy way out too easy. But I understand now: That's separate from how I feel about the warriors themselves, and about my husband. I'm proud of him. I'm proud of the work he does. He's found his way to give something back, to make the world a better, slightly gentler place. I think about the faces of the Marines I saw while waiting with Frank before he left for the ship, the Marines he cares for. They stood around in their camouflage utilities. They were surrounded by piles of green backpacks and duffle bags. They played with Rosie. They were so young. Somebody's brother.

Somebody's son.

The first night the embryos were inside me, I woke up with heartburn. It continued off and on the next day, and the day after that I started to bloat up, too, thick and tight around the middle. By the evening of the second day, my body felt too tight and bloated to stand up straight; I couldn't take a deep breath. That night my squeezed intestines cramped with gas, which made me want to curl up, but that forced more burning stomach acid up into my squeezed esophagus. I was pacing around the dark living room hunched in half, when my knees started to give way and my vision dimmed around the edges. I got down on the floor fast, my skin clammy. After a minute I went upstairs to the bathroom. When it happened again, I lay on the tile floor feeling nauseated.

All this would have been easier to bear if I were eight months pregnant with a growing baby to explain the distension and discomfort of my body. But with only microscopic embryos in me, the discomfort was made worse by the fear that my ovaries were on their way to exploding.

To implant, embryos need progesterone, but because of the unnatural way the IVF process works, your body's not producing any naturally. So you either have to take three shots of Profasi in the large muscle of the buttock every third night, or you can opt for nightly shots of progesterone-in-oil, which is like injecting a big aching wad of peanut butter into your butt every night for two weeks, and, if you wind up pregnant, for a few more weeks after that.

Since I'd taken the drug before with no problems, Dr. Nash put me on Profasi. It's a lot more convenient, but it also sends 1.3 percent of patients into ovarian hyperstimulation syndrome, which can cause the ovaries to explode, the lungs to drown in fluid, and the heart to arrest. The signs that this is starting to happen is fluid retention or bloating, weight gain, dizziness, and nausea.

Frank woke up and found me on the bathroom floor. He held my hand. He brought me antacids, and that helped a little. I went back to bed. I slept sitting up. A couple times I heard his voice beside me in the dark. "Are you all right?"

"I'm okay now," I said.

The next morning Rosie lay beside me on the bed, quiet and companionable. I called Dr. Nash. It looked like I'd be switching to those uncomfortable nightly shots of progesterone-in-oil, and I was actually happy about it. In the meantime I was able to control the heartburn and cramps by nibbling, very slowly, on an apple, and drinking Gatorade.

That night I threw up the Gatorade.

The next day on the phone Dr. Nash suggested one of those power drinks for senior citizens, which was like drinking sweetened condensed milk straight. By evening I'd had enough and switched to water. At 3 A.M. I threw all that up, too.

Having your muscles convulse when everything inside is under so much pressure is amazingly painful. I was nine pounds heavier and looked four months pregnant. I was having trouble breathing. When the chest pains started, Frank woke up Dr. Nash.

Driving out to the main clinic in the gray dawn, Frank was angry. "This is not worth it. Nothing is worth all this."

It was worth it to me, but I was too weak to argue, could only whimper miserably, "I'm afraid I'll lose the embryos. I'm afraid I'm going to lose my one chance." I couldn't understand why he was so angry. It felt like he was angry at me, but that wasn't it at all.

He kneaded the steering wheel, his jaw knotted. "I'm afraid I'm going to lose my wife."

From the clinic, Dr. Nash sent me to the hospital. A nurse put white surgical support hose on my legs to prevent blood clots. An IV dripped clear liquid into my veins. "Go to class," I whispered to Frank. "Go work on the house, take care of Rosie."

"You're sure you don't want me to stay with you?"

"I'm surrounded by nurses. Dr. Nash said I'll be okay."

I lay on a gurney, rolled here, rolled there, parked in a corridor. I drifted with the pain. At the clinic they'd hinted this changed nothing, that my chances of hanging on to the embryos inside me were still the same as before. I didn't believe them. I let go of hope, felt it swirl away from me and it was okay. Peacefully I drifted on. Someone told me they were going to have to put a shunt in my abdomen to drain the fluid. "Okay," I murmured. They told me they couldn't give me the usual anesthesia because I might be pregnant, just a little topical. "Okay," I murmured. I had no idea what was coming.

They put a small cuff on my finger to track the amount of oxygen in my blood and a bigger cuff on my arm to track my blood pressure and heart rate. My other arm, the one with the IV, was tied down and covered up. The doctor, a new doctor I'd never seen before, was on that side, muttering to his assistant. On the other side of me a nurse tried to distract me with conversation. "So," she said, "any other children? Pets?"

I tried to think. "A dog."

"What's his name?"

The doctor squirted cold jelly onto my abdomen.

"Rosie."

He was using ultrasound to locate the biggest pocket of fluid. The nurse was saying something about a cat named Rosie; I was trying to figure out where the cat came from. The doctor was poking hard into my side with an instrument of some sort, strong pressure and a sharp, pricking feeling. He did it twice. It hurt. It went away.

Fine. I could handle that.

"And before you know it summer will be here," the nurse chattered. "What's your favorite season?"

The doctor continued muttering and clinking his tools.

"The change."

"What change?"

I summoned up the energy to say, "Between seasons," and the doctor yelled, "Don't breathe!" and punched my side with something that sent a blowtorch of pain from my abdomen to my shoulder. I jerked and gasped and he shouted again, "Don't breathe! Relax!" The nurse echoing him, "Don't hold your breath! Relax! Relax!"

The pain withdrew. I lay there gasping, listening to them tell me not to breathe next time and not to tense up. I said hoarsely, "A little warning ahead of time would have been helpful."

The doctor muttered about having to do it again now. The nurse suggested I take a deep breath and let it out slowly as he went in. "Hold my hand and squeeze it," she said.

I gripped her hand. I took a deep breath. I started to let it out slowly.

This time the pain was worse. Again the doctor shouted at me to relax. I hung on to the table with my tied-down hand and squeezed the nurse's hand with the other until the pain finally stopped.

The nurse was panting. I gulped for air and peered at the doctor. He was fiddling with something at my side and shaking his head. "Going to have to make another puncture," he grumbled, and turned away to rustle and clink with his assistant.

My eyes burned. I tried to take a deep breath. I just wanted to steady myself, control my feelings, the only things that were mine to control anymore, but my lungs didn't have enough space to expand. The tears welled up.

265

"Oh dear," said the nurse, and stroked my forehead, for which I loved her and hated her because it made me feel small and weak and that wasn't how I wanted to feel right then. A sob slipped out. The doctor glanced at me with a puzzled frown, as if he'd just noticed there was a person there.

"She's upset," the nurse said. And he said, helpfully, "Don't be upset."

There were a lot of things I wanted to say to that doctor. Mostly I wanted someone to untie my hand on that side so I could punch him.

When I had recovered myself, the doctor tried again. The pain, two waves of it, was duller this time. With the first wave I felt something hot and wet running down my side before he stopped it. With the second wave I felt something like a red-hot wire twisting around inside me. I heard whimpering. I suppose it was me. After the doctor muttered and fiddled around some more, he patted my tied-down hand and gave me a big grin. "Good luck!"

I whimpered, "Thank you," as he swept out of the room.

Hearing myself say that, I wanted my hand untied so I could just punch myself.

Back in my room I discovered I now had a spigot in my side. A tube ran from the spigot to a collection bag clamped to my calf. I appeared to be dispensing Kool-Aid. The woman in the next bed moaned. Frank came and went, solicitous and brooding. Every time I moved, that hot wire felt like it was being drawn across my middle. I didn't move much. A lot of flowers arrived, my father, too, kissing me on the cheek, filling up the room, saying he was glad I hadn't been discharged yet because he'd have been pissed if he'd driven all the way out here for nothing. He handed me a five-hundred-page book. "Just how long do you think I'm going to be here?" I laughed—carefully, without moving.

I had time to stare out the window and wonder why this had

happened to me. If God was big enough to underlie the entire universe, I could believe God could control every little careening bump of every atom. But from my possum's perspective, the universe looked random. There was no reason that I could see. I just counted myself lucky that the bump that hit me wasn't a direct hit from a mortar shell.

I lifted a spoonful of clear broth to my nose. It had been nearly seventy-two hours since I'd last eaten anything I could keep down. I breathed in. *Aaaah.* I sipped the broth. The flavor exploded in my mouth. Oh what transcendent bliss. Nothing before or since has ever tasted so perfect, so satisfyingly savory; it almost made all the pain worthwhile. I slurped up spoonful after spoonful. I popped delectably squiggly cubes of lemon Jell-O into my mouth, the meaning of the universe squishing between my tongue and the roof of my mouth. I wiggled my feet. Hooded in their white surgical hose, with a peekaboo hole over the toes like a face, they looked like virginal ninjas. I almost cried when half a bowl of broth and four Jell-O cubes left me too full to eat more.

If God created the world the way it is on purpose, the evidence suggests God must not care about good and evil the same way we do. Pregnancy or ovarian hyperstimulation or mortar shell, good, bad, or hideous—did God care which one hit me? I was beginning to think not. In addition, if God deliberately created me the way I am, with a free will, then the only thing God must care about is whether or not I choose to respond to each bump with the part of God that's in me, my finger tip reaching out to touch God's.

I didn't feel very in touch with that part. I had let myself get too busy, in constant motion. The part of me that wanted to punch Dr. Evil—I don't think that was the Light leading me.

But when I was still and alone on the gurney in the corridor, floating on a steady river of pain, I had been able to let go of what I wanted and just drift with what came my way. I wondered if I would be able to do that when I was feeling fine again, without the pain to focus me.

Two and a half days later, Dr. Nash sent me home. Beth and Rollie came over. "How are you, doll?" She stuck out her lower lip in sympathy and gave me a careful hug.

"Look." Moving gingerly, I lifted my dress—my favorite baggy comfort dress I always wore on days I'd rather be in bed—and showed off the spigot. "While I was away, I got my connector to the central pod."

Beth was impressed. "I'm so jealous."

A day later, I went back to have it taken out. This time I drew Dr. Good. Like Dr. Evil, he was a radiologist, but their specialty was the only thing they had in common.

"Wow!" Dr. Good squeezed my shoulder. "You look so much better I hardly recognize you." I didn't recognize him at all. As far as I knew I'd never seen him before. He disconnected the clamp apparatus, peeled off the bandages, and braced himself for a mighty tug. "Ready?"

I nodded, dutifully starting to let out my breath.

He said, "One, two, *three!*" And he simply slipped it out.

It had about a two-inch tail of turquoise tubing. It left behind a hole the size of a fat pinhead. The sight of it made me laugh. Today, I have to really hunt to find the scar.

When I got back home, I called the clinic to check in. Dora answered the phone, and Dora, beautiful Dora, who always gently hit the vein on the first try, who had never hurt me with a needle, said a painful thing. She exclaimed, "When I heard you'd gone into hyperstimulation I got so excited for you! Most hyperstim patients wind up pregnant!"

I wanted to cover my ears, but it was too late. I had begun to hope again.

Tanker ships throb up from the Gulf of Mexico into the Port of

Houston, their holds filled with oil. We import more than half the oil we use in this country. There's no way to drill or conserve our way out of that hole. Maybe Landon was right. Maybe simply quitting cold-turkey is the only solution.

Gary and I cruise over to the port to have a look, but since the terror attacks it's not open to unofficial gawkers anymore. So Rosie and I leave Gary waving from his front porch and move on.

Beneath the hood of the Corvette, inside each of the engine's eight cylinders, a tiny drop of gas is mixed with air, compressed, and ignited, the force of thousands of explosions per minute driving us east past petrochemical plants, scribbled tangles of pipe, and eerie flames. What sounds like a solid roar is really thousands of distinct, individual eruptions of power, a miniature war with shells bursting all around.

In the tall green sugar cane fields of the Louisiana delta, a lumbering tractor hauls a load of cane up the road to an ancient-looking processing plant that steams gently on the edge of a ramshackle town. Between the road and a simple white clapboard A.M.E. church, a young man with a scarred and twisted face gardens in the sun. A billboard looms, a huge photograph of a smiling man in a white collar like Frank's, and the headline: We Priests Have a Happy Life. Join Us!

In an absurd world, hard work and religion both hold out the promise of finding some meaning and maybe even some happiness. So does war.

During the First World War, the average British soldier had a better than 50 percent chance of being killed, wounded, or taken prisoner. The average French soldier's odds were worse—more than three hundred thousand of them died in the first two months alone. During bombardments that shook the earth, men couldn't hear themselves scream while they waited to be obliterated. Sometimes they were, sometimes they weren't; there was no real defense against shells; death was random, survival a matter of luck. And yet despite this and all the

269

other miseries of war, very few deserted or mutinied. For more than four years, millions of men simply fought on and on.

"I adore war. It is like a big picnic without the objectlessness of a picnic. I've never been so well or so happy," said poet and decorated British officer Julian Grenfell, not long before he was killed by a shell in 1915. World War I's soldier-poets wrote eloquently of war's attractions. Sigmund Freud said war "strips us of the later accretions of civilization and lays bare primal man in each of us." The instinct to make war is perhaps as ancient and irrational as the drive to make babies, as universal as the longing to know why we are here—the longing for the Light, for God. Neither communism nor materialism have managed to put an end to spiritual yearning. Even the sufferings of war fail to stop people from having babies. If making war is as fundamental a part of being human as longing for God and making babies, part of the natural order, how can we ever hope to replace it with permanent peace? What's the point of even trying?

The engine roars.

PSYCHIC POWERS

Starting date 10/29/01 . . . waxing gibbous moon . . . pit stop in New Orleans = one day

Beauuuuuutiful . . . sweeeeeet . . ." The empathic advisor strokes my palm, her hands warm in the cool night air. "You have—" She turns her head to cough. "You have a very long, very deep—" Cough, cough. "Excuse me. I'm sorry."

"I wish I had a cough drop to give you." I feel for her. The cough is throwing off her spiel.

She brightens. "Ha! I just remembered!" She lets go of my hand. "I think I have some Life Savers." She digs through her purse.

I lean back in the folding chair. The shadowy plaza in front of the cathedral in New Orleans' rickety, gaudy, wrought-iron French Quarter is ringed with readers of palms, tarot cards, and crystals who each set out a small table, a couple of chairs, some candles, and they're in business. I picked this one because she looked accessible to a first-timer— no high priestess getup, no scary fingernails, and, except for one scented candle, no props. Just sensible, no-nonsense fortunetelling.

She takes my hand again. "Beauuuutiful." Her tongue juggles the Life Saver. "Yes, you have a long, deep soul mate line." She squints at my palm in the flickering candlelight. "You like to dance when you're alone. You're intuitive about other people. You feel responsible for their upsets, you're very nurturing."

I smile on the outside like I'm satisfactorily impressed. Inside I'm rolling my eyes because I guess on some level I had kind of hoped there would be more to it than this. I assume there's as much to palm reading as there is to astrology. My astrological chart, which my mother had done for me when I was a kid, was based on the exact minute of my birth and actually describes me pretty accurately. It makes sense to me that it would, because if God underlies everything in the universe, then everything in the universe is connected, from distant stars to the palm of my hand.

But this woman hasn't "read" anything in my palm that she couldn't have guessed by watching me closely, from the way I walked when I first approached her to the cheap wedding band I'm wearing that looks like it was probably bought years ago when I was younger and poorer.

"Mmm . . . beauuutiful, sweeeet." She turns my hand, looks at the back. "You had a big stress about two months ago. Take the B vitamins, take the zinc."

Uh huh. The whole country had a big stress about two months ago on September 11. Stress shows up in the nail bed. I raise my eyebrows at her, still smiling.

Having established her credentials for accuracy, she starts getting into the advice. She tells me I should trust my intuition, that I shouldn't forget to dance when I'm under stress, that I have a loooong life line. I'll live to be ninety-five, to be exact. Sounds good to me.

"And you're very fertile." She traces my palm with her finger. "So be careful unless you're sure. One main line and three coming off it. Four all together, but mainly one."

I stare at her, my smile fading.

"But even if you don't choose to get pregnant with them, they'll still be with you, around you. Maybe not as children. Maybe not as *your* children."

It took three stabs to get the blood for the pregnancy test. That seemed like a bad omen since Dora was doing the stabbing. While we watched the syringe fill with red, she said, "The woman who was next to you at the transfer asked about you."

"I'll bet she did," I laughed. "How is she?"

"She had her beta test yesterday. Positive." Dora patted my hand and smiled as if that meant mine would be, too, but my heart sank. Three of us had transfers that day. Each of us had at best a one-in-three chance of becoming pregnant. One of us was now pregnant. It wasn't rational, it wasn't even statistically accurate, but I felt as if she'd stolen my chance at pregnancy.

I went home to wait. Despite the bad omen, it was hard not to fantasize about being pregnant, about the possibility of twins. I worked hard at the mental discipline of pessimism. Every time I thought about the test result or life after the test result, I selfconsciously channeled my thoughts toward a negative result: the back bedroom finished as a study, not a child's room; freedom to travel; the ability to pay off debt; no stress over whether I was dragging Frank into something he wasn't meant for. I sat at the computer. I did busy work, mindless work, anything to make the time go by till one o'clock.

One o'clock came and went.

One-thirty.

Two.

At 2:04 the phone rang. My stomach was flipping. I heard Frank hurrying down the stairs as I picked up the phone.

"Hello Kristin, how are you?" Dr. Nash asked.

"My stomach's flipping."

And then he said what I had expected him to say but hoped he wouldn't. He said it fast, like he knew I needed him to get it over with. He was afraid the beta test was negative. He was very sorry.

"That's what I was expecting to hear." It came out automatically.

"Yeah, our numbers are good, but they can't be 100 percent." He'd said it a thousand times.

My polite, automatic mouth continued without me. "Can I stop the progesterone-in-oil, cold turkey?"

"Yes, that would be fine."

"And can we meet with you sometime to talk about what happened? I'd like to know what that means for any future attempts."

"Sure, that's a normal part of the cycle."

And then he said again he was sorry, and regards to Francis.

I sat there with the silent phone at my ear. Francis? Apparently he didn't even remember Frank's name because the only place Frank was Francis was on official paperwork. No one ever called him Francis. I looked at the receiver in my hand. I could see the doctor filing us away with the rest of the negatives, under H.

I looked up. Frank was standing at the foot of the stairs. He came across the room then. I had never had a baby, not a real one. But in my imagination she had been real. I had been pregnant with hope for four years, and she had just died. Hope is a curse.

Frank folded me into his arms. "You know, I would have been upset if you'd been pregnant."

I nodded silently against his warm neck, musky and sweet.

"But like you know, if I'm really honest, I have to admit that deep down inside I would have been happy."

He was holding me as if I might break. When he said that, I did.

The Vette crunches slowly along a drive in the cathedral's cemetery. Last night I walked the narrow streets of the French Quarter, listened to jazz, drank beer, and ate jambalaya and handmade donuts buried under a burg of powdered sugar before finally riding the trolley back to the Garden District to fall asleep with Rosie beneath a twelve-foot ceiling in a hushed, antebellum hotel. Now the morning sun casts sharp shadows among tombs the size of back yard playhouses. They line the drives and pathways like a miniature, crumbling city of stone.

We get out of the car. The hum of a nearby elevated highway rises and falls. The place smells of fish. Rosie sniffs the tombs as if the smell is far more complex, as if she's sorting through wafting reams of information.

With two hundred million olfactory cells compared to my measly five million, her sense of smell is so powerful sometimes it seems like she has a sixth sense, a connection with an unknown world we humans can only guess at. Once when she and I had walked into the house in D.C., she took one whiff and exploded with her deepest bark of alarm, all the fur standing up on her back. She charged upstairs hunting for the repairman who had come and gone while we were out, leaving behind a little bit of himself in the air.

I walk among the tombs. Some are well cared for, some falling down; weeds grow on the flat roof of one. Each represents a single family's hope of life in the face of death. I sniff this air, try to imagine that instead of fish it smells of babies and the future. Hope depends on the imagination, which depends on the unconscious, which connects us with something deep and ancient that runs through us all.

Despite a complete lack of evidence, I continue to hope there's more to death than what I can see. I die a little every day, but thanks to hope I soldier on. It occurs to me, too, there's actually evidence to support the hope that there are peaceful alternatives to war, proven realistic alternatives. Thousands of years of Chinese history are full of sly examples of ruthless invaders who overran China but in the end were absorbed by the people they had supposedly defeated. Similarly, in the last century when the fascists in Germany and Japan came to power, there may have been nonviolent ways to stop them, even after the moderates on all sides screwed up. World War II went on for six years, destroyed entire cities, and killed as many as sixty million people, fully half of them civilians. If Europe and Asia had actively but peacefully resisted the Germans and Japanese the way Gandhi's Indians later resisted the British, could the death toll and destruction have been any worse?

I take comfort in these possibilities. Hope may be a curse, but hopelessness is unbearable. Too much hope and you're crushed by the inevitable disappointment; too little and you're flattened just the same.

Peace is that place in the middle between fantasy and despair, a place that's the width of a tightrope.

> Have I mentioned that after being in the desert, when I got back on board and saw your picture again on my desk, I was surprised at how my heart did something when I saw your face. With time, the memories grow a little softer, and when you see a picture, you suddenly realize how important it is to actually see your partner.

I pull out my wallet and finger through the credit cards and receipts and various IDs. The picture I carry is a little dog-eared, my two-dimensional soul mate smiling at me in his black dress uniform, two gold lieutenant's stripes and a cross on each cuff. Looking at his picture, my heart fills with love, too, but it has no scent, no laugh, no warm, sweet-smelling skin or annoying habits. Despite the daily emails, I feel in love with a phantom.

I lean against the side of the Vette and wait for Rosie to finish sniffing. I want my real husband back. I try to imagine him coming home, how wonderful it will be to feel him hold me again. It doesn't feel real.

Frank held me on the couch while he called my family, one by one, and our friends. After my sisters hung up with Frank, they called each other and cried.

I decided I had cried enough. I washed my face. We went to a movie, something dark and funny and unsentimental. We splurged on dinner out.

But in the quiet darkness of our bed that night, with nothing to distract me, sobs curled me tight as a fetal ball. Frank wrapped his arms around me; he kissed my forehead. Grief, like all pain, is wordless and timeworn; it does not judge; it just is. I let its current carry me. I let it spin me, bewilder me, love me, and as I did I felt Frank kiss my cheek, my neck, my shoulders. His arousal touched me. When the rush of tears had worn away the sharpest edges of my curled-up heart, whorled and hushed as a snail, I uncurled and wrapped myself around him.

THE ROAD TO DOG ZEN

Starting date 10/30/01 . . . full moon . . . odometer 132,341 . . . route: northeast through Mississippi, Alabama, and Tennessee to a pit stop in Bowling Green, Kentucky, then east through West Virginia and Virginia, and home to Washington, D.C. = five days, 1500 miles

Heading north out of New Orleans, the road comes upon Lake Pontchartrain, 630 square miles of water that should force it to go around, but hearing the rest of America calling to it from the far shore, the road steps out on faith and shoots straight across, transformed into a flat causeway.

The Vette speeds just above the surface. The windows are down, Rosie's nose in the wind. For twenty-four miles, we're surrounded by the changeable sameness of the water. We are in the middle of a liquid desert.

Out in the desert, you can feel God up close. There's nothing around to distract you. Just the vast empty wastes of sand, rock, distant plateaus, the quiet just before the twilight breeze stirs the tents, the dark vacuum of space holding the diamonds of the night sky. One day back when we were in Egypt, I spent hours on a little hill, listening to the wind, wondering what the future held,

> looking out across the desert. I sang
> hymns to myself as I tried to get back
> in touch with what was important.

Rosie pulls her head in and bumps my shoulder with her nose before lying down.

A couple of days after the pregnancy test, Frank and Rosie and I had driven down to Florida to visit my mother. "Honey," Mom asked, "would you mind keeping Rosie off the new wood floor in the kitchen and dining room? I hate for it to get scratched up right away."

It was a perfectly reasonable request, but it reminded me I had a dog, not a child. No one would ever come home to visit me the way I had come home to visit my mother, and within half an hour of arriving I was hiding in the guest room.

Frank slipped in. "Oh," he said when he saw my red eyes and red nose. "We thought you were sleeping."

I shook my head.

He looked worried. "Did I do something?"

I shook my head. "Nobody did anything. It's just my crummy life."

"Do you want me to go away?"

"No."

I avoided my sisters. They didn't feel like my sisters anymore—they felt like somebody else's mother. They'd call, and I'd let the machine take it.

The clinic's therapist said, "You're a writer. Write them a letter." So I did. I quoted the therapist a lot.

July 1998
Dear Ingrid & Erin,
I'm sending you both the same letter because I want to say the same thing to both of you. First, I love you

both and feel lucky to have two such loving, thoughtful sisters who have been so supportive through the years of my infertility treatment. Most especially I have appreciated your willingness to give me the room I need to heal after this latest round of treatment, even though I know it must have been hard for you. And believe me, I need a lot of room. The emotional fallout has been far, far greater than I ever imagined, and it's the main reason why I'm hesitating about whether or not to try again, which Frank and I have been talking about.

Among the most difficult are the feelings of alienation I feel toward both of you, who mean so much to me. I met with the therapist today, and she explained that such feelings—envy, jealousy, bitterness toward others, alienation—happen in situations like infertility because normally, when there's something we want and we can't have it, we either convince ourselves we don't want it or we try harder to get it. Neither of those options apply here, because I can't convince myself I don't want children and I can't possibly try any harder. So I envy you, and I don't like myself for envying you, and until I can deal with that I'd rather not inflict it on you.

Anyway, I am leaning toward trying again, but the thought of diving back in is not exciting or invigorating. It's depressing actually, because the way my therapist described it, it's like going back to war after only a couple weeks of R&R. You want to win the war, but war is hell, and who wants to go back to hell? But I think it beats the alternative, which feels like quitting before the war is decisively over.

I'd appreciate your prayers. If this next try fails, if

there is a next try, I am hoping I can get myself spiritually to the point where I can look to the future with joyful anticipation of what in the world God has planned for me.

    I love you both,
    Kristin

When my sisters received that letter, they called each other and cried again.

I sweated in the back yard dirt, got it blooming. Out front, I dug in the brick planter Frank had built between the house and the sidewalk.

Frank pushed open the front door. "Could you come in and help me with something?"

I brushed off my hands.

He closed the door behind me, shutting us off from the sidewalk. He put his arms around me. "I just wanted to give you a hug and tell you I love you."

Dr. Nash opened with a sympathetic, "Well, darn."

I had waited two and a half weeks to meet with him so I could work up enough self-control to maintain some dignity, but sympathy dissolves self-control like sugar in tea. I steeled myself. "So where do we stand? Do we know anything more than before?"

He took the hint and rattled off facts and statistics. I had hoped he would say, "Well, it's hopeless," so I could just peacefully give up. But no, the odds were in fact slightly better, because now he knew I had eggs, that my eggs fertilized, that the embryos looked great, that my uterus and endometrium looked great, none of which he knew before.

I absorbed this. "We're really struggling with whether or not to try again. I need some time to get over this last one. If I knew I'd have a baby at the end of it, I'd plunge right in again, no hesitation. But with the odds against it . . ."

Dr. Nash seemed to be waiting for my point. What was my point?

"Frank's leaving for the Navy in three months. Can we freeze his sperm to try again after he's gone?"

Frank shifted and made a low, ominous sound.

Dr. Nash said he wouldn't recommend it; the rate of success with frozen sperm was half that of fresh. "I don't mean to make light of your need to take time to heal from this last attempt, but if you think you might try again, I would try to heal faster."

The elevator doors closed. Frank watched the lighted numbers count backward. "Why did you tell him we're struggling over whether or not to try again?"

"Because we are."

"There's no more insurance."

"We can borrow against our life insurance. But money's not the real issue and you know it."

"For God's sake, Kristin, you want to know for certain whether you're meant to have children, but some things just aren't knowable."

The elevator doors dinged open.

Somewhere in the middle of all this the Light was shining, I was sure of it. If I could just find it in the darkness, everything would become clear, way would open, and all I'd have to do was follow the Light. No stumbling, no flailing around, and at the other end I would emerge re-energized and at peace, instead of worn ragged like now.

"To promote peace, nations and their leaders have to take the long view, anticipate problems, avoid sowing the seeds of injustice. Once the grievances tip the scale from hope to despair, it's almost impossible to avoid war."

My spiritual friends listened, watching me or gazing thoughtfully into space.

"To promote inner peace, maybe individuals have to take the long view, too, the *really* long view—the view from eternity. The evidence of the world indicates that God cares more about the fight against evil than evil itself, how we live the journey rather than whether or not we reach the destination. When I was in the hospital, it occurred to me that maybe all the Light cares about is whether or not I live more fully in the Light, and that I should express my love for God and God's love for me through the world around me. Whether or not I have a baby isn't necessarily relevant to that larger goal."

We sat in silence for a while. I'd left Frank sitting in silence on the patio in a misty evening rain, too depressed about the prospect of another possible attempt to go inside and work on the back bedroom. I didn't feel much different. Before I started trying to become a mother, back when I was younger and knew everything, I heard about a friend of a friend, a woman and her husband who lived on what he made and every year spent her entire annual salary on IVF attempts. That was $60,000 a year. Every year. For ten years. She wound up with a baby in the end, "but my God," I remember saying with a self-righteous gasp, "think how many needy children she could have adopted for that amount of money."

It's bad karma to judge other people's dreams. It's like begging the universe to set you up. Now I was no longer stunned by the amount of money she had spent. What took my breath away was the emotional price I now knew she must have paid.

To my spiritual friends I said, "I don't feel like God has abandoned me. But I don't feel peaceful. I think that's why I'm not ready to stop. I haven't arrived at a peaceful place yet. I just don't know if I have the strength to get there."

Afterward, as I turned the key in the ignition and listened to the old Honda squeal to life, I heard a rumble. An even older Corvette muscled its way up the street, somewhere between '74 and '76, I thought, tipped off by its vertical rear window and rubber bumpers. There goes my car, I thought wistfully, then amended that: *My* car would be a '78. That was the year I got my driver's license and first started noticing Vettes. Maybe one day I'd do it—just go out and buy one.

I watched this Corvette round the corner fast and tight, and there it went, gone. One day. Maybe. But even the cheapest Corvettes are expensive to maintain, and so are children. If I invested in another IVF cycle and wound up with a baby, I probably wouldn't be able to afford the car.

I put the Honda into drive.

I took a trip. Frank and I both knew I'd come home with a decision.

I flew out to Iowa and soaked up the nurturing normalcy of Aunt Beth's farm life. I meant to tell her about my infertility and ask her advice, but it was such a relief to escape to a place where my infertility wasn't on the agenda that I couldn't bring myself to spoil it.

I rented a car. I drove from Iowa to Kansas, to see an old friend, another sensible Midwesterner, recently divorced. Her I told, and we wallowed in each other's pain. One morning she woke up giggling. She dreamed she and I were walking down the street. I was carrying a heavy, bulky shopping bag filled with tampons that were big cottony wads, homemade and environmentally friendly, and a big heavy reusable porcelain applicator. I was hauling it around with me everywhere I went. Her dream self told my dream self, "Kristin, you need to put that down."

"So what do you think?" she asked.

"I think it's weird when other people dream your dreams for you."

"Do you think God was talking to you through my subconscious?"

"That, or it was your good sense talking to me through your subconscious. It sounds like the kind of practical advice you would give."

Frank picked me up at the airport. The Honda's air conditioner wheezed tepid air at us, both of us sweating. I lifted my damp hair off my neck. "I want to put this baby burden down."

He nodded, suspicious.

"But I can't till I feel some peace about it." I let my hair drop, leaned my head against the headrest. "And there's only one way that's going to happen."

He nodded again, his worst fears confirmed. We drove on, him with his hands hanging from the wheel, me slumped in the passenger seat, united in our resignation. All around us traffic on the Beltway gasped in the heat, the sunlight on chrome too bright, the passing buildings blurred, the trees huddled, all of us drained and waiting for this summer to be over.

I'm inside the Corvette assembly plant in Bowling Green, Kentucky. While Rosie waits outside in the Vette, I watch gleaming new Vettes without drive trains glide past union men and union women, some in jeans and t-shirts, some in clown faces or witch's hats. They'll turn out 135 Corvettes on this, the last day of public tours "due to the present situation" following the attacks in September. It's October 31, and Rosie and I are getting close to home.

These new Vettes can blow the doors off mine, and suck down half the gas doing it. They get better all the time. One day they'll invent an engine for an American sports car that doesn't use gasoline at all. If cars can improve, why can't people?

The Pennsylvania Friends improved. After the greed of some Quaker and non-Quaker colonists caused injustices that led the Native Americans in Pennsylvania to resort to violence, after the Quaker legislators resigned so their nonpacifist neighbors could defend themselves, Friends didn't stay out of the fighting that followed.

They sheltered Indians fleeing the violence. They prevented massacres of their native neighbors. They have continued to provide relief to the victims of war ever since. Their reputation as honest players gets them in where others can't go: After World War I, while the British maintained their blockade of Germany, the only group allowed in to feed starving German children was the Quakers. They helped over a million children survive, among them my ten-year-old Oma, who as she sat down in her school auditorium and filled up on food for the first time in years, looked up at a banner, "Provided by the Quakers in America," and never forgot.

Watching the new Corvettes come together, I finally come to a little bit of clearness. The destination of eliminating war completely is like a hazy purple mountain I can see on the horizon while walking across the world's biggest desert. Even if it's not a mirage, I'll die before I get there. The sight of it leaves me passive with despair. But if I look around the moment in time where I am, if I focus on the journey rather than the destination and endeavor to live "in virtue of that life and power which takes away the occasion for all wars," even if I fail, I can hang on to a little hope and keep on going as way opens, one step at a time. I can't think of a better spiritual home for me than a religious way that was started by a man who made shoes for people's feet, a man who walked all over England to share the hope of equality and peace. For better or worse, I am a Quaker.

The Pennsylvania Quakers' story actually began more than eighty years before that war broke out. George Fox, who founded the Religious Society of Friends, was visiting Quaker colonists in North Carolina when someone made the argument that the Light did not live in the Indians. Fox, who believed the human conscience was guided by the Light, asked a nearby Indian if he felt ashamed when he lied. The man answered that why yes, he did. That was proof enough for Fox, and for most Friends, that there was That of God in everyone, Indians and Europeans alike.

Not long after that, when the first generation of English Friends began colonizing Pennsylvania, William Penn learned the local language and gave Indians the same respect he gave Europeans. He and his Quaker colonists negotiated and paid for land, even though their English king had already "given" it to them. They honored treaties. While the other colonies suffered constant Indian wars, the Pennsylvania Quakers and their Indian neighbors lived side by side in peace, a peace that lasted for seventy years. Just because perfection is impossible doesn't mean we can't improve. The nonviolent approach has worked before and it can work again.

Human greed and violence probably mean we'll always need warriors to protect us from the consequences of our mistakes. But human greed and violence mean we'll also always need courageous people of conscience to save us from our own worst selves. The world needs both Quakers and Marines. So does my marriage. And within myself, so do I.

As the second IVF cycle began, I called my sisters and asked them to bring their children up for the weekend. Late at night, when Frank was upstairs puttering around the back bedroom construction zone and the kids were asleep on the living room floor, Ingrid and Erin and I sat around the kitchen eating ice cream and talking, reminiscing, each of us contributing our piece of our collective memory. It was just like when we were teenagers, except we didn't have the energy to stay up as late as we used to.

I sat down at my desk every morning to work. I helped Frank finish up the last of the house projects. I accompanied him to the naval air station across the river and came home with a military dependent ID card. I invited all our friends over for a goodbye party for him. I injected myself with fertility drugs three times a day. I was having a life, not just trying to have a baby. I was following Rosie's example, living in the present. I needed to plan for the future, I needed to learn from the past, but I couldn't live in either place—they didn't exist. The only thing that was real was here and now.

I started to notice childless role models. Jesus. Thich Nhat Hanh. Mother Teresa. Uncle Hans. The woman I call my second mom and her husband as well. Dolly Parton. Janet Reno, who, when she was eventually done serving as Attorney General, would buy a red pickup and drive across the country. And a slightly older couple at Frank's church, professionally powerful and personally humble, who comforted me one Sunday with just a few words about the myth we carry around in our heads, that we all have some kind of right to a perfect little baby. Even so, near the end of my twenty-four hours of bed rest after the transfer, I lay there looking at the ceiling, smiling and thinking: I have embryos floating in me.

A week later, Frank reported to Naval Chaplains School in Rhode Island.

My pod-sister Beth and my second mom took over the final week of shooting me up with progesterone-in-oil every night. No hyperstim dramatics the second time around. On the day of the pregnancy test, Erin drove up to be with me. She and her husband were back together again, but their separation had left its mark—like Oma, Erin knew what it meant to be sad. She left Lydia with her husband and came to me the way I had gone to her. She was waiting when I got back from the main clinic, where it had taken three people fifteen minutes and six tries to get my blood. I hugged her, wearing Sesame Street Band-Aids on both elbows and the backs of both hands.

This time it was a nurse who called. As I held the phone to my ear, a single word whispered through my mind: Corvette, Corvette, Corvette . . . Erin and I sat on the couch and talked through our tears and eventually turned to venting about politics. Then she drove home to her husband and daughter in Richmond and I lost myself in a book about someone with a much shittier life than mine.

Frank had to call from a pay phone. "Well?"

"It's okay, I'm not pregnant."

"How are you doing? Are you okay?"

"Pretty well, actually. I'm sad but I'm not grieving like last time."

He was quiet.

"Are you okay?" I asked.

I heard him sigh. Then: "I think I'm kind of sad."

I gazed out the sliding-glass door at my garden, still blooming despite the heat. For a moment it shimmered as if it were the heat and not tears. I blinked hard.

"I've been talking with some of the other guys here, and somebody pointed out that if we had twins they could be friends for each other whenever we move. And if the infant stage got to me, I could always re-up for sea duty until they were in school."

All of a sudden I didn't have to blink anymore. I laughed.

"So now you're going to go buy your Corvette?"

"I'm applying for a loan tomorrow."

The Vette rolls east through bluegrass country, thoroughbreds grazing. Nine thousand miles ahead of us, Frank's ship is once again rolling east, too, moving through the Suez Canal, headed for the Indian Ocean. He'd never really traveled till he met me, had never been out of the country. He sends me an email.

> My list of countries so far: Canada, Antigua, St. Martin, Scotland, Ireland, England, France, West Germany and East Germany back when there were two, Austria, Luxembourg, Belgium, Italy, Crete, Turkey, Egypt, Spain, Bahrain, United Arab Emirates, Kuwait, and that little French island we landed on for a half-hour when we flew to Antigua.
>
> Some of these were with you, some with the Navy, some were only to pass through on a train, or stand on a pier, but I can claim them. I never thought I would be a world traveler.

The person I love is being swept further and further away by forces bigger than both of us. I've been thinking thoughts like this for six weeks, but now they go by like cars on the highway. By now driving has become a form of centering prayer for me. Like Rosie, I'm able to drop at will into the car's bubble of white noise, the Zen of the road. I absorb what flows out of the radio, the television, the newspapers, the email on my screen, draw conclusions when I can, and try to stay unruffled by things I can't control.

```
All for now. So glad you have been
safe so far. All the news of the
anthrax shit really made me con-
cerned. Please continue to be care-
ful. Really glad you have been able
to realize a dream.
```

The earth shoves itself up into the crumpled old ridges and hollows of the Appalachians; the road twists its way through. In the mined hills of West Virginia, the Vette rumbles past a mountain of coal. Dump trucks tip out their loads in black hillocks, and yellow bulldozers plow them up the slope, then beep slowly back down. I pull into a gas station where two people slow their cars to tell me the gas at that station is for county vehicles only. There is no sign anywhere to indicate this, everyone just knows. That's how many strangers come through here.

I could happily lose myself in America the land, America the people; there's no law, natural or manmade, that says I can't be a pacifist and a patriot, too. I stop to buy a red-white-and-blue bandanna and tie it around Rosie's neck. After six weeks and ten thousand miles, I know I could go on like this forever, living each day in this endlessly new and interesting limbo with only my dog for company. All my life I've been happiest and most optimistic when I'm going somewhere, but in order for my inner self to get anywhere, my outer self has to stop and be still, which doesn't often happen in my real life. During the past six weeks, the Vette has let me do both. Sitting in the driver's seat I'm essentially still, yet I'm also in motion. Now, with Virginia and Washington, D.C., just over the horizon, I don't want to stop.

I guess I could keep going. But I'm ready to choose not to.

Dr. Nash bustled around his desk and reached up to wrap me in an enthusiastic hug. "If you ever change your mind and want to try again, we'll always be here for you."

On my way out, Dora called from behind the counter, "Are we going to see you again?"

I stopped at the door. "No, I'm moving on."

She hurried across the softly lit lobby and gave me a hug, too, her thin arms squeezing me tight. "We're going to miss you around here," she sniffed. I left before we both started crying.

Outside on the bright downtown sidewalk I took a deep breath of exhaust fumes and crisp autumn air. I felt as if I'd been let out of prison.

I found my dream Corvette in the woods of Virginia's Northern Neck. It gleamed midnight blue in the sunlight. When I started it up, the engine didn't whine—it rumbled. When I took it for a test drive, it roared down the back roads like a nimble tank with rockets strapped underneath. A couple of days later, after arranging a complicated series of rides with my sisters, I put Rosie in the Vette for the first time and hit the road for home.

We're almost there. We roll through northern Virginia back to Washington, D.C., where after years of on-again-off-again IVF, Beth is two months pregnant. It shouldn't have happened: In the middle of the cycle, on the morning of September 11, she was at her job in northern Virginia. Against the tide of fleeing government workers and the police and soldiers suddenly guarding the bridges, she couldn't get back into the city, couldn't get home to her drugs till the next morning. She missed a whole day's worth of injections.

I'm smiling for her as if my team has won. I don't even feel wistful—it's her life, not mine. Mine has taken me across the country and back,

back to where the Pentagon has become a tourist attraction. On a balmy autumn afternoon I park the Vette and lead Rosie into a murmuring crowd on the grassy median across from the ruined fifth side.

I'm not prepared for the way it hits me. It was shocking the first time I saw it when I drove by at the start of my trip, but at fifty-five miles an hour it was there and then gone. Now, standing still and staring at it, Rosie pressing against my leg, the sight hits me in my stomach. I find myself squinting at the world. I find myself wishing to be alone.

Next to me, a Japanese couple takes turns smiling for their photo op. I'm not making this up. I couldn't make this up. I squint at them, offended. But they are tourists. During the course of their American vacation, the photo op will have become such a rote activity they may not even be aware they are smiling.

So this next part I make up. I imagine them returning home, developing the pictures, showing them to their friends. If one of their friends should ask, "Why are you smiling in front of a place where people died?" they would frown and say, "but we do not remember smiling."

Going forward, as a Quaker I try to keep it simple and travel light. I try to make deliberate decisions about what to keep in my life and what to discard.

The last IVF cycle had produced more good embryos than the first one. Even after we had put the best back inside me—four that time instead of three—there had still been some good ones left over.

Dr. Nash had asked, "Do you want to discard the rest like last time? Or watch them for freezing just in case?"

I knew I should tell him, "Discard."

"Watch them for freezing," I said.

Even when I found out it was another twelve hundred dollars to freeze and store them for a year, and that beyond a year their quality would rapidly deteriorate, even when I found out only two went on to reach the blastocyst stage necessary for freezing, I still couldn't bring myself to say, "Discard."

They were only two. The odds of a successful cycle with only two frozen embryos, assuming they both survived the unfreezing process, were so low it would never be worth it for me even if I'd been tempted to try.

But I also couldn't throw them away. After the year came and went, I would occasionally think I should really call the lab and make sure they've disposed of them. I've never gotten around to it. I prefer to imagine them out there somewhere, frozen in time, our two children forever.

JOY RIDE

Starting date 3/10/02 . . . waning crescent moon . . . odometer 136,015 . . . route: from Richmond down through the Carolinas and back = five days, 1,067 miles

I used to work in television. But I rarely watched it. I certainly never subscribed to cable television. "It's addictive," I always said. "Too many choices suck you in."

Then the planes crashed. Frank shipped out. I felt powerless. But knowledge was power, and at first the broadcast networks' wall-to-wall coverage satisfied my need to know. Gradually, though, the evening news anchors went back to anchoring just the evening news, gave up the airtime they'd seized from Oprah and the cast of *General Hospital*. It became clear: For the long term, only cable could quench my thirst for news.

At first, it was just quick hits. A few minutes in the lobby at the post office. Then it was a half-hour at my sister's house in Richmond. An hour in a hotel room while traveling across the country. I thought I could control it. You always do. Before I knew it, I was watching often enough to develop strong opinions about cable's talking heads: shouters in need of duct tape, young studs in silly take-me-seriously glasses, smug cheerleaders who'd grown up to read the news. But when Aaron Brown on CNN refused to join the media madness and cover the latest news about O.J.—when Brown just smiled his lopsided smile and refused to utter so much as the initials "O" and "J," even though his production crew was goading him by running the old footage of the White Bronco Chase over his shoulder—I fell in love.

Back home, I begin arranging to accidentally wind up in front of others' cable-connected television sets weeknights around ten. I like the soothing sound of his humane and humble voice. I like his glasses. I email Frank: "If you don't come back, I'm going to have Aaron Brown's love child."

Just before Christmas, Frank hoists his pack alongside his assistant and bodyguard, a lanky, fast-talking Arizonan named Brad. They climb aboard a CH-46 helicopter crowded with Marines that thunders over the water toward Pakistan, another 46 visible through the open door, wind whipping past their helmets. That night a C-130 transport plane flies them into Afghanistan and Frank steps onto the tarmac at Kandahar Airport where the Marines are digging in. CNN is there.

I'm watching the news. It's Christmas Eve. Without warning, there he is, a second and a half of my husband inside a cavelike, war-damaged terminal on the other side of the world, leading Marines in a hymn. I leap to my feet. I shout. I run around the living room. I am as deliriously beside myself as Rosie is every time I return home from an errand, because once Frank left the ship and went ashore I couldn't picture where he'd gone, couldn't imagine it. It was as if he'd died: He existed on some other level, but I had no way of knowing where that existence was or what it looked like.

Now that I've seen him on TV, seen the candlelight flickering on the rough terminal walls like the Roman catacombs, he's resurrected in my imagination, alive and real again.

When the phone rings soon after, it's Frank, calling me from Afghanistan on one of the "morale phones" provided to the troops for the holidays. Hearing his voice, I'm instantly reminded how he talks, how he walks, how he laughs, how he always leaves the trash can in front of the toilet for me to trip over in the dark—the real physical Frank. And I realize how inexact and inadequate written words are. All these months he's sent me thousands of words via email, but they didn't add up to the real Frank. They left me plenty of space to construct a fantasy Frank, no more real than the television image of Aaron Brown.

Frank lives with Brad in a two-man tent. He lives without running water, goes without a shower the entire month he's there. He eats food out of foil pouches. He fights off the cold and the cameramen who want to make him famous for washing his underwear in a bucket and hanging it to dry on barbed wire. He avoids land mines on his daily visitation rounds to his congregation in their fighting holes. He's counseling a Marine when a burn barrel explodes; he and Brad run to the wounded. The night the airport comes under attack, they run through the dark to the medical tent to be there for casualties as gunfire crackles in the distance, rounds skipping off the runway fifty meters out. There are no casualties, so he and Brad sit outside the tent and watch bright green and red tracer rounds stitching the darkness. Mortar platoons light up the night with illumination flares. Frank watches as flames spring up in a few places where falling rounds catch the brush on fire, listens to the thumping snarl of Cobra attack helicopters overhead.

I'm on the road, driving back to North Carolina after spending Christmas at my mother's, when a C-130 goes down in Pakistan, killing everyone on board. All day as I drive I listen for news on the radio. I know when Frank's at sea he hops rides on helicopters to visit his battalion's Marines on other ships. I know not all his Marines are at Kandahar, but I tell myself it doesn't seem very likely that he'd be traveling around. Besides, there were only seven people on the plane. I tell myself odds are, even if he and his assistant were traveling around, they probably weren't on it. I tell myself to breathe as I round the corner onto our street.

There, in front of the house we rent, the street is empty. At last I can get a deep breath. There's no nondescript government sedan waiting for me. But I know somewhere that sedan has pulled up in front of seven other houses.

When the C-130 went down in Pakistan, Frank and Brad *were* in Pakistan. They'd been checking on a group of Marines on guard at an airfield, and were waiting to hop a ride on another C-130 back to Kandahar.

By February Frank's back on the ship. By March his ship's heading west, heading for home, and I'm back on the road.

Rosie, Annali, and I have been passing the billboards for a couple hundred miles—a king-sized three-dimensional hot dog (headline: "You Never Sausage a Place!"), a genuine wrecked car ("Smash Hit!")—till Annali's on the edge of her seat.

"Look!" She points. "There's another one! 'Honeymoon Suite—Heir Conditioned!'" She laughs. Annali, after all, just turned nine.

When we finally blast into South Carolina, a monster sombrero on top of a two-hundred-foot tower rises over the horizon. "Behold," I declare, "one of the wonders of the world."

We have arrived at South of the Border. It started out as a beer stand. Today it's a complex: motel, gas 'n' go, restaurants, carnival rides, putt-putt golf, fireworks outlet, supermarket-sized tchotchke shops, a giant neon cartoon Mexican whose legs straddle the road like an arch. If you ride the elevator to the top of the tower, as Annali and I do, you can walk around the sombrero's brim and look out at miles and miles of desolate red-clay-piney-woods nothingness. You will look out and you will be grateful for the exotic amusements below your feet—the museum of concrete garden statues, the miniature train, even Big Bertha.

Bertha's a painted head in the pinball arcade; her flabby, fabric body hangs below. Annali stands in front of Big Bertha and lobs balls at the hole that is Bertha's mouth, complete with padded lips. A canned voice bellows, "Feed me! Feed me! I'm honnngry!" and whenever a ball makes it in, Bertha belches. Annali scores a plastic eyeball on a suction cup, which she licks and wears on the middle of her forehead for the rest of the day.

Next door, we feed ourselves southern-fried tacos in a concrete and cinderblock cavern that looks like it could seat a dozen tour busloads and then be hosed down afterward. But since this is a Monday afternoon in the off-season, the only other people in there are a tattooed man who'd ridden in on a motorcycle and a sunburned woman in a tube top who'd been hanging on behind. Like us, they're here because it's on the way.

I'm turning forty this week. It's hard to believe it's been nearly eight years since I first started trying to have a baby. The moon seems to circle in and out of the earth's shadow faster and faster, its rhythmic sunlit sickle scything down the years. The solar system and I are both halfway to going dark, but before it burns out, the sun has over five billion years left to it; if I'm lucky, if the palm reader was right, I have forty or fifty.

Before I'm another month older, Frank's ship will drop anchor off the North Carolina coast. Seven months after he left, Rosie and I will be waiting for him to arrive from the ship in the hot, crowded parking lot in front of battalion headquarters. Marines in desert tan will pour off buses and out of Humvees. Rosie will ignore them all. But every once in a while a man will walk by in woodland green and Rosie will jump up, look from him to me to him; the last time she saw Frank, he was wearing woodland green. When Frank finally climbs out of a Humvee, he'll be wearing desert tan. Rosie will look right past him till he's almost on top of her. Then she'll catch his scent. Her ears, her nose, her whole body will strain toward him, and then realizing it really is Frank, she'll tuck her ears and yelp and bound around him, then back to me, then to him, tangling all of us together in her leash. He'll get down to greet her and she'll lick his face, his neck, his ears, his hands, over and over again. He'll be thinner, tanner; there will be circles under his eyes. He'll reach up and take my hand and I'll feel his grip in mine and it will be just like that moment on the phone when I first heard his voice after so long—I'll know everything one person can know about another, and he'll know the same about me. That night I'll take off the locket he gave me and put it away, and we'll lie side by side in the dark with Rosie at our feet, our fingers touching, just listening to each other breathe.

But before that happens, way will open for Annali and me to spend a week on the road. Annali has always been game for adventure, but Ingrid's a homebody. "Show her the world," she'll say to me.

Annali is the eldest child, like I am. She was the first of Ingrid's and Erin's children that I carried around on my hip, as she reached entranced for a fluttering leaf; the first one I pushed, staring up from her stroller, past the dinosaurs in the Smithsonian Museum of Natural History. A couple days ago as the moon was waning, I strapped Annali into a booster in the co-pilot's seat, shoved Rosie into the back of the Vette, and hit the gas. Destination: the Carolinas, my sometime home.

After South of the Border we zoom the back roads, engine roaring, shouting along with Annali's Backstreet Boys CD while Rosie pants into the wind and barks. I am mistress of ceremonies, emcee of the world flying past our windows. We screech to a stop in a small town that smells of glue. Once upon a time Frank and I lived in a parsonage next to a church outside this town. I've spotted a diner I know, tucked into a crooked side street in the shadow of a steam-spewing furniture factory.

Here, Annali can walk in, sit down, and get her first real taste of the very best in genuine southern cooking—Three Overcooked Vegetables and a Meat. She runs her finger down the menu, fills in the blanks with three vegetables (black-eyed peas, greens, and cooked apples—what the regional dietary classification system lacks in accuracy it makes up for in elegant simplicity) and a meat (chicken-fried steak), plus corn bread and hushpuppies on the side. She gives the cook the extravagant compliment of eating most of it, except for a few hushpuppies, which she saves for Rosie, who's waiting in the car. "Hush, puppy," she says.

During our Carolina travels we visit a paper mill, stumble across a pair of procreating ducks, zoom past "the world's largest chair," which is three stories tall, and also "the world's largest peach," which is a water tower outside the town of Gaffney that's shaped like a peach and looks like Big Bertha's butt. In a motel that night at bath time, Annali makes up a song about it. It goes like this: "Naked . . . naked . . . naked . . ." And then the big finale, where she turns her back to her audience (Rosie and me) and wiggles her bottom: "Gaff-uh-nee peach!"

By the end of the week we're roaring along singing, "Hey, hey, we're the Monkees," the music of *my* childhood. "You know what?" Annali announces after the fiftieth round of "I'm a Believer," "I'm not tired of you yet."

All of a sudden something strange peeks above the piney woods ahead. It looks like jumbo jewelry in motion.

Annali catches her breath; I hit the brakes.

It's whirligigs, a pasture full. They sprout twenty, thirty feet high, patchwork windmills and air ships constructed from scrap metal, old state-line signs, and defunct gas station parts, all turning and tinkling in the wind. In the trees across the road, outside a barn, we see sparks flying. We get out of the car and find an old man with knotted hands welding together another massive, magical whirligig. He talks with Annali about how he found the parts for his creations, about the eight dogs he's buried over the years. He opens the gate into the pasture and Annali follows Rosie through, head tilted back, eyes wide.

Watching her reminds me of a trip I took with Oma. When I was about Annali's age, Oma took me across the Atlantic on my first trip to Germany, where she'd grown up. In my memory, the castles and cobblestone streets and cathedral-like forests will always be a magical, fairy tale world.

Oma's been gone for years now. After that massive stroke left her unaware of the world around her, for two long weeks my mother sent dispatches from Oma's final crossing: "Today she smiled as if she was dreaming . . . last night she lifted her hand as if something was there . . . this morning she's gone." Goodbye forever. I miss my Oma. But the things she told me live on in me, and when I think about that trip we took together thirty years ago, it's like waving hello to her.

I look across the pasture at Annali. She's standing beneath a fantastical merry-go-round, squinting up through her little disposable camera at a scrap-metal cowboy riding a tricycle over her head.

Some miles ago she turned to me in her booster seat and said, "Aunt Kiki, I've been thinking. Since you can't have any children, if you want to, we could pretend I'm your daughter, just while we're on our trip."

I squirmed, a little uncomfortable. "Sure," I said, "that would be fun."

A minute later she spoke up again, very formal this time. "So, uh, Mom, there's something I've been wanting to ask you about."

I gave it my best June Cleaver, with a southern twist. "Honey, you can ask me anything you like."

After a long pause, she giggled, embarrassed. "Actually, I didn't want to ask anything." She scrunched up her face, earnestly casual. "I just like saying that. You know, calling you Mom."

Then she reached over and gave me a hug, Rosie tried to get in on it from behind our seats, and for a moment I had a little trouble seeing the road.

Across the pasture now, Annali lowers the camera and sees me watching her. She lifts her hand and waves.

After five days and a thousand miles, the sliver of moon has melted and gone. I'm another week older, another week closer to being gone myself, and Annali and I are rumbling back up into Virginia. We say goodbye. She gallops back to her family, shouting about whirligigs.

Rosie and I get back on the road home—home, where we'll wait for Frank. Night has fallen, black and moonless; the new moon, her dark side facing the earth, has set with the sun. In the Vette's puny headlights I can see only the leading edge of the road as it unrolls out of the vast night ahead. Tomorrow the moon will slowly begin opening like an eye, widening to reflect the Light and illuminate the darkness before slowly closing again. Way opens, way closes, and then way opens again, circling around and around as I drive on, the moon and the starry patchwork of constellations all turning and tinkling in the solar wind.

AUTHOR'S NOTE

This is a true story—it is both true and a story. Everything really happened, but some of the events have been simplified or compressed in time. All of the characters are real live people. Most of them let me use their real names, but some didn't, and the names of people from the past who played only small roles have also been changed. A few characters, such as motel clerks, are composites of several real people. Some of the conversations are composites, too, while others record almost word for word what was really said or as best as I could remember what was said when I wrote it down in my journal at the time.

When summarizing complex medical and military data, historical events, Quakerism, and other religious ways, I've tried to be as accurate as possible. But summary leaves out the nuances, and with them goes some accuracy. If you're interested in exploring these subjects in more detail, you may find the following books a helpful place to start: Jared Diamond's *Guns, Germs, and Steel: The Fates of Human Societies,* Robert Lawrence Smith's *A Quaker Book of Wisdom,* and Thich Nhat Hanh's *Peace Is Every Step: The Path of Mindfulness in Everyday Life.* For more information and support on infertility, contact the national nonprofit infertility association RESOLVE, www.resolve.org. A more detailed reading list can be found at www.kristinhenderson.com.

ACKNOWLEDGMENTS

I will be forever grateful to editors Tom Shroder and Lynn Medford of the *Washington Post* for helping me first turn a piece of my life into an article; to my agent Sam Stoloff for believing that article could be turned into a book; and to Seal Press editor Leslie Miller for making that book happen while encouraging me to dig deeper and ask the Big Questions.

I could not have asked those questions without the moral support of the Poison Clan Literary Collective, especially the poetic Toad; the fearless first-draft feedback of my friend Ken Forsberg; and the guidance of my writers group—Randi Einbinder, Rochelle Hollander Schwab, Catherine Petrini, and Leslie Kostrich, my much-cherished critic-at-large who never hesitates to tell me when I can do better.

I am especially grateful to my wonderful friends and family for allowing me to include them in these pages, and for their patient and generous help while I was writing, including Reva Griffith, who shared her family research. I also owe a debt of education to more knowledgeable people than I, who have shared their wisdom and scholarship in books.

Most of all, my gratitude goes to my brave and trusting husband, without whose support this book would not have been possible. As I write this, he is once again far from home with his Marines, this time in Iraq. Thanks to him I now know that in the midst of war, there is some peace in knowing you are loved.

ABOUT THE AUTHOR

KRISTIN HENDERSON lives in Washington, D.C., where her essays are regularly featured in the *Washington Post*. Her short fiction has appeared in various literary journals, and has been nominated for a Pushcart Prize. She's a member of the National Writers Union and an amateur autocross racer. More trip photos, a map, reading list, discussion topics, and informational links are available at www.kristinhenderson.com.

Selected Titles from Seal Press

Atlas of the Human Heart by Ariel Gore. $14.95, 1-58005-088-3. Ariel Gore spins the spirited story of a vulnerable drifter who takes refuge in the fate and the shadowy recesses of a string of glittering, broken relationships.

The Chelsea Whistle by Michelle Tea. $14.95, 1-58005-073-5. In this gritty, confessional memoir, Michelle Tea takes the reader back to the city of her childhood: Chelsea, Massachusetts—Boston's ugly, scrappy little sister and a place where time and hope are spent on things not getting any worse.

Growing Seasons: Half-baked Garden Tips, Cheap Advice on Marriage and Questionable Theories on Motherhood by Annie Spiegelman. $14.95, 1-58005-079-4. A celebration of family in all its comfort and complexity.

Unreliable Truth: On Memoir and Memory by Maureen Murdock. $14.95, 1-58005-083-2. A fascinating exploration of memory and identity, and an exacting look at how memoir is crafted.

Drive: Women's True Stories from the Open Road edited by Jennie Goode. $15.95, 1-58005-066-2. This collection of women's experiences on the road fills a void in road literature and will move readers to take their own journeys.

East Toward Dawn: A Woman's Solo Journey Around the World by Nan Watkins. $14.95, 1-58005-064-6. After the loss of her son and the end of a marriage, the author sets out in search of joy and renewal in travel.

The Boxer's Heart: Lessons from the Ring by Kate Sekules. $14.95, 1-58005-077-8. A brilliantly candid memoir and first-ever guide to the world of women's boxing.

Seal Press publishes many books of fiction and nonfiction by women writers. Please visit our Web site at **www.sealpress.com**.